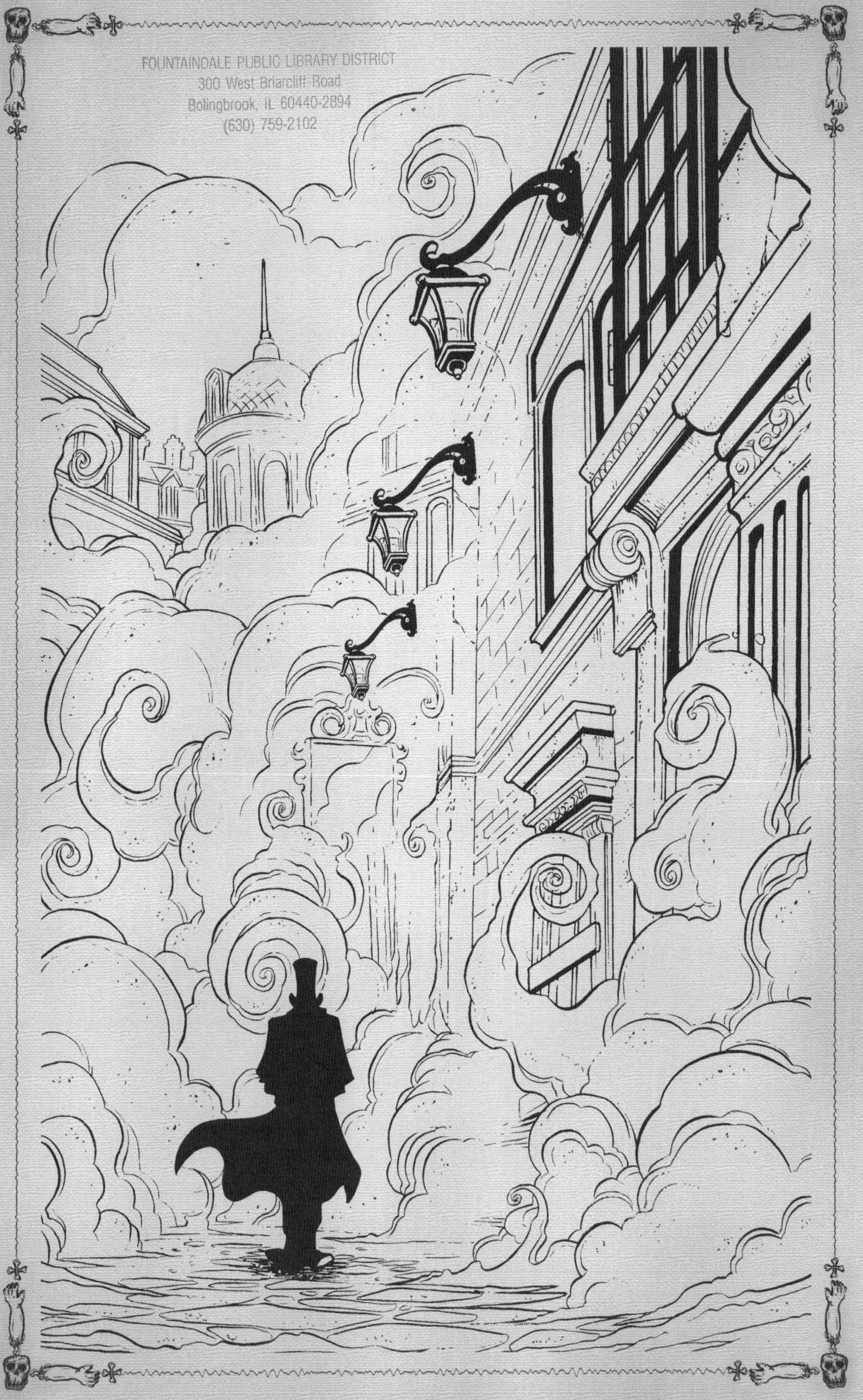

A ZOMBIES CHRISTMAS CAROL

IN SEQUENTIAL ART

BEING

An Undead Story of Christmas

BY

CHARLES DICKENS
(Deftly Adapted by JIM McCANN)

PRESENTING

A
CHRISTMAS
PRESENT
BY

A
CHRISTMAS
PAST AND FUTURE
BY

PENCILS
DAVID BALDEON

PENCILS
JEREMY TREECE

INKS
JORDI TARRAGONA

INKS
ROGER BONET

COLORS
FERRAN DANIEL

COLORS
JORGE GONZALEZ

With the Letters of **JEFF ECKLEBERRY**

PRODUCTION
DAMIEN LUCCHESE

EDITOR
JOHN DENNING

SENIOR EDITOR
MARK PANICCIA

Special Thanks to **DAVID GABRIEL**

COLLECTION EDITOR
CORY LEVINE

EDITORIAL ASSISTANTS
JAMES EMMETT & JOE HOCHSTEIN

ASSISTANT EDITORS
MATT MASDEU, ALEX STARBUCK & NELSON RIBEIRO

EDITORS, SPECIAL PROJECTS
JENNIFER GRÜNWALD & MARK D. BEAZLEY

SENIOR EDITOR, SPECIAL PROJECTS
JEFF YOUNGQUIST

SENIOR VICE PRESIDENT OF SALES
DAVID GABRIEL

SVP OF BRAND PLANNING & COMMUNICATIONS
MICHAEL PASCIULLO

EDITOR IN CHIEF
AXEL ALONSO

CHIEF CREATIVE OFFICER
JOE QUESADA

PUBLISHER
DAN BUCKLEY

EXECUTIVE PRODUCER
ALAN FINE

ZOMBIES CHRISTMAS CAROL. Contains material originally published in magazine form as ZOMBIES CHRISTMAS CAROL #1-5. First printing 2011. ISBN# 978-0-7851-5772-4. Published by MARVEL WORLDWIDE, INC., a subsidiary of MARVEL ENTERTAINMENT, LLC. OFFICE OF PUBLICATION: 135 West 50th Street, New York, NY 10020. Copyright © 2011 Marvel Characters, Inc. All rights reserved. $24.99 per copy in the U.S. and $27.99 in Canada (GST #R127032852); Canadian Agreement #40668537. All characters featured in this issue and the distinctive names and likenesses thereof, and all related indicia are trademarks of Marvel Characters, Inc. No similarity between any of the names, characters, persons, and/or institutions in this magazine with those of any living or dead person or institution is intended, and any such similarity which may exist is purely coincidental. **Printed in the U.S.A.** ALAN FINE, EVP - Office of the President, Marvel Worldwide, Inc. and EVP & CMO Marvel Characters B.V.; DAN BUCKLEY, Publisher & President - Print, Animation & Digital Divisions; JOE QUESADA, Chief Creative Officer; JIM SOKOLOWSKI, Chief Operating Officer; DAVID BOGART, SVP of Business Affairs & Talent Management; TOM BREVOORT, SVP of Publishing; C.B. CEBULSKI, SVP of Creator & Content Development; DAVID GABRIEL, SVP of Publishing Sales & Circulation; MICHAEL PASCIULLO, SVP of Brand Planning & Communications; JIM O'KEEFE, VP of Operations & Logistics; DAN CARR, Executive Director of Publishing Technology; SUSAN CRESPI, Editorial Operations Manager; ALEX MORALES, Publishing Operations Manager; STAN LEE, Chairman Emeritus. For information regarding advertising in Marvel Comics or on Marvel.com, please contact John Dokes, SVP Integrated Sales and Marketing, at jdokes@marvel.com. For Marvel subscription inquiries, please call 800-217-9158. **Manufactured between 8/1/2011 and 8/29/2011 by R.R. DONNELLEY, INC., SALEM, VA, USA.**

10 9 8 7 6 5 4 3 2 1

STAVE 1:

Marley's Hungry Death

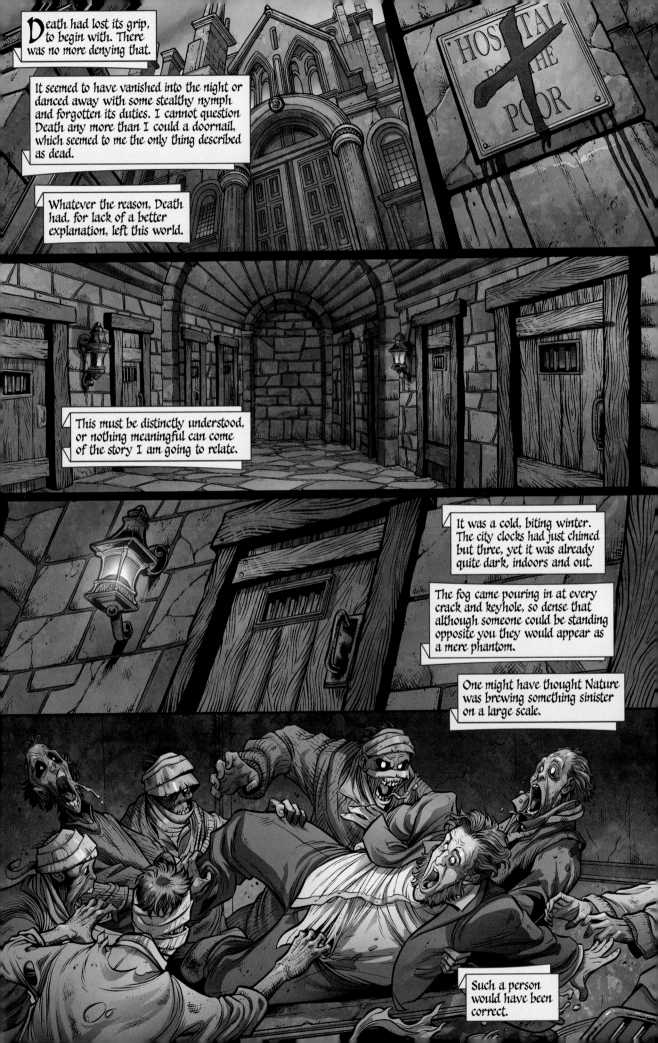

Death had lost its grip, to begin with. There was no more denying that.

It seemed to have vanished into the night or danced away with some stealthy nymph and forgotten its duties. I cannot question Death any more than I could a doornail, which seemed to me the only thing described as dead.

Whatever the reason, Death had, for lack of a better explanation, left this world.

HOSPITAL FOR THE POOR

This must be distinctly understood, or nothing meaningful can come of the story I am going to relate.

It was a cold, biting winter. The city clocks had just chimed but three, yet it was already quite dark, indoors and out.

The fog came pouring in at every crack and keyhole, so dense that although someone could be standing opposite you they would appear as a mere phantom.

One might have thought Nature was brewing something sinister on a large scale.

Such a person would have been correct.

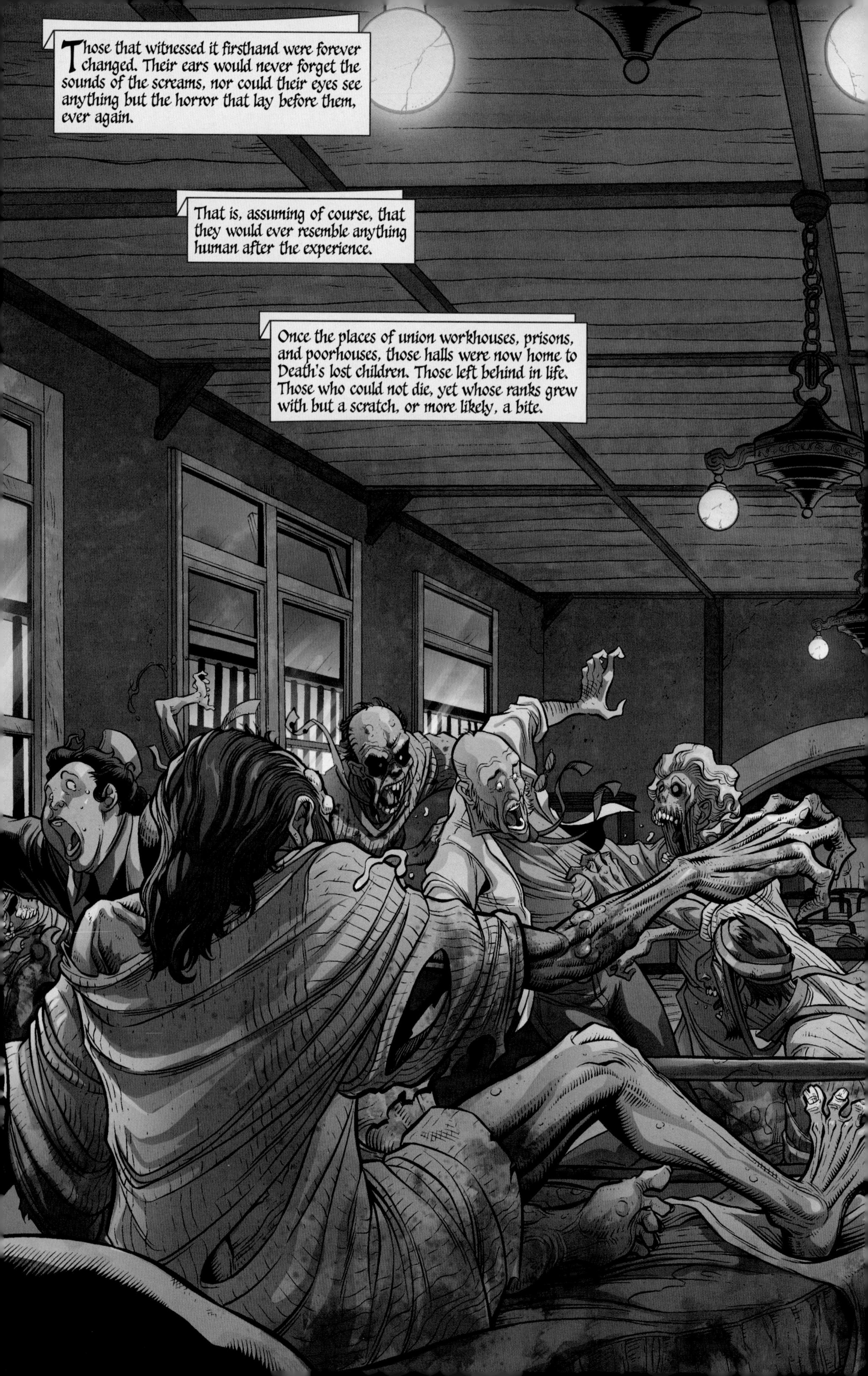
Those that witnessed it firsthand were forever changed. Their ears would never forget the sounds of the screams, nor could their eyes see anything but the horror that lay before them, ever again.
That is, assuming of course, that they would ever resemble anything human after the experience.
Once the places of union workhouses, prisons, and poorhouses, those halls were now home to Death's lost children. Those left behind in life. Those who could not die, yet whose ranks grew with but a scratch, or more likely, a bite.

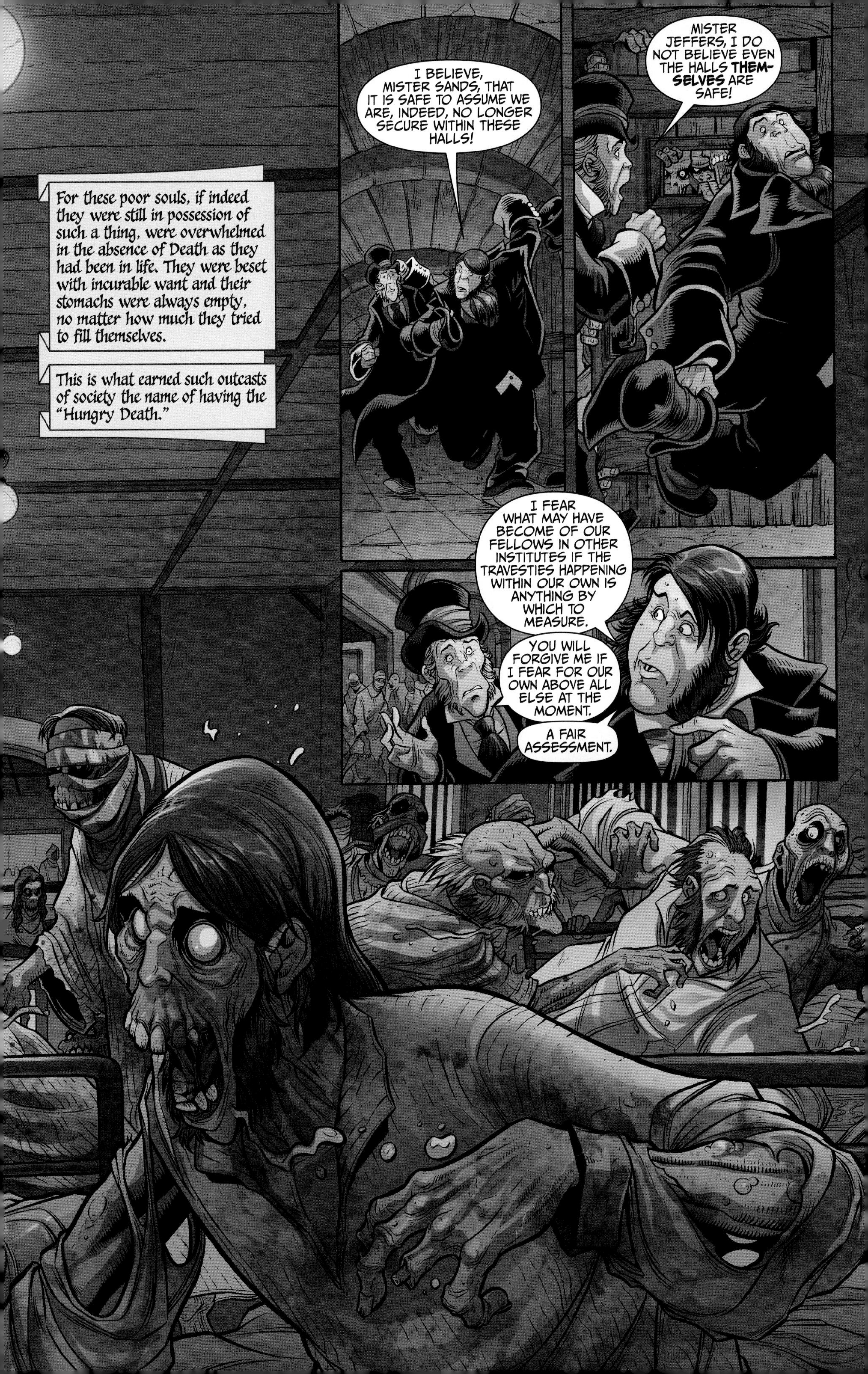
For these poor souls, if indeed they were still in possession of such a thing, were overwhelmed in the absence of Death as they had been in life. They were beset with incurable want and their stomachs were always empty, no matter how much they tried to fill themselves.
This is what earned such outcasts of society the name of having the "Hungry Death."
I BELIEVE, MISTER SANDS, THAT IT IS SAFE TO ASSUME WE ARE, INDEED, NO LONGER SECURE WITHIN THESE HALLS!
MISTER JEFFERS, I DO NOT BELIEVE EVEN THE HALLS **THEMSELVES** ARE SAFE!
I FEAR WHAT MAY HAVE BECOME OF OUR FELLOWS IN OTHER INSTITUTES IF THE TRAVESTIES HAPPENING WITHIN OUR OWN IS ANYTHING BY WHICH TO MEASURE.
YOU WILL FORGIVE ME IF I FEAR FOR OUR OWN ABOVE ALL ELSE AT THE MOMENT.
A FAIR ASSESSMENT.

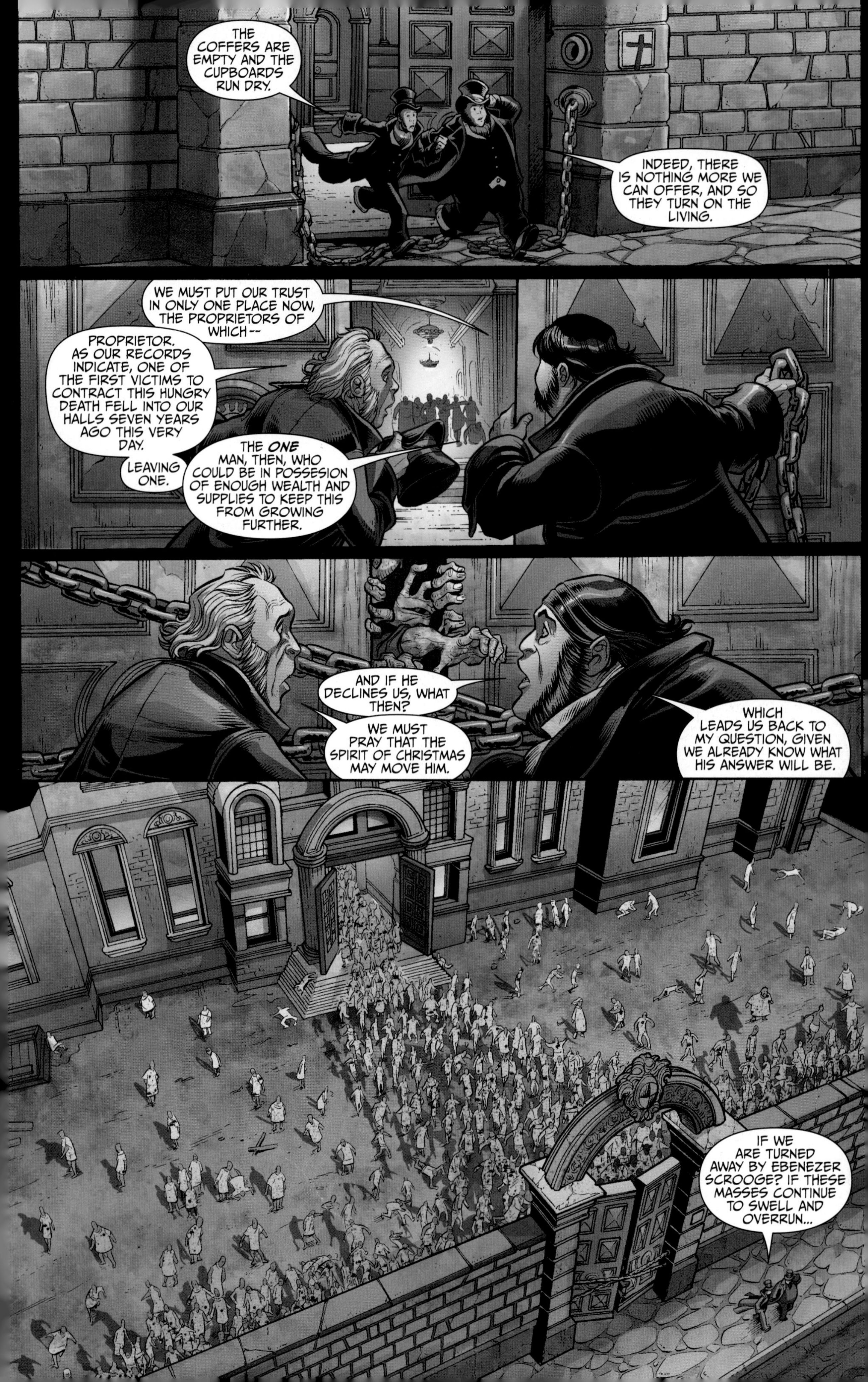
THE COFFERS ARE EMPTY AND THE CUPBOARDS RUN DRY.
INDEED, THERE IS NOTHING MORE WE CAN OFFER, AND SO THEY TURN ON THE LIVING.
WE MUST PUT OUR TRUST IN ONLY ONE PLACE NOW, THE PROPRIETORS OF WHICH--
PROPRIETOR. AS OUR RECORDS INDICATE, ONE OF THE FIRST VICTIMS TO CONTRACT THIS HUNGRY DEATH FELL INTO OUR HALLS SEVEN YEARS AGO THIS VERY DAY.
LEAVING ONE.
THE ONE MAN, THEN, WHO COULD BE IN POSSESION OF ENOUGH WEALTH AND SUPPLIES TO KEEP THIS FROM GROWING FURTHER.
AND IF HE DECLINES US, WHAT THEN?
WE MUST PRAY THAT THE SPIRIT OF CHRISTMAS MAY MOVE HIM.
WHICH LEADS US BACK TO MY QUESTION, GIVEN WE ALREADY KNOW WHAT HIS ANSWER WILL BE.
IF WE ARE TURNED AWAY BY EBENEZER SCROOGE? IF THESE MASSES CONTINUE TO SWELL AND OVERRUN...

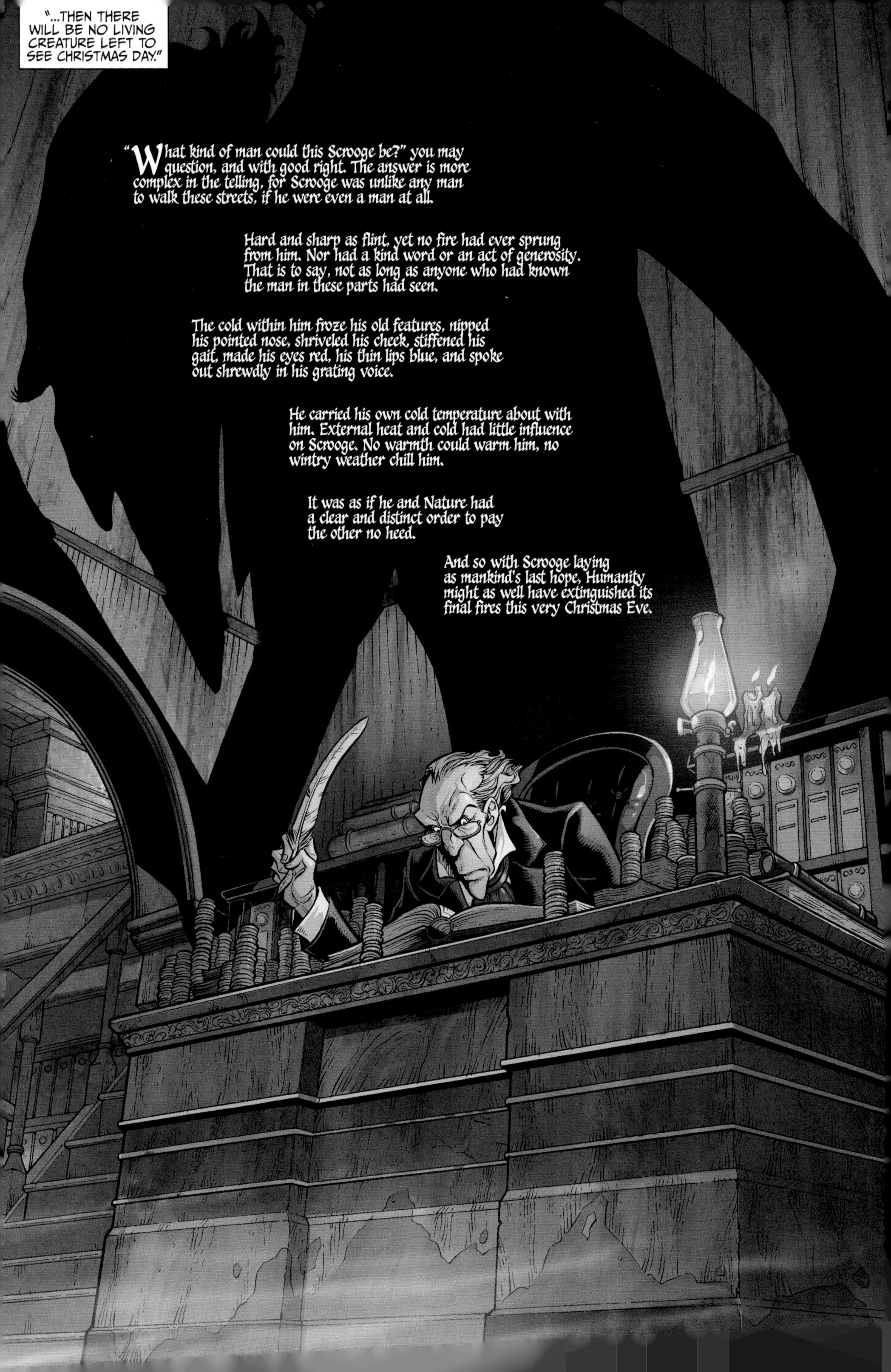
"...THEN THERE WILL BE NO LIVING CREATURE LEFT TO SEE CHRISTMAS DAY."
"What kind of man could this Scrooge be?" you may question, and with good right. The answer is more complex in the telling, for Scrooge was unlike any man to walk these streets, if he were even a man at all.
Hard and sharp as flint, yet no fire had ever sprung from him. Nor had a kind word or an act of generosity. That is to say, not as long as anyone who had known the man in these parts had seen.
The cold within him froze his old features, nipped his pointed nose, shriveled his cheek, stiffened his gait, made his eyes red, his thin lips blue, and spoke out shrewdly in his grating voice.
He carried his own cold temperature about with him. External heat and cold had little influence on Scrooge. No warmth could warm him, no wintry weather chill him.
It was as if he and Nature had a clear and distinct order to pay the other no heed.
And so with Scrooge laying as mankind's last hope, Humanity might as well have extinguished its final fires this very Christmas Eve.

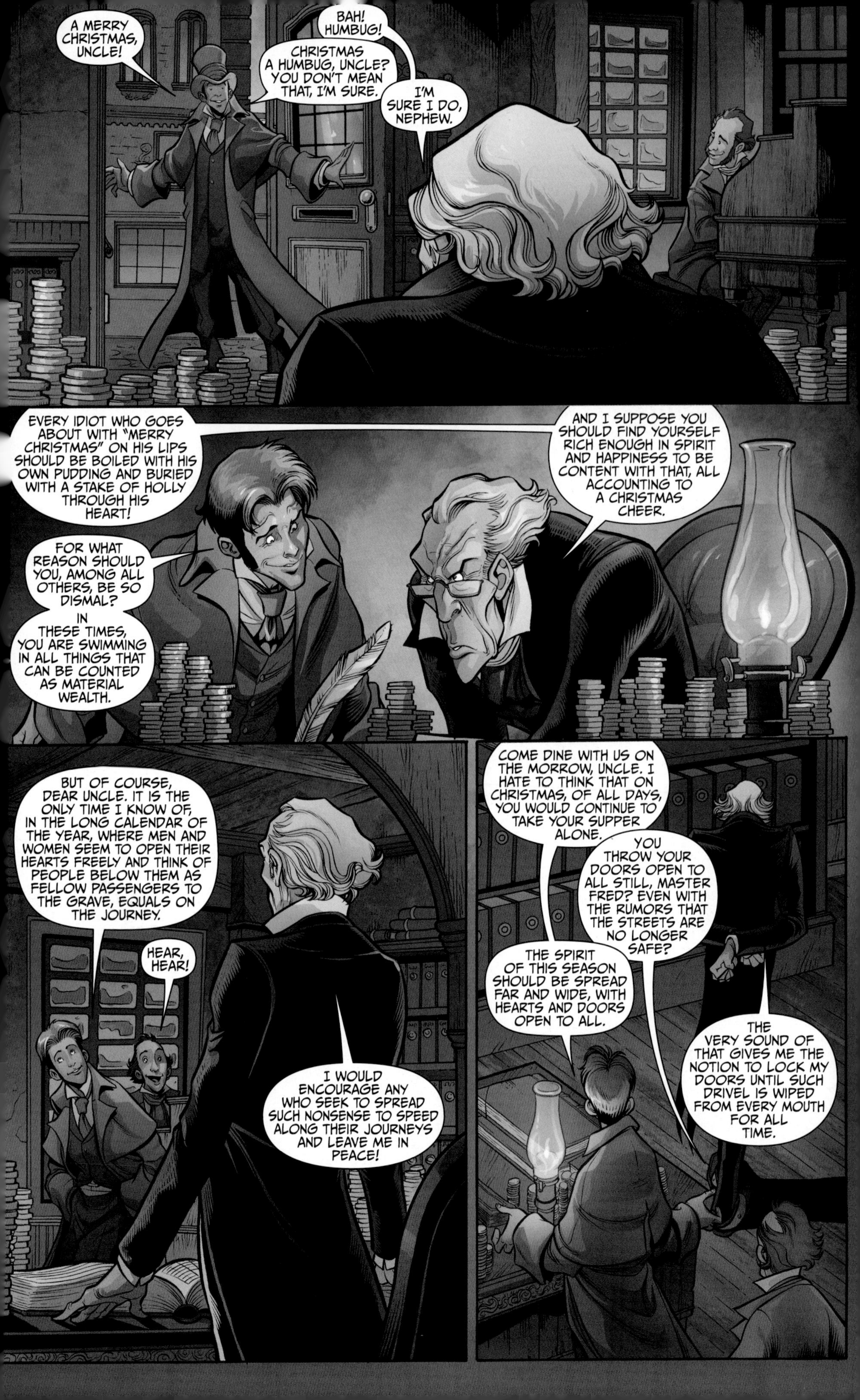
A MERRY CHRISTMAS, UNCLE!
BAH! HUMBUG!
CHRISTMAS A HUMBUG, UNCLE? YOU DON'T MEAN THAT, I'M SURE.
I'M SURE I DO, NEPHEW.
EVERY IDIOT WHO GOES ABOUT WITH "MERRY CHRISTMAS" ON HIS LIPS SHOULD BE BOILED WITH HIS OWN PUDDING AND BURIED WITH A STAKE OF HOLLY THROUGH HIS HEART!
FOR WHAT REASON SHOULD YOU, AMONG ALL OTHERS, BE SO DISMAL?
IN THESE TIMES, YOU ARE SWIMMING IN ALL THINGS THAT CAN BE COUNTED AS MATERIAL WEALTH.
AND I SUPPOSE YOU SHOULD FIND YOURSELF RICH ENOUGH IN SPIRIT AND HAPPINESS TO BE CONTENT WITH THAT, ALL ACCOUNTING TO A CHRISTMAS CHEER.
BUT OF COURSE, DEAR UNCLE. IT IS THE ONLY TIME I KNOW OF, IN THE LONG CALENDAR OF THE YEAR, WHERE MEN AND WOMEN SEEM TO OPEN THEIR HEARTS FREELY AND THINK OF PEOPLE BELOW THEM AS FELLOW PASSENGERS TO THE GRAVE, EQUALS ON THE JOURNEY.
HEAR, HEAR!
I WOULD ENCOURAGE ANY WHO SEEK TO SPREAD SUCH NONSENSE TO SPEED ALONG THEIR JOURNEYS AND LEAVE ME IN PEACE!
COME DINE WITH US ON THE MORROW, UNCLE. I HATE TO THINK THAT ON CHRISTMAS, OF ALL DAYS, YOU WOULD CONTINUE TO TAKE YOUR SUPPER ALONE.
YOU THROW YOUR DOORS OPEN TO ALL STILL, MASTER FRED? EVEN WITH THE RUMORS THAT THE STREETS ARE NO LONGER SAFE?
THE SPIRIT OF THIS SEASON SHOULD BE SPREAD FAR AND WIDE, WITH HEARTS AND DOORS OPEN TO ALL.
THE VERY SOUND OF THAT GIVES ME THE NOTION TO LOCK MY DOORS UNTIL SUCH DRIVEL IS WIPED FROM EVERY MOUTH FOR ALL TIME.

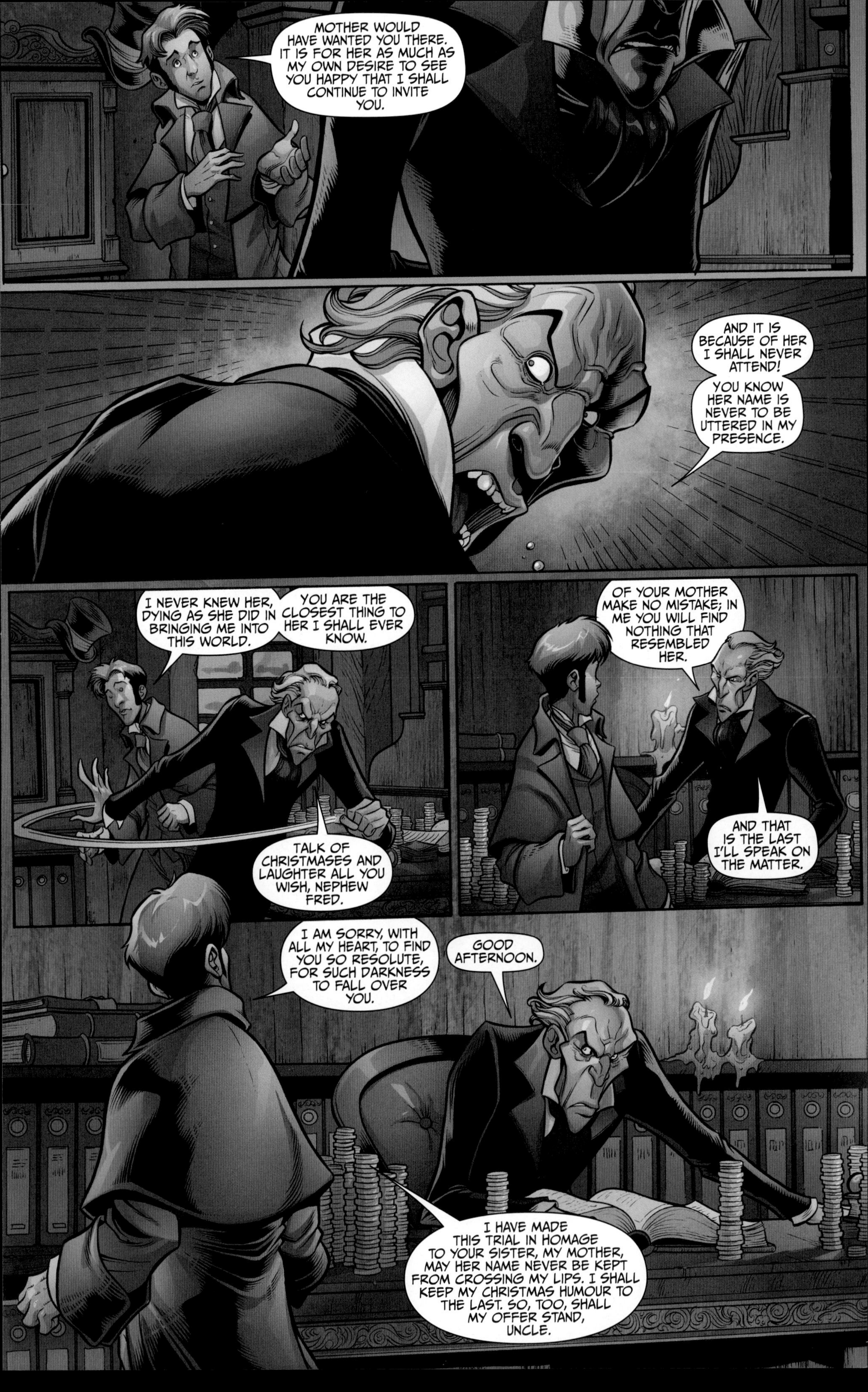
MOTHER WOULD HAVE WANTED YOU THERE. IT IS FOR HER AS MUCH AS MY OWN DESIRE TO SEE YOU HAPPY THAT I SHALL CONTINUE TO INVITE YOU.
AND IT IS BECAUSE OF HER I SHALL NEVER ATTEND!
YOU KNOW HER NAME IS NEVER TO BE UTTERED IN MY PRESENCE.
I NEVER KNEW HER, DYING AS SHE DID IN BRINGING ME INTO THIS WORLD.
YOU ARE THE CLOSEST THING TO HER I SHALL EVER KNOW.
TALK OF CHRISTMASES AND LAUGHTER ALL YOU WISH, NEPHEW FRED.
OF YOUR MOTHER MAKE NO MISTAKE; IN ME YOU WILL FIND NOTHING THAT RESEMBLED HER.
AND THAT IS THE LAST I'LL SPEAK ON THE MATTER.
I AM SORRY, WITH ALL MY HEART, TO FIND YOU SO RESOLUTE, FOR SUCH DARKNESS TO FALL OVER YOU.
GOOD AFTERNOON.
I HAVE MADE THIS TRIAL IN HOMAGE TO YOUR SISTER, MY MOTHER, MAY HER NAME NEVER BE KEPT FROM CROSSING MY LIPS. I SHALL KEEP MY CHRISTMAS HUMOUR TO THE LAST. SO, TOO, SHALL MY OFFER STAND, UNCLE.

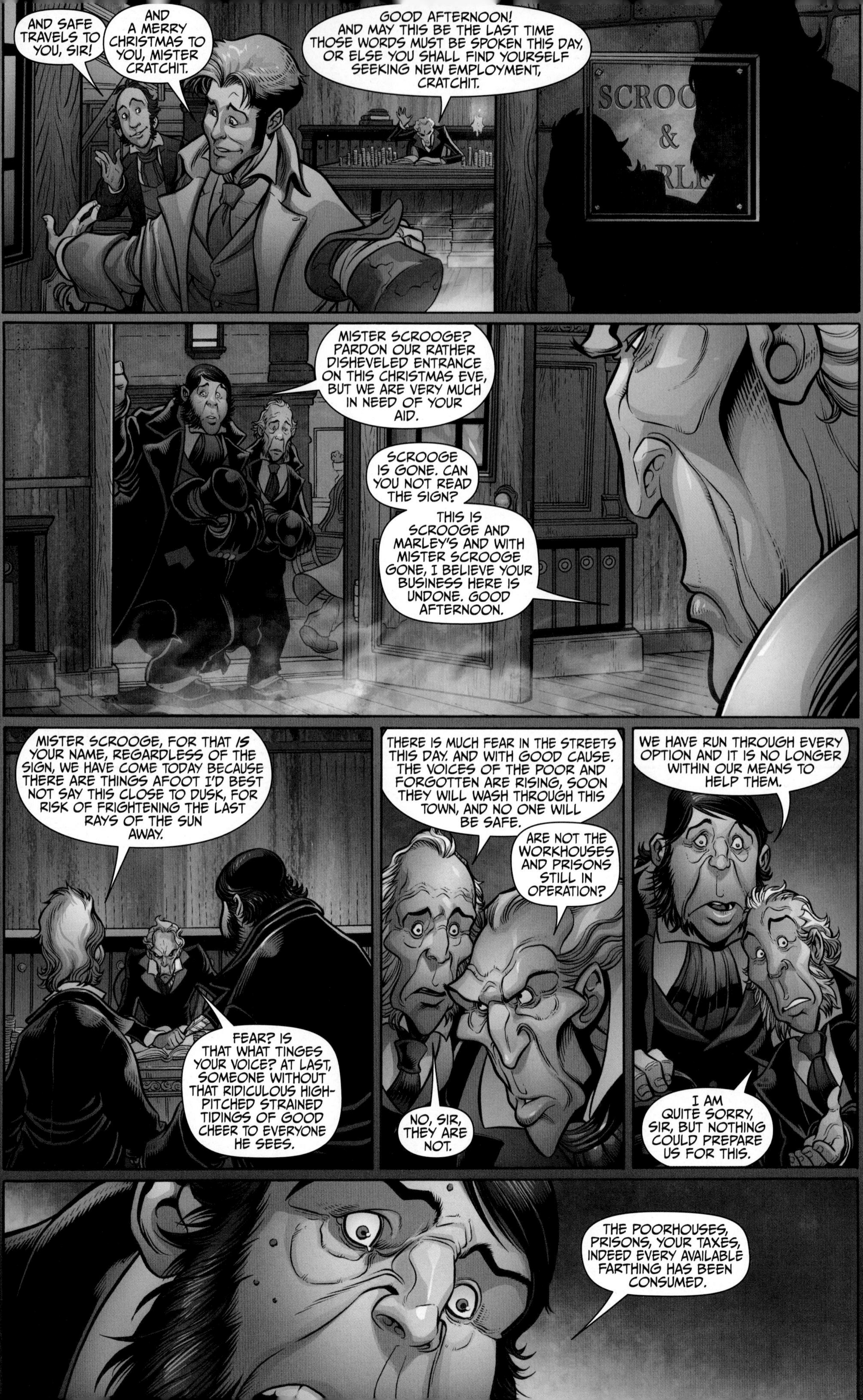
AND SAFE TRAVELS TO YOU, SIR!
AND A MERRY CHRISTMAS TO YOU, MISTER CRATCHIT.
GOOD AFTERNOON! AND MAY THIS BE THE LAST TIME THOSE WORDS MUST BE SPOKEN THIS DAY, OR ELSE YOU SHALL FIND YOURSELF SEEKING NEW EMPLOYMENT, CRATCHIT.
SCROO
&
ARLE
MISTER SCROOGE? PARDON OUR RATHER DISHEVELED ENTRANCE ON THIS CHRISTMAS EVE, BUT WE ARE VERY MUCH IN NEED OF YOUR AID.
SCROOGE IS GONE. CAN YOU NOT READ THE SIGN?
THIS IS SCROOGE AND MARLEY'S AND WITH MISTER SCROOGE GONE, I BELIEVE YOUR BUSINESS HERE IS UNDONE. GOOD AFTERNOON.
MISTER SCROOGE, FOR THAT *IS* YOUR NAME, REGARDLESS OF THE SIGN, WE HAVE COME TODAY BECAUSE THERE ARE THINGS AFOOT I'D BEST NOT SAY THIS CLOSE TO DUSK, FOR RISK OF FRIGHTENING THE LAST RAYS OF THE SUN AWAY.
FEAR? IS THAT WHAT TINGES YOUR VOICE? AT LAST, SOMEONE WITHOUT THAT RIDICULOUS HIGH-PITCHED STRAINED TIDINGS OF GOOD CHEER TO EVERYONE HE SEES.
THERE IS MUCH FEAR IN THE STREETS THIS DAY. AND WITH GOOD CAUSE. THE VOICES OF THE POOR AND FORGOTTEN ARE RISING, SOON THEY WILL WASH THROUGH THIS TOWN, AND NO ONE WILL BE SAFE.
ARE NOT THE WORKHOUSES AND PRISONS STILL IN OPERATION?
NO, SIR, THEY ARE NOT.
WE HAVE RUN THROUGH EVERY OPTION AND IT IS NO LONGER WITHIN OUR MEANS TO HELP THEM.
I AM QUITE SORRY, SIR, BUT NOTHING COULD PREPARE US FOR THIS.
THE POORHOUSES, PRISONS, YOUR TAXES, INDEED EVERY AVAILABLE FARTHING HAS BEEN CONSUMED.

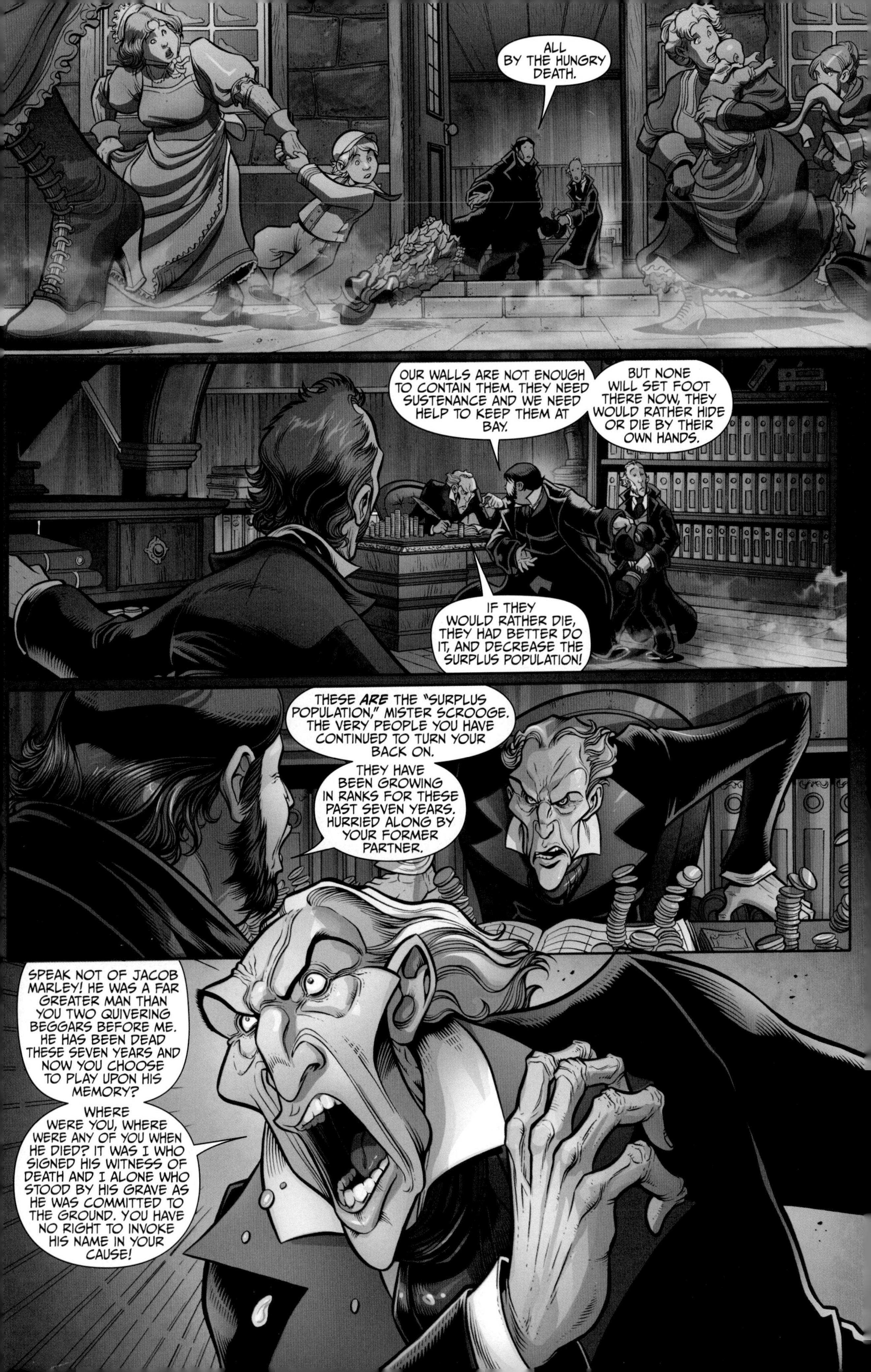
ALL BY THE HUNGRY DEATH.
OUR WALLS ARE NOT ENOUGH TO CONTAIN THEM. THEY NEED SUSTENANCE AND WE NEED HELP TO KEEP THEM AT BAY.
BUT NONE WILL SET FOOT THERE NOW, THEY WOULD RATHER HIDE OR DIE BY THEIR OWN HANDS.
IF THEY WOULD RATHER DIE, THEY HAD BETTER DO IT, AND DECREASE THE SURPLUS POPULATION!
THESE ARE THE "SURPLUS POPULATION," MISTER SCROOGE. THE VERY PEOPLE YOU HAVE CONTINUED TO TURN YOUR BACK ON.
THEY HAVE BEEN GROWING IN RANKS FOR THESE PAST SEVEN YEARS. HURRIED ALONG BY YOUR FORMER PARTNER.
SPEAK NOT OF JACOB MARLEY! HE WAS A FAR GREATER MAN THAN YOU TWO QUIVERING BEGGARS BEFORE ME. HE HAS BEEN DEAD THESE SEVEN YEARS AND NOW YOU CHOOSE TO PLAY UPON HIS MEMORY?
WHERE WERE YOU, WHERE WERE ANY OF YOU WHEN HE DIED? IT WAS I WHO SIGNED HIS WITNESS OF DEATH AND I ALONE WHO STOOD BY HIS GRAVE AS HE WAS COMMITTED TO THE GROUND. YOU HAVE NO RIGHT TO INVOKE HIS NAME IN YOUR CAUSE!

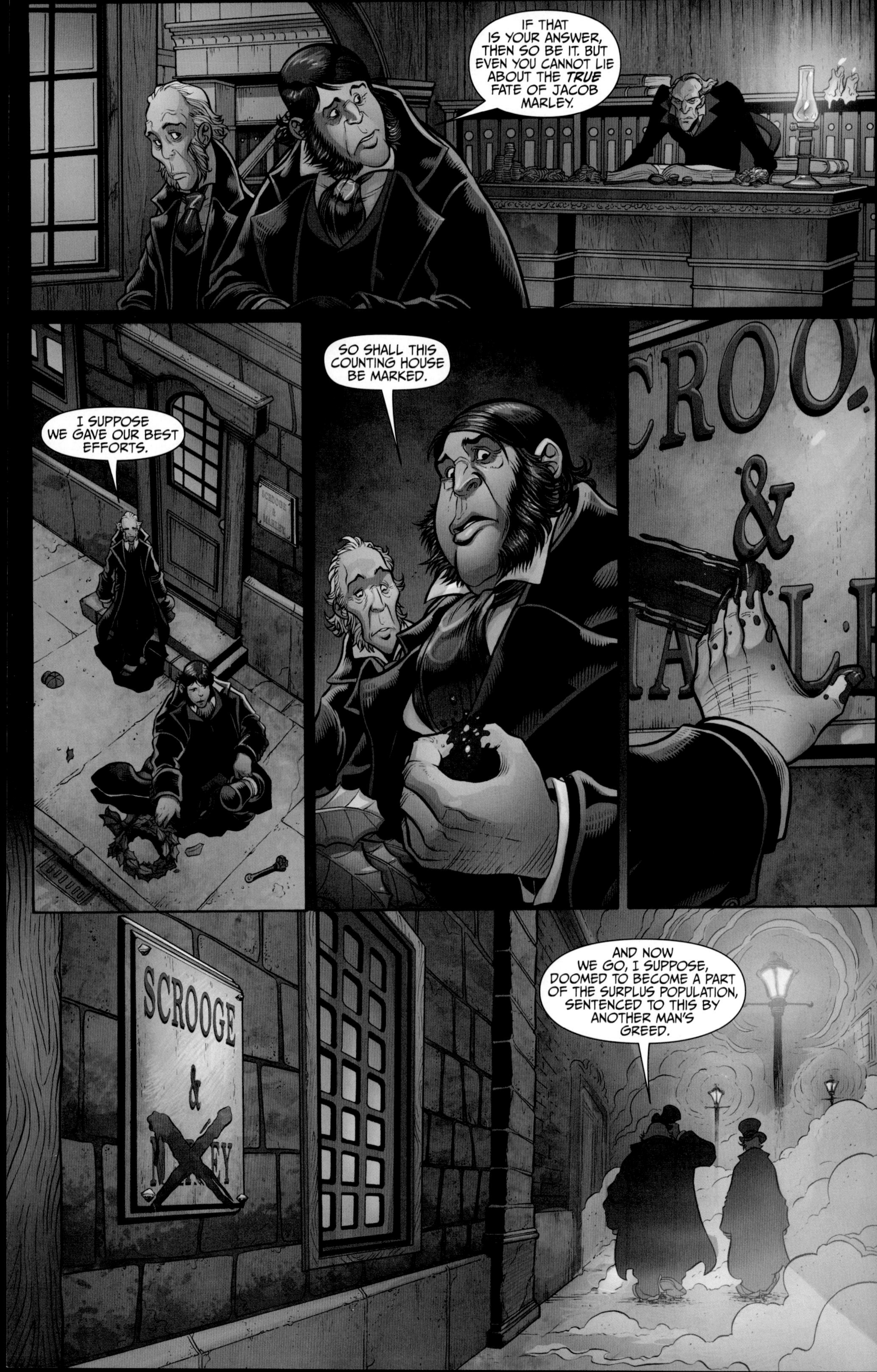
IF THAT IS YOUR ANSWER, THEN SO BE IT. BUT EVEN YOU CANNOT LIE ABOUT THE *TRUE* FATE OF JACOB MARLEY.
I SUPPOSE WE GAVE OUR BEST EFFORTS.
SO SHALL THIS COUNTING HOUSE BE MARKED.
SCROOGE & MARLEY
AND NOW WE GO, I SUPPOSE, DOOMED TO BECOME A PART OF THE SURPLUS POPULATION, SENTENCED TO THIS BY ANOTHER MAN'S GREED.

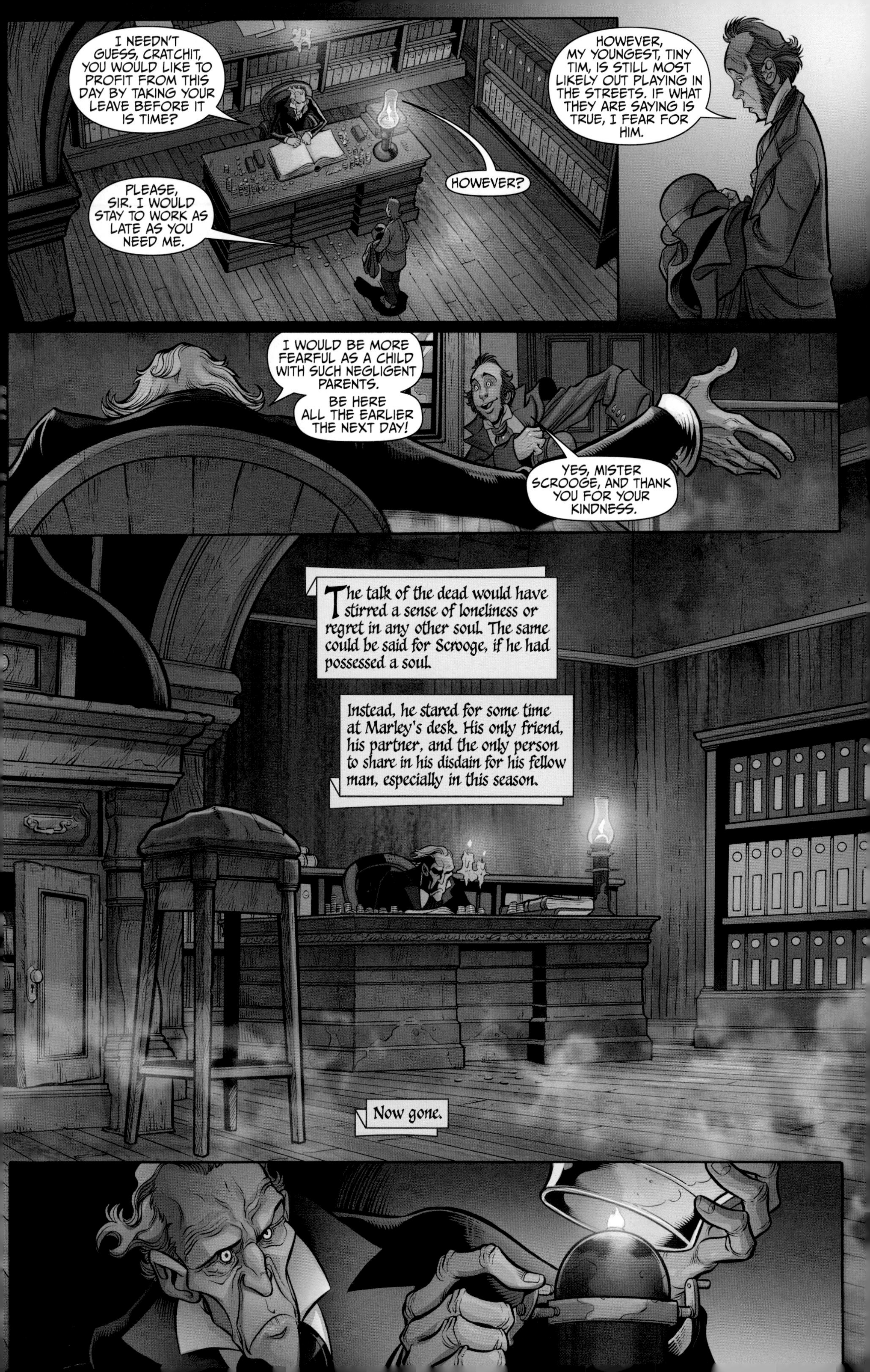
I NEEDN'T GUESS, CRATCHIT, YOU WOULD LIKE TO PROFIT FROM THIS DAY BY TAKING YOUR LEAVE BEFORE IT IS TIME?
PLEASE, SIR. I WOULD STAY TO WORK AS LATE AS YOU NEED ME.
HOWEVER?
HOWEVER, MY YOUNGEST, TINY TIM, IS STILL MOST LIKELY OUT PLAYING IN THE STREETS. IF WHAT THEY ARE SAYING IS TRUE, I FEAR FOR HIM.
I WOULD BE MORE FEARFUL AS A CHILD WITH SUCH NEGLIGENT PARENTS.
BE HERE ALL THE EARLIER THE NEXT DAY!
YES, MISTER SCROOGE, AND THANK YOU FOR YOUR KINDNESS.
The talk of the dead would have stirred a sense of loneliness or regret in any other soul. The same could be said for Scrooge, if he had possessed a soul.
Instead, he stared for some time at Marley's desk. His only friend, his partner, and the only person to share in his disdain for his fellow man, especially in this season.
Now gone.

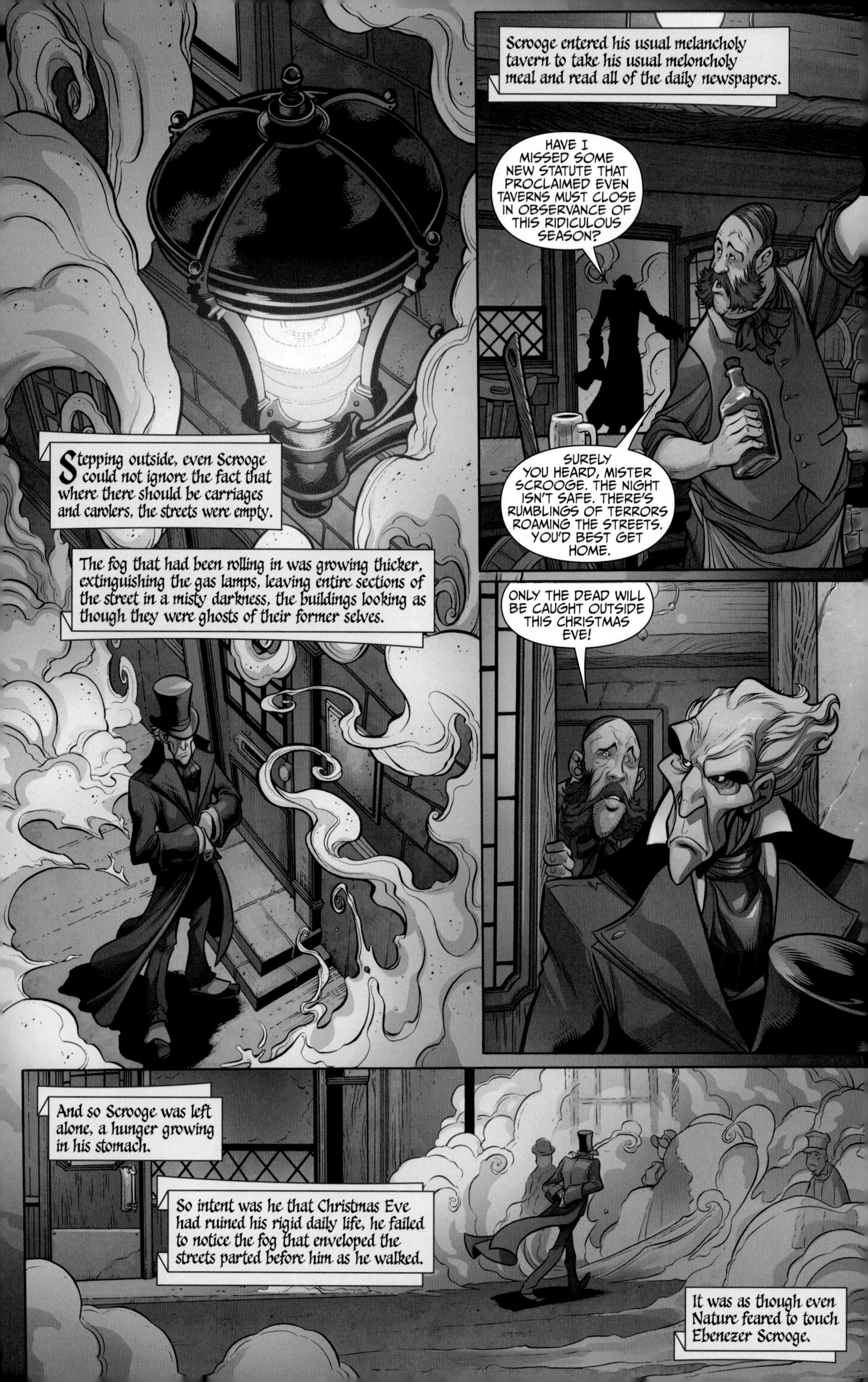
Stepping outside, even Scrooge could not ignore the fact that where there should be carriages and carolers, the streets were empty.
The fog that had been rolling in was growing thicker, extinguishing the gas lamps, leaving entire sections of the street in a misty darkness, the buildings looking as though they were ghosts of their former selves.
Scrooge entered his usual melancholy tavern to take his usual meloncholy meal and read all of the daily newspapers.
HAVE I MISSED SOME NEW STATUTE THAT PROCLAIMED EVEN TAVERNS MUST CLOSE IN OBSERVANCE OF THIS RIDICULOUS SEASON?
SURELY YOU HEARD, MISTER SCROOGE. THE NIGHT ISN'T SAFE. THERE'S RUMBLINGS OF TERRORS ROAMING THE STREETS. YOU'D BEST GET HOME.
ONLY THE DEAD WILL BE CAUGHT OUTSIDE THIS CHRISTMAS EVE!
And so Scrooge was left alone, a hunger growing in his stomach.
So intent was he that Christmas Eve had ruined his rigid daily life, he failed to notice the fog that enveloped the streets parted before him as he walked.
It was as though even Nature feared to touch Ebenezer Scrooge.

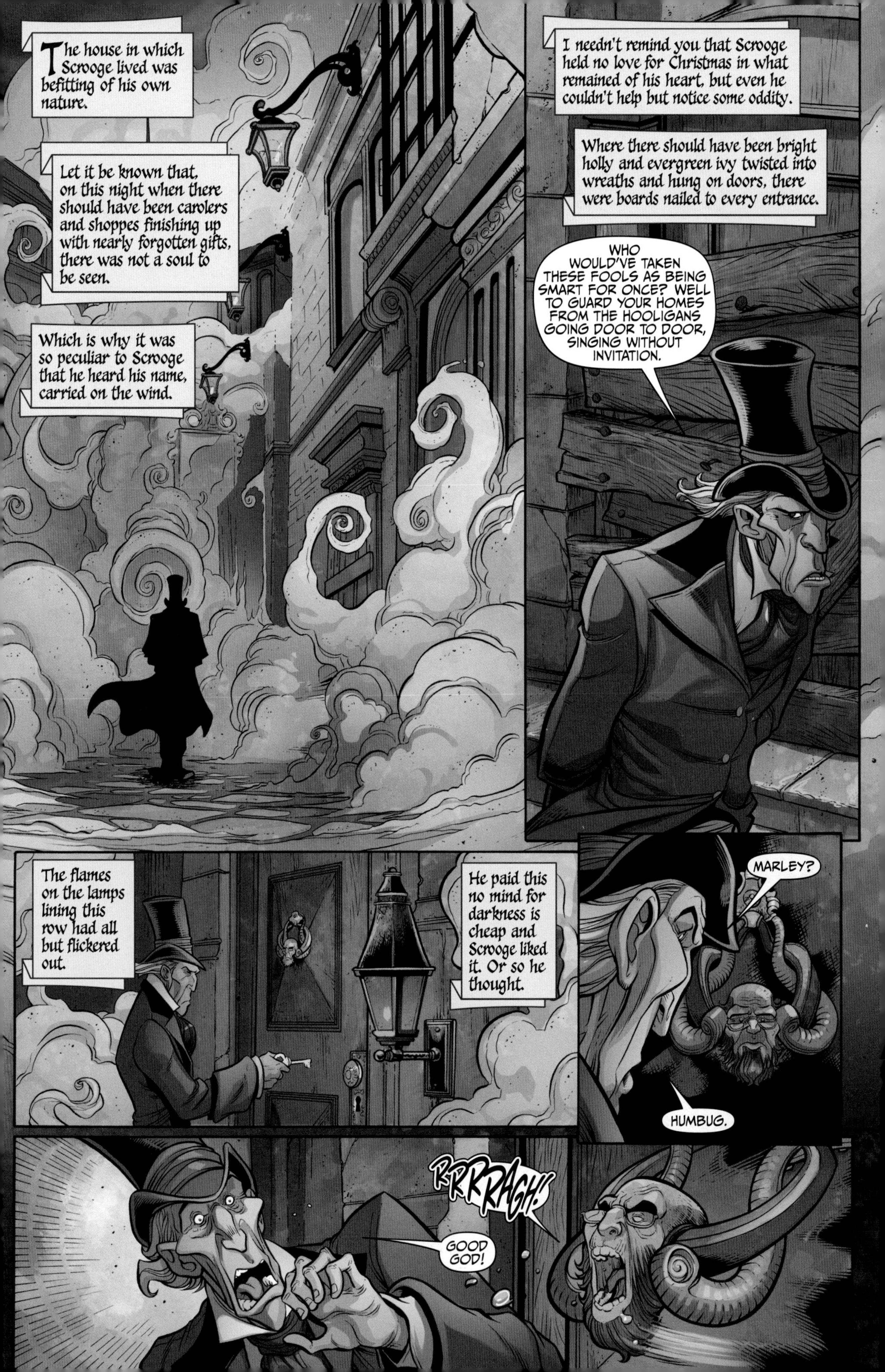
The house in which Scrooge lived was befitting of his own nature.
Let it be known that, on this night when there should have been carolers and shoppes finishing up with nearly forgotten gifts, there was not a soul to be seen.
Which is why it was so peculiar to Scrooge that he heard his name, carried on the wind.
I needn't remind you that Scrooge held no love for Christmas in what remained of his heart, but even he couldn't help but notice some oddity.
Where there should have been bright holly and evergreen ivy twisted into wreaths and hung on doors, there were boards nailed to every entrance.
WHO WOULD'VE TAKEN THESE FOOLS AS BEING SMART FOR ONCE? WELL TO GUARD YOUR HOMES FROM THE HOOLIGANS GOING DOOR TO DOOR, SINGING WITHOUT INVITATION.
The flames on the lamps lining this row had all but flickered out.
He paid this no mind for darkness is cheap and Scrooge liked it. Or so he thought.
MARLEY?
HUMBUG.
RRRRAGH!
GOOD GOD!

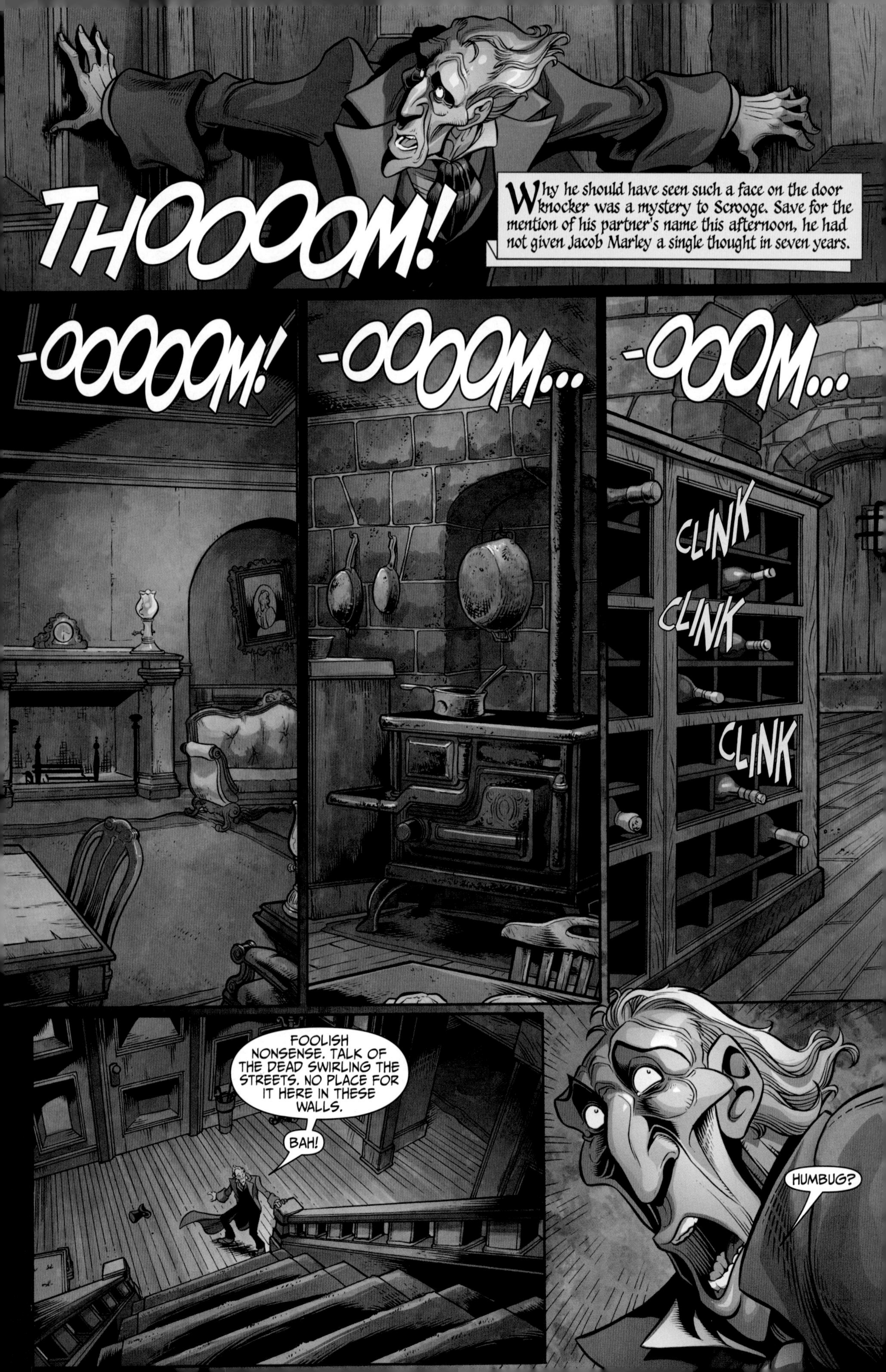
THOOOOM!
Why he should have seen such a face on the door knocker was a mystery to Scrooge. Save for the mention of his partner's name this afternoon, he had not given Jacob Marley a single thought in seven years.
-OOOOOM!
-OOOOM...
-OOOM...
CLINK
CLINK
CLINK
FOOLISH NONSENSE. TALK OF THE DEAD SWIRLING THE STREETS. NO PLACE FOR IT HERE IN THESE WALLS.
BAH!
HUMBUG?

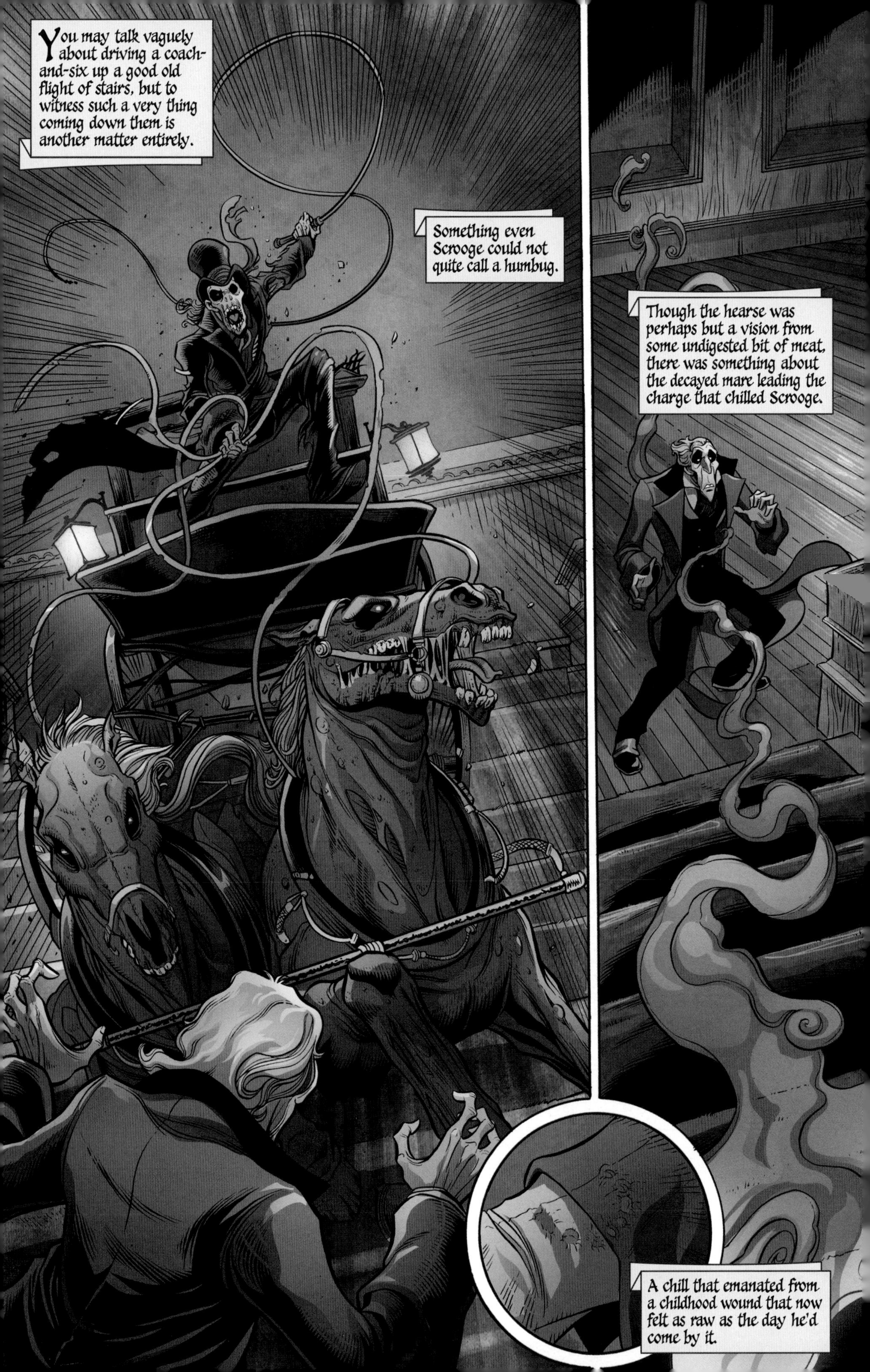
You may talk vaguely about driving a coach-and-six up a good old flight of stairs, but to witness such a very thing coming down them is another matter entirely.
Something even Scrooge could not quite call a humbug.
Though the hearse was perhaps but a vision from some undigested bit of meat, there was something about the decayed mare leading the charge that chilled Scrooge.
A chill that emanated from a childhood wound that now felt as raw as the day he'd come by it.

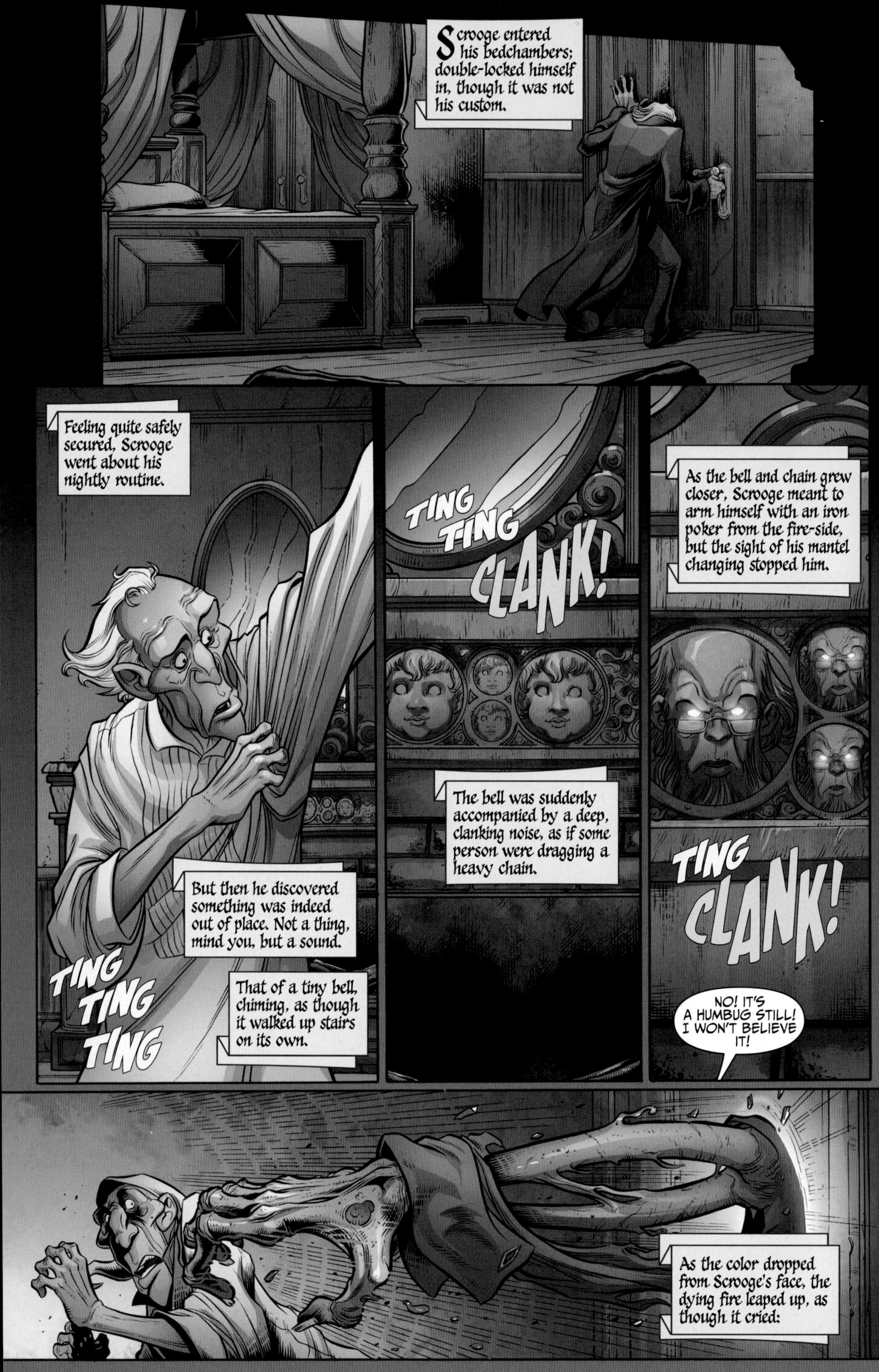
Scrooge entered his bedchambers; double-locked himself in, though it was not his custom.
Feeling quite safely secured, Scrooge went about his nightly routine.
But then he discovered something was indeed out of place. Not a thing, mind you, but a sound.
That of a tiny bell, chiming, as though it walked up stairs on its own.
TING TING TING
TING TING CLANK!
The bell was suddenly accompanied by a deep, clanking noise, as if some person were dragging a heavy chain.
As the bell and chain grew closer, Scrooge meant to arm himself with an iron poker from the fire-side, but the sight of his mantel changing stopped him.
TING CLANK!
NO! IT'S A HUMBUG STILL! I WON'T BELIEVE IT!
As the color dropped from Scrooge's face, the dying fire leaped up, as though it cried:

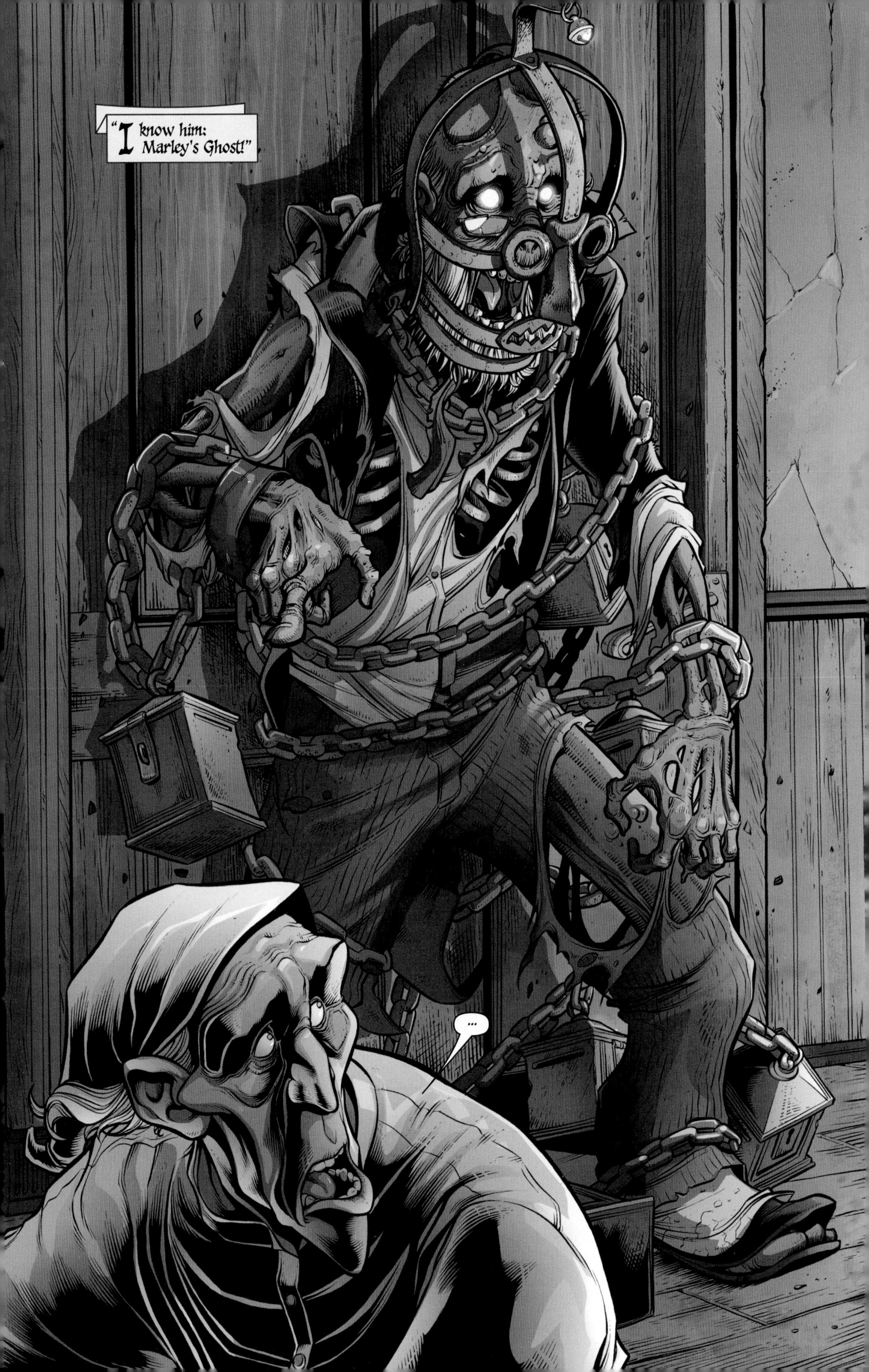
"I know him: Marley's Ghost!"
...

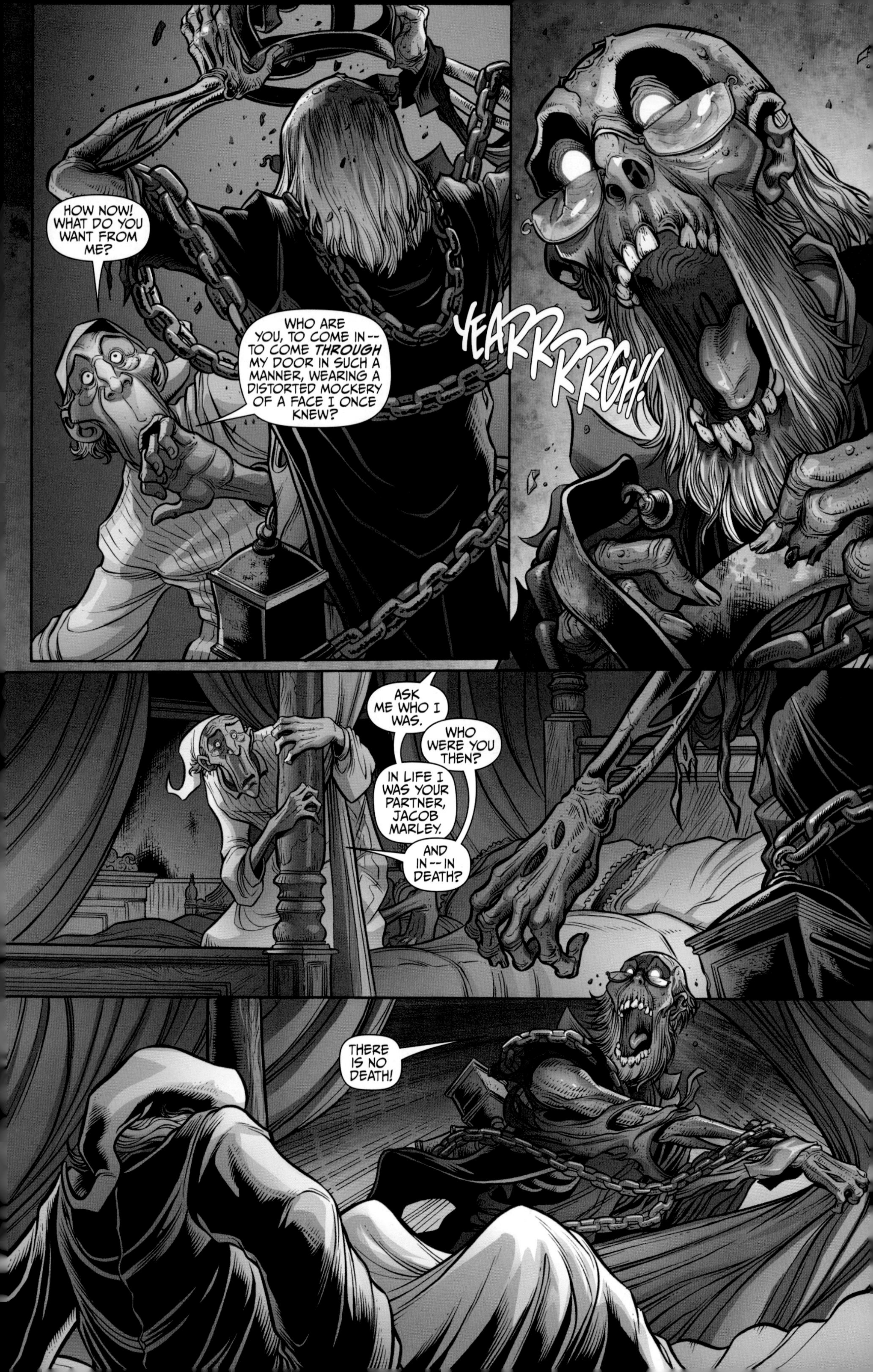
HOW NOW! WHAT DO YOU WANT FROM ME?
WHO ARE YOU, TO COME IN-- TO COME *THROUGH* MY DOOR IN SUCH A MANNER, WEARING A DISTORTED MOCKERY OF A FACE I ONCE KNEW?
YEARRRRGH!
ASK ME WHO I WAS.
WHO WERE YOU THEN?
IN LIFE I WAS YOUR PARTNER, JACOB MARLEY.
AND IN--IN DEATH?
THERE IS NO DEATH!

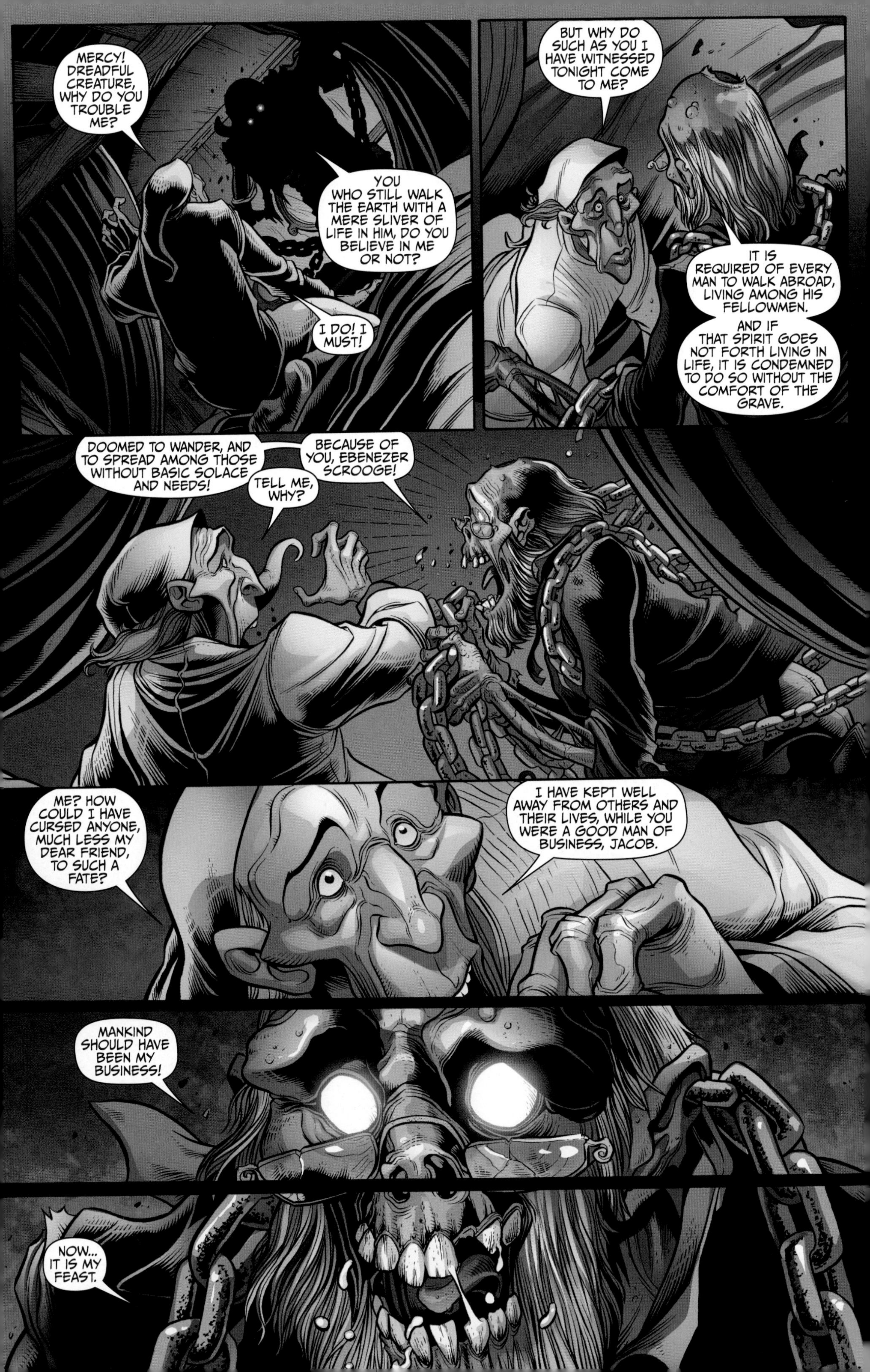
MERCY! DREADFUL CREATURE, WHY DO YOU TROUBLE ME?
YOU WHO STILL WALK THE EARTH WITH A MERE SLIVER OF LIFE IN HIM, DO YOU BELIEVE IN ME OR NOT?
I DO! I MUST!
BUT WHY DO SUCH AS YOU I HAVE WITNESSED TONIGHT COME TO ME?
IT IS REQUIRED OF EVERY MAN TO WALK ABROAD, LIVING AMONG HIS FELLOWMEN.
AND IF THAT SPIRIT GOES NOT FORTH LIVING IN LIFE, IT IS CONDEMNED TO DO SO WITHOUT THE COMFORT OF THE GRAVE.
DOOMED TO WANDER, AND TO SPREAD AMONG THOSE WITHOUT BASIC SOLACE AND NEEDS!
BECAUSE OF YOU, EBENEZER SCROOGE!
TELL ME, WHY?
ME? HOW COULD I HAVE CURSED ANYONE, MUCH LESS MY DEAR FRIEND, TO SUCH A FATE?
I HAVE KEPT WELL AWAY FROM OTHERS AND THEIR LIVES, WHILE YOU WERE A GOOD MAN OF BUSINESS, JACOB.
MANKIND SHOULD HAVE BEEN MY BUSINESS!
NOW... IT IS MY FEAST.

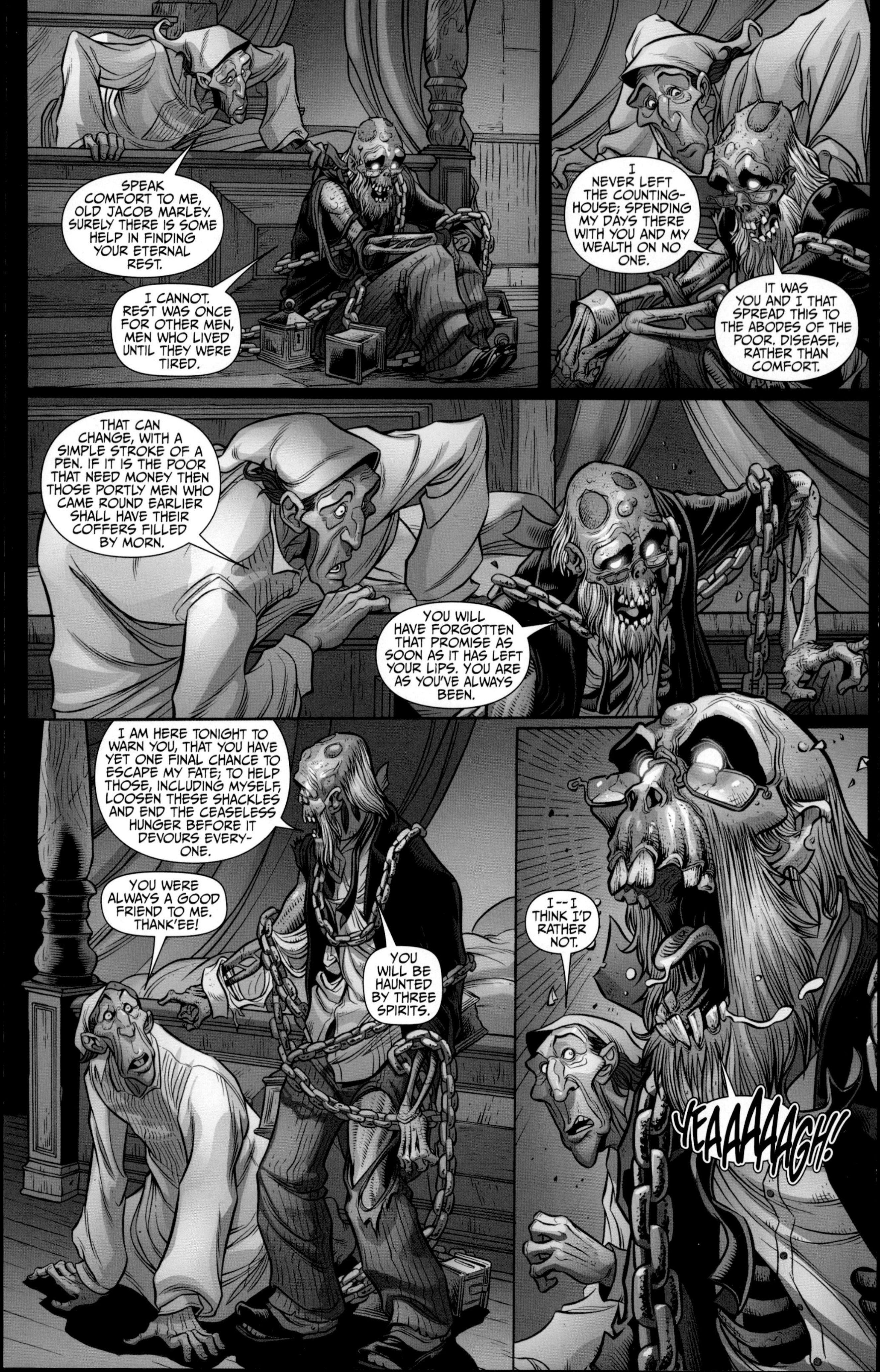
SPEAK COMFORT TO ME, OLD JACOB MARLEY. SURELY THERE IS SOME HELP IN FINDING YOUR ETERNAL REST.
I CANNOT. REST WAS ONCE FOR OTHER MEN, MEN WHO LIVED UNTIL THEY WERE TIRED.
I NEVER LEFT THE COUNTING-HOUSE; SPENDING MY DAYS THERE WITH YOU AND MY WEALTH ON NO ONE.
IT WAS YOU AND I THAT SPREAD THIS TO THE ABODES OF THE POOR. DISEASE, RATHER THAN COMFORT.
THAT CAN CHANGE, WITH A SIMPLE STROKE OF A PEN. IF IT IS THE POOR THAT NEED MONEY THEN THOSE PORTLY MEN WHO CAME ROUND EARLIER SHALL HAVE THEIR COFFERS FILLED BY MORN.
YOU WILL HAVE FORGOTTEN THAT PROMISE AS SOON AS IT HAS LEFT YOUR LIPS. YOU ARE AS YOU'VE ALWAYS BEEN.
I AM HERE TONIGHT TO WARN YOU, THAT YOU HAVE YET ONE FINAL CHANCE TO ESCAPE MY FATE; TO HELP THOSE, INCLUDING MYSELF, LOOSEN THESE SHACKLES AND END THE CEASELESS HUNGER BEFORE IT DEVOURS EVERY-ONE.
YOU WERE ALWAYS A GOOD FRIEND TO ME. THANK'EE!
YOU WILL BE HAUNTED BY THREE SPIRITS.
I--I THINK I'D RATHER NOT.
YEAAAAAGH!

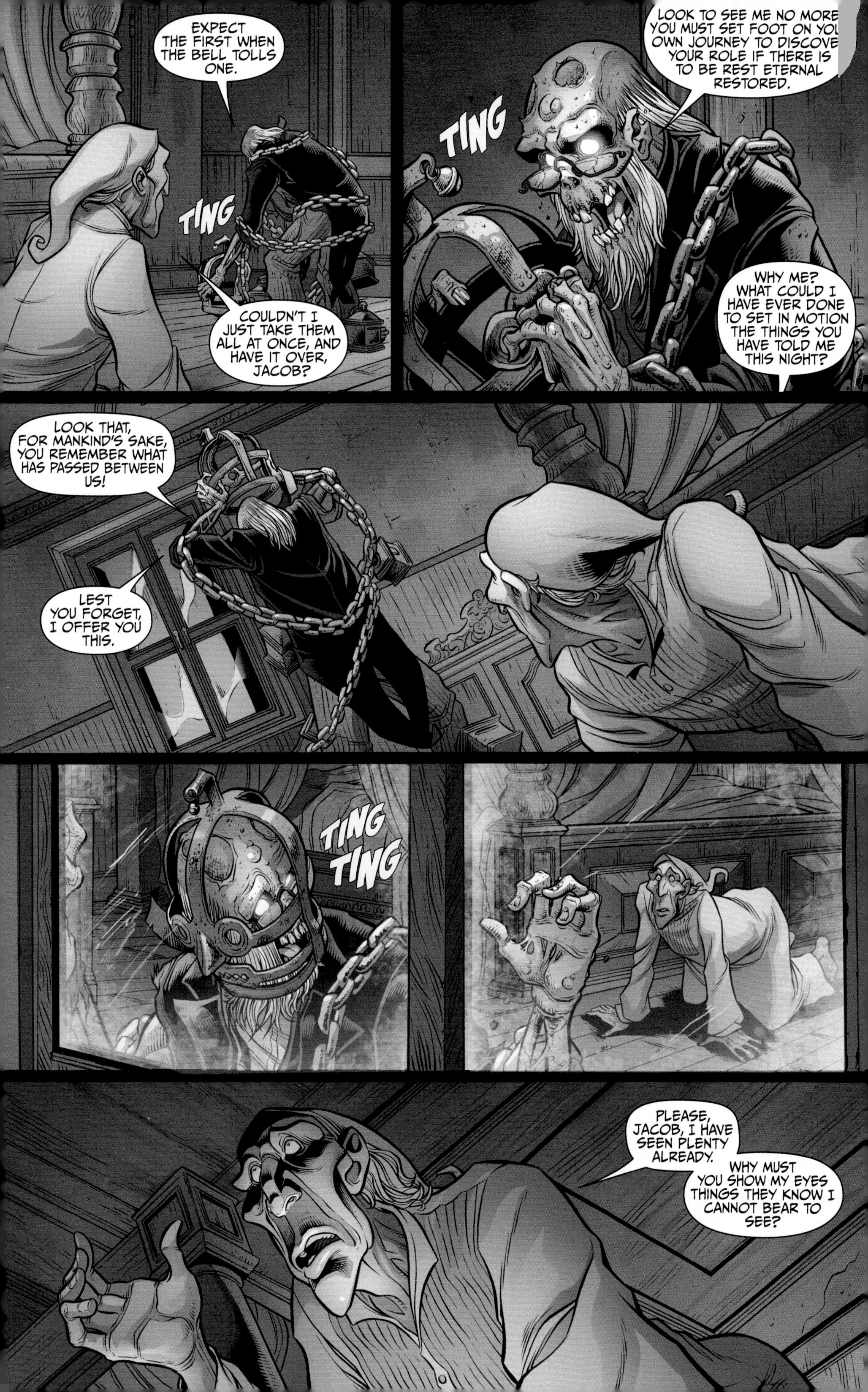
EXPECT THE FIRST WHEN THE BELL TOLLS ONE.
TING
COULDN'T I JUST TAKE THEM ALL AT ONCE, AND HAVE IT OVER, JACOB?
LOOK TO SEE ME NO MORE. YOU MUST SET FOOT ON YOUR OWN JOURNEY TO DISCOVER YOUR ROLE IF THERE IS TO BE REST ETERNAL RESTORED.
TING
WHY ME? WHAT COULD I HAVE EVER DONE TO SET IN MOTION THE THINGS YOU HAVE TOLD ME THIS NIGHT?
LOOK THAT, FOR MANKIND'S SAKE, YOU REMEMBER WHAT HAS PASSED BETWEEN US!
LEST YOU FORGET, I OFFER YOU THIS.
TING
TING
PLEASE, JACOB, I HAVE SEEN PLENTY ALREADY.
WHY MUST YOU SHOW MY EYES THINGS THEY KNOW I CANNOT BEAR TO SEE?

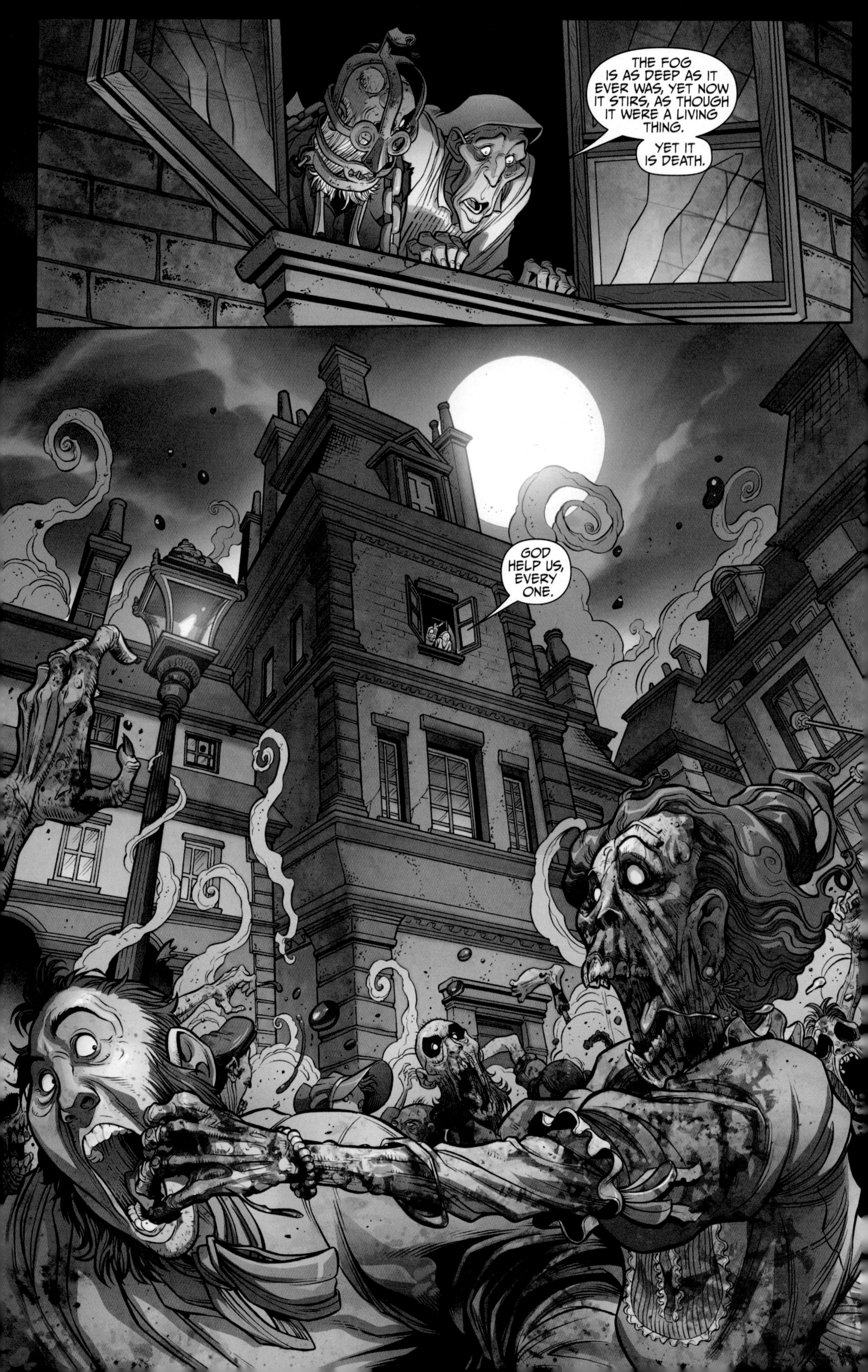
THE FOG IS AS DEEP AS IT EVER WAS, YET NOW IT STIRS, AS THOUGH IT WERE A LIVING THING.
YET IT IS DEATH.
GOD HELP US, EVERY ONE.

STAVE 2:

The Beginnings of the Hungry Death

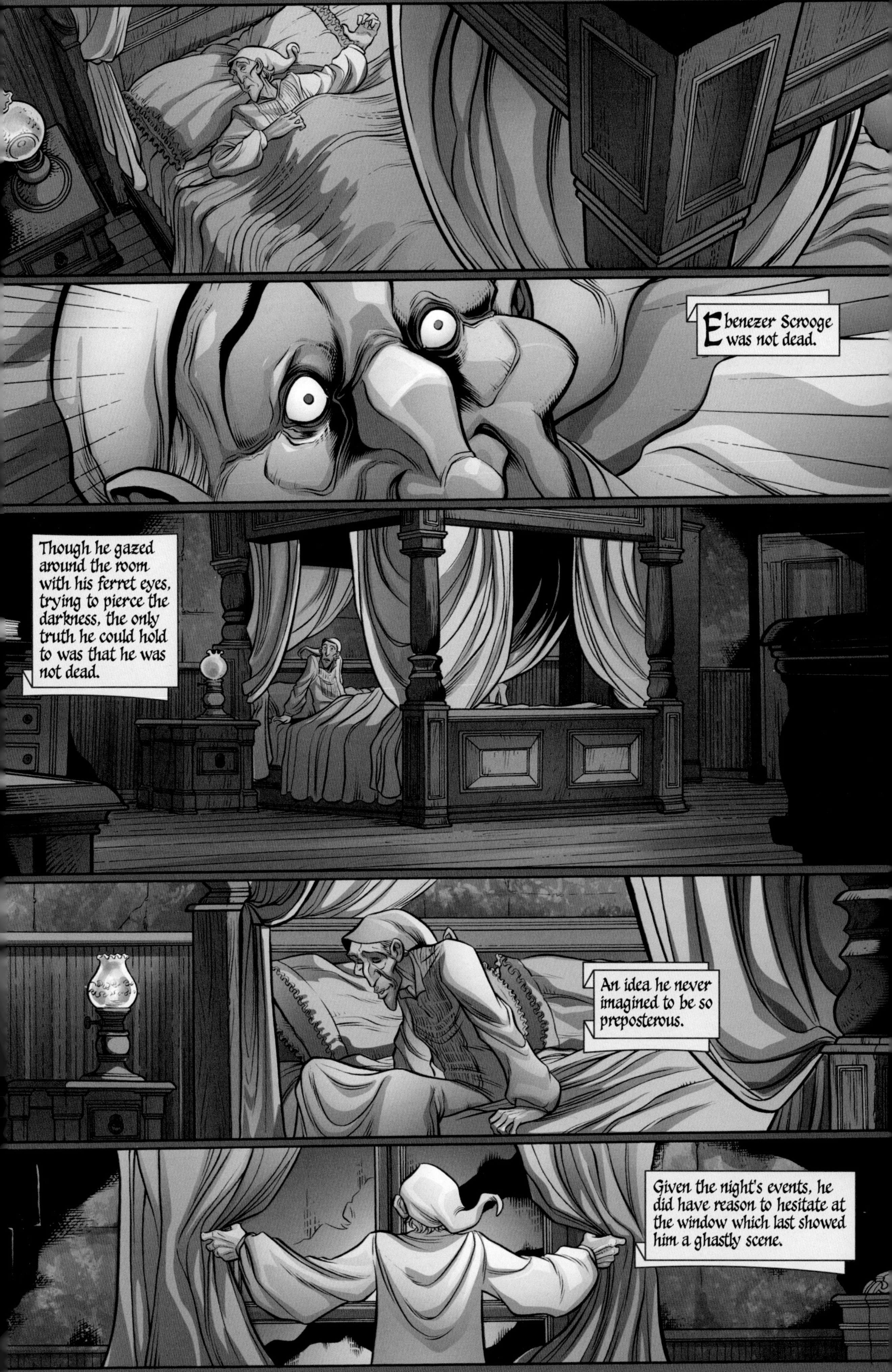
Ebenezer Scrooge was not dead.
Though he gazed around the room with his ferret eyes, trying to pierce the darkness, the only truth he could hold to was that he was not dead.
An idea he never imagined to be so preposterous.
Given the night's events, he did have reason to hesitate at the window which last showed him a ghastly scene.

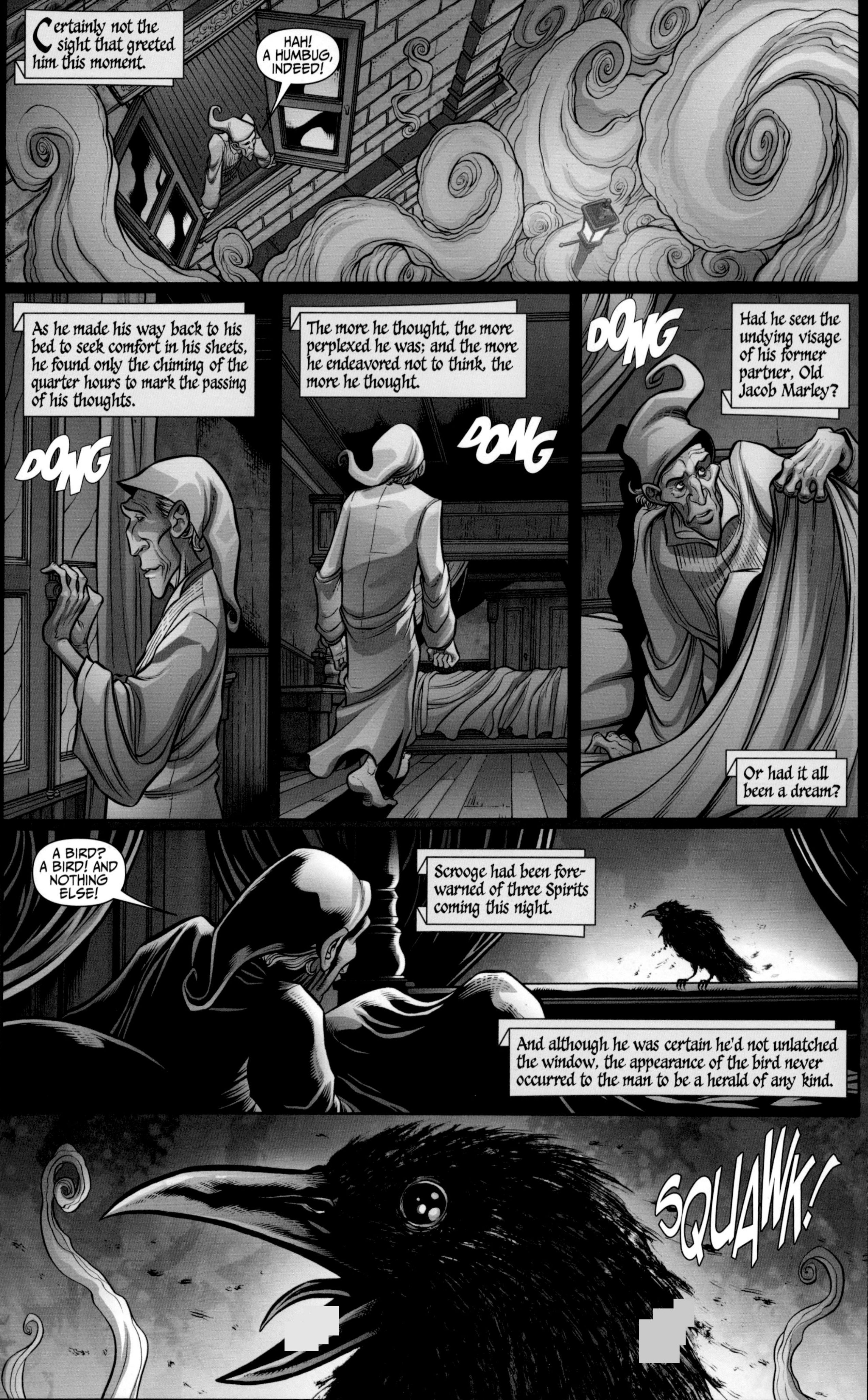
Certainly not the sight that greeted him this moment.
HAH! A HUMBUG, INDEED!
As he made his way back to his bed to seek comfort in his sheets, he found only the chiming of the quarter hours to mark the passing of his thoughts.
DONG
The more he thought, the more perplexed he was; and the more he endeavored not to think, the more he thought.
DONG
DONG
Had he seen the undying visage of his former partner, Old Jacob Marley?
Or had it all been a dream?
A BIRD? A BIRD! AND NOTHING ELSE!
Scrooge had been fore-warned of three Spirits coming this night.
And although he was certain he'd not unlatched the window, the appearance of the bird never occurred to the man to be a herald of any kind.
SQUAWK!

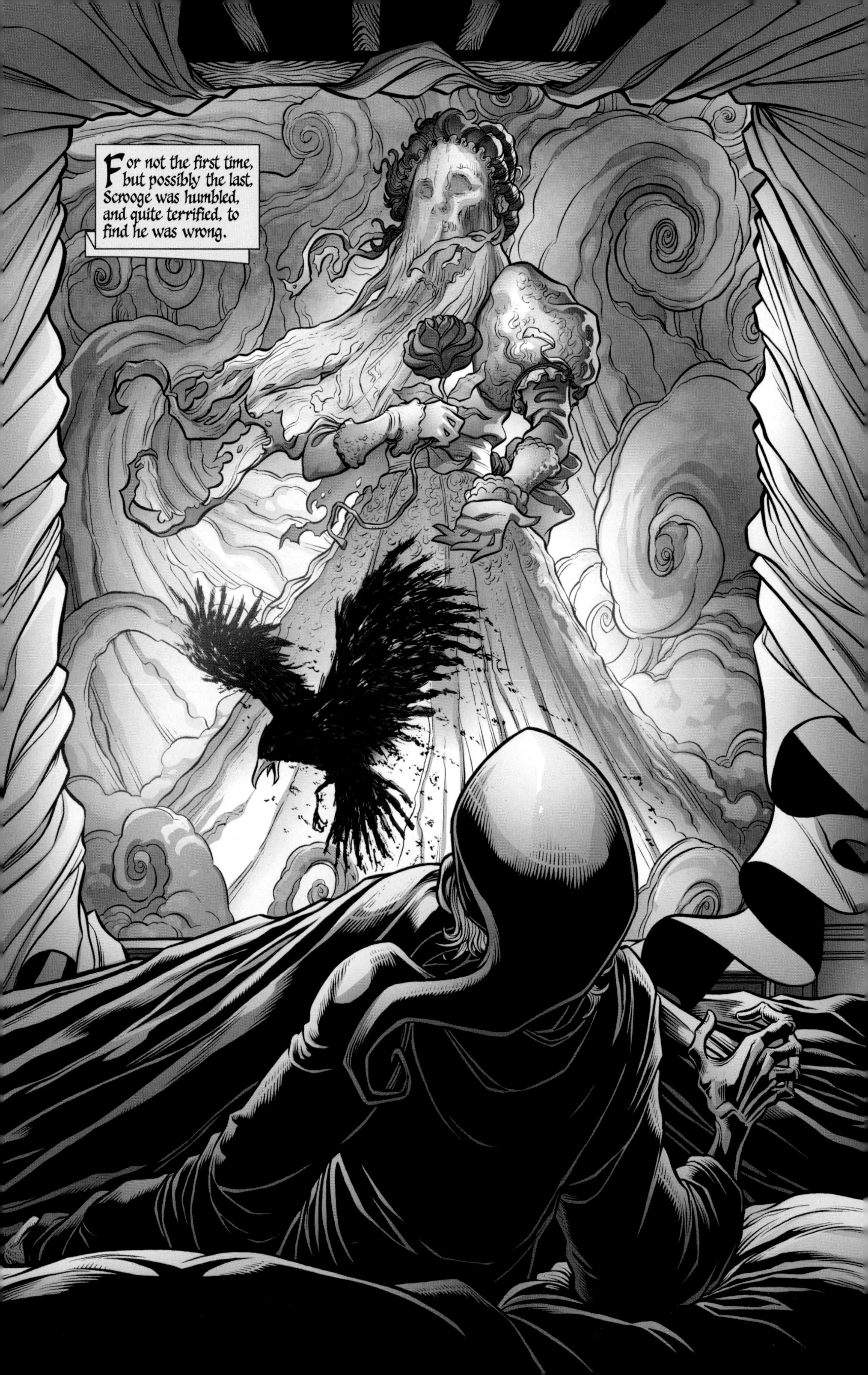
For not the first time, but possibly the last, Scrooge was humbled, and quite terrified, to find he was wrong.

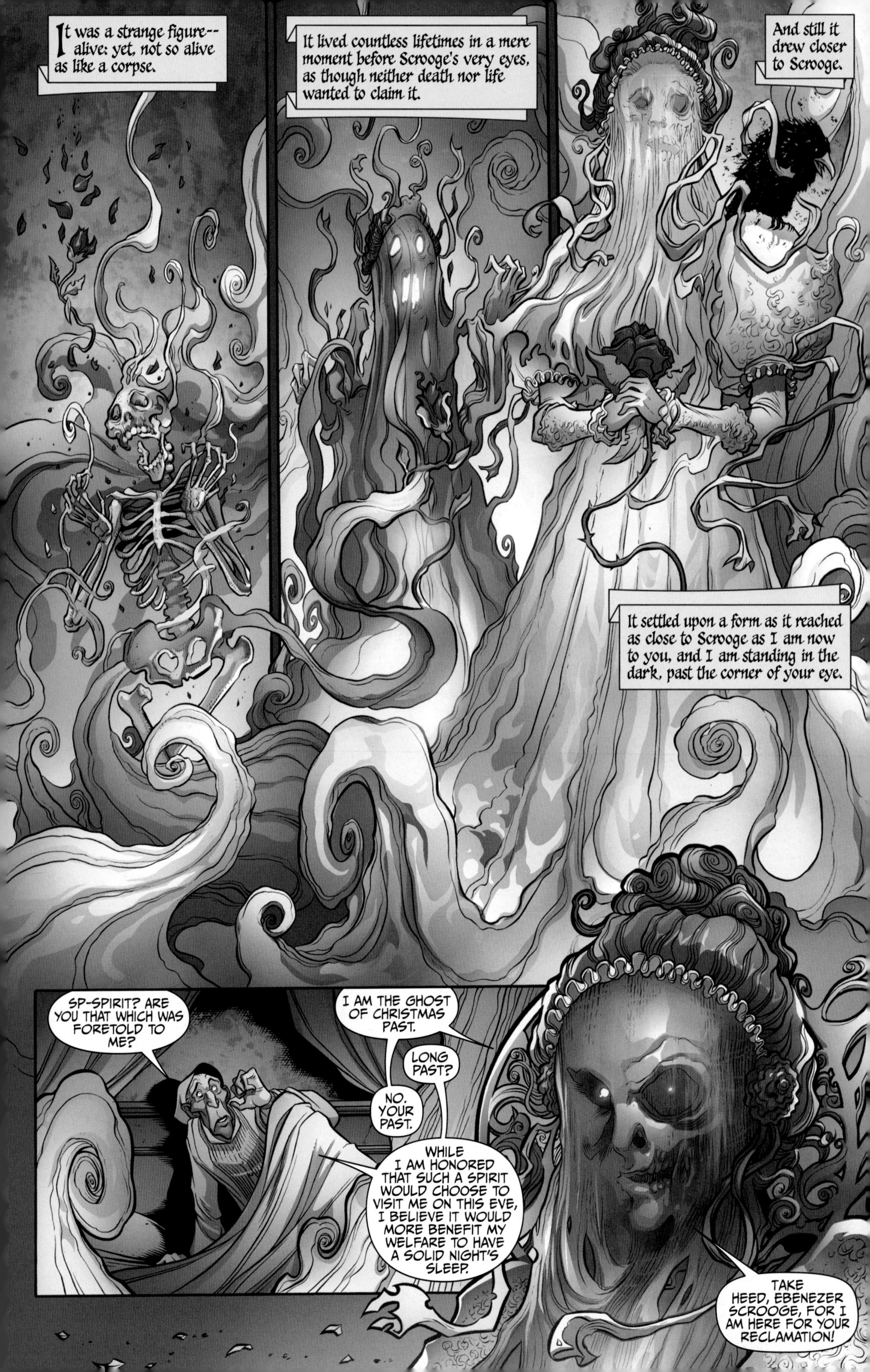
It was a strange figure-- alive: yet, not so alive as like a corpse.
It lived countless lifetimes in a mere moment before Scrooge's very eyes, as though neither death nor life wanted to claim it.
And still it drew closer to Scrooge.
It settled upon a form as it reached as close to Scrooge as I am now to you, and I am standing in the dark, past the corner of your eye.
SP-SPIRIT? ARE YOU THAT WHICH WAS FORETOLD TO ME?
I AM THE GHOST OF CHRISTMAS PAST.
LONG PAST?
NO. YOUR PAST.
WHILE I AM HONORED THAT SUCH A SPIRIT WOULD CHOOSE TO VISIT ME ON THIS EVE, I BELIEVE IT WOULD MORE BENEFIT MY WELFARE TO HAVE A SOLID NIGHT'S SLEEP.
TAKE HEED, EBENEZER SCROOGE, FOR I AM HERE FOR YOUR RECLAMATION!

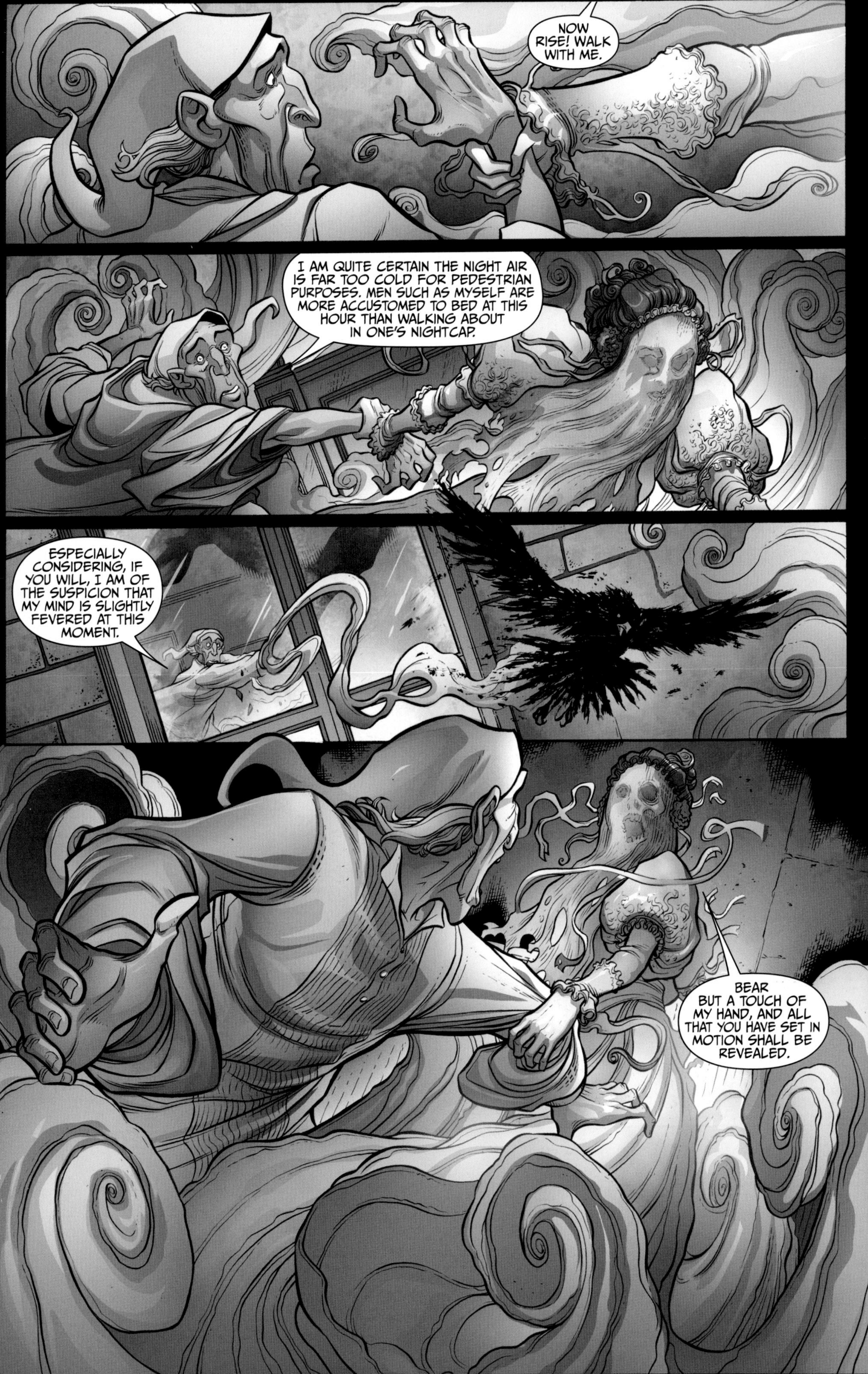
NOW RISE! WALK WITH ME.
I AM QUITE CERTAIN THE NIGHT AIR IS FAR TOO COLD FOR PEDESTRIAN PURPOSES. MEN SUCH AS MYSELF ARE MORE ACCUSTOMED TO BED AT THIS HOUR THAN WALKING ABOUT IN ONE'S NIGHTCAP.
ESPECIALLY CONSIDERING, IF YOU WILL, I AM OF THE SUSPICION THAT MY MIND IS SLIGHTLY FEVERED AT THIS MOMENT.
BEAR BUT A TOUCH OF MY HAND, AND ALL THAT YOU HAVE SET IN MOTION SHALL BE REVEALED.

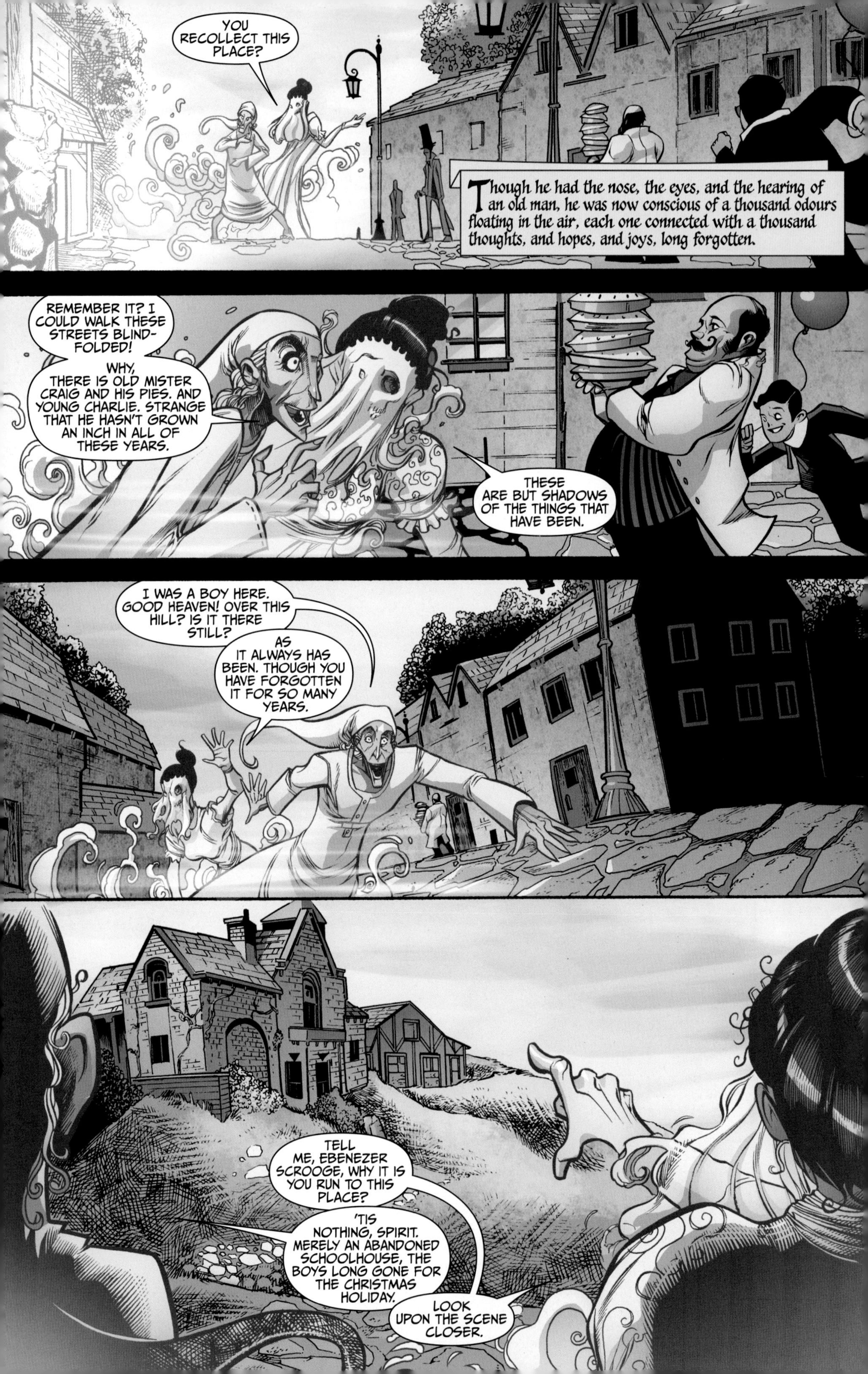
YOU RECOLLECT THIS PLACE?
Though he had the nose, the eyes, and the hearing of an old man, he was now conscious of a thousand odours floating in the air, each one connected with a thousand thoughts, and hopes, and joys, long forgotten.
REMEMBER IT? I COULD WALK THESE STREETS BLIND-FOLDED!
WHY, THERE IS OLD MISTER CRAIG AND HIS PIES. AND YOUNG CHARLIE. STRANGE THAT HE HASN'T GROWN AN INCH IN ALL OF THESE YEARS.
THESE ARE BUT SHADOWS OF THE THINGS THAT HAVE BEEN.
I WAS A BOY HERE. GOOD HEAVEN! OVER THIS HILL? IS IT THERE STILL?
AS IT ALWAYS HAS BEEN. THOUGH YOU HAVE FORGOTTEN IT FOR SO MANY YEARS.
TELL ME, EBENEZER SCROOGE, WHY IT IS YOU RUN TO THIS PLACE?
'TIS NOTHING, SPIRIT. MERELY AN ABANDONED SCHOOLHOUSE, THE BOYS LONG GONE FOR THE CHRISTMAS HOLIDAY.
LOOK UPON THE SCENE CLOSER.

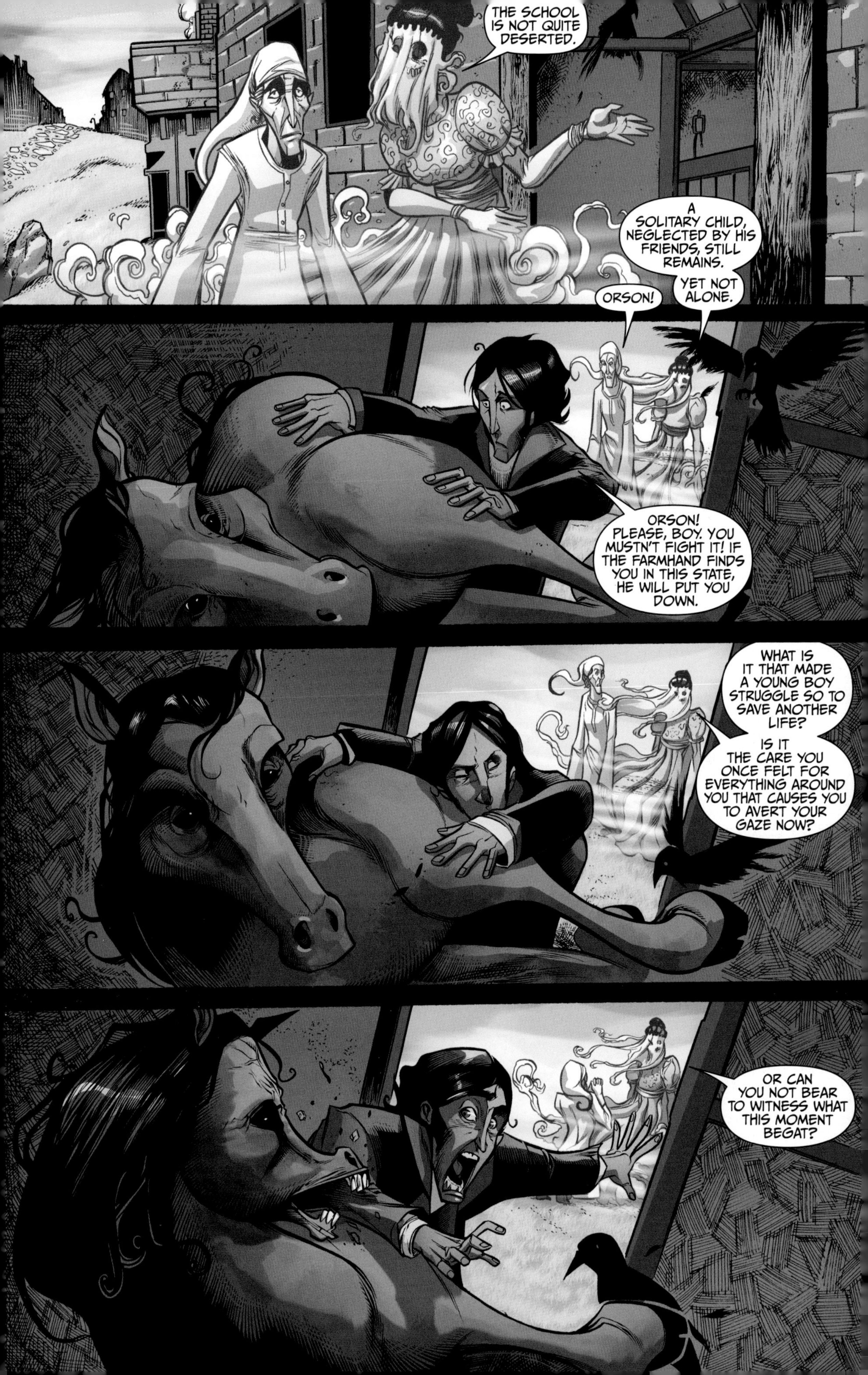
THE SCHOOL IS NOT QUITE DESERTED.
A SOLITARY CHILD, NEGLECTED BY HIS FRIENDS, STILL REMAINS.
YET NOT ALONE.
ORSON!
ORSON! PLEASE, BOY. YOU MUSTN'T FIGHT IT! IF THE FARMHAND FINDS YOU IN THIS STATE, HE WILL PUT YOU DOWN.
WHAT IS IT THAT MADE A YOUNG BOY STRUGGLE SO TO SAVE ANOTHER LIFE?
IS IT THE CARE YOU ONCE FELT FOR EVERYTHING AROUND YOU THAT CAUSES YOU TO AVERT YOUR GAZE NOW?
OR CAN YOU NOT BEAR TO WITNESS WHAT THIS MOMENT BEGAT?

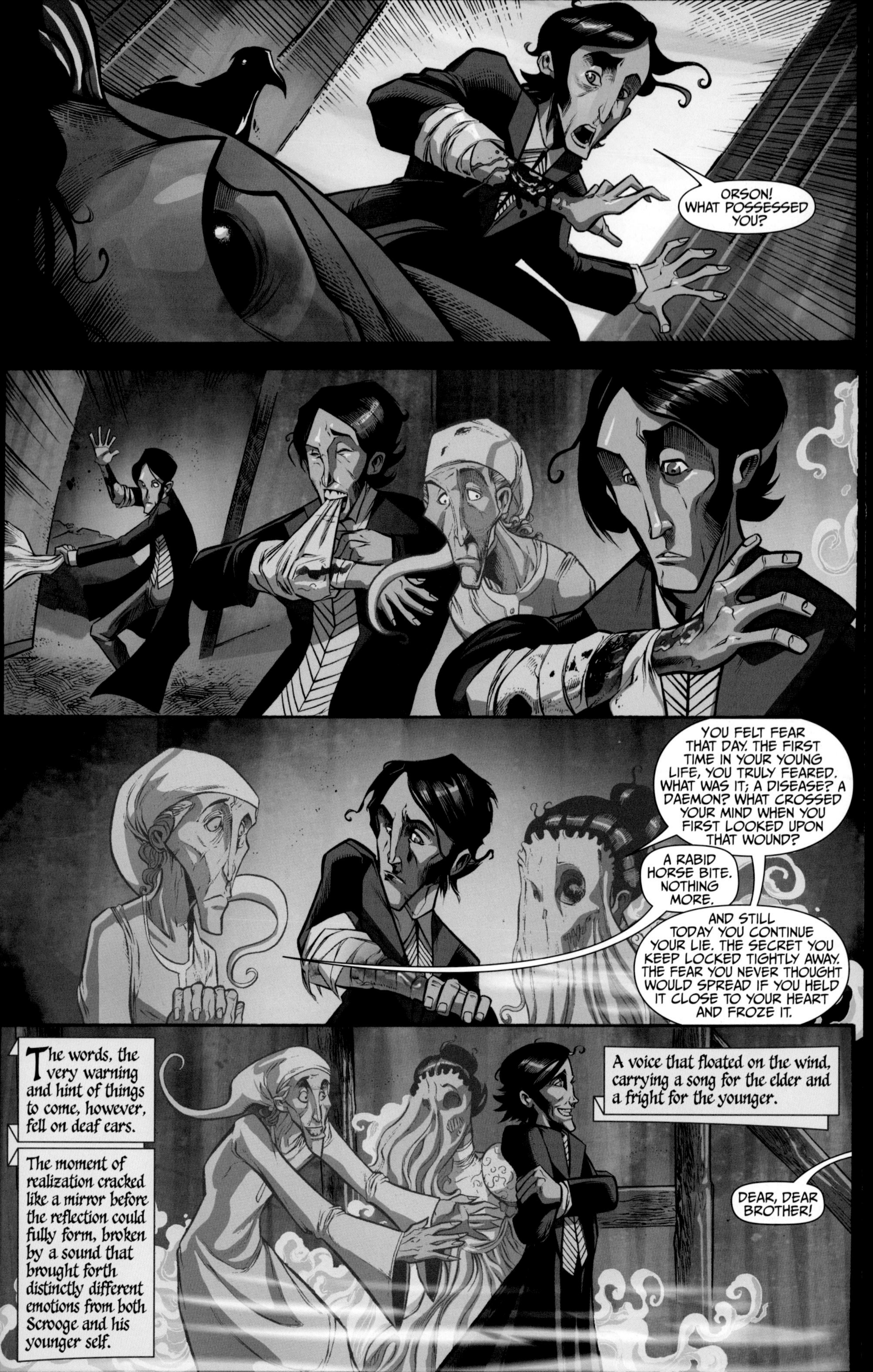
ORSON! WHAT POSSESSED YOU?
YOU FELT FEAR THAT DAY. THE FIRST TIME IN YOUR YOUNG LIFE, YOU TRULY FEARED. WHAT WAS IT; A DISEASE? A DAEMON? WHAT CROSSED YOUR MIND WHEN YOU FIRST LOOKED UPON THAT WOUND?
A RABID HORSE BITE. NOTHING MORE.
AND STILL TODAY YOU CONTINUE YOUR LIE. THE SECRET YOU KEEP LOCKED TIGHTLY AWAY. THE FEAR YOU NEVER THOUGHT WOULD SPREAD IF YOU HELD IT CLOSE TO YOUR HEART AND FROZE IT.
The words, the very warning and hint of things to come, however, fell on deaf ears.
The moment of realization cracked like a mirror before the reflection could fully form, broken by a sound that brought forth distinctly different emotions from both Scrooge and his younger self.
A voice that floated on the wind, carrying a song for the elder and a fright for the younger.
DEAR, DEAR BROTHER!

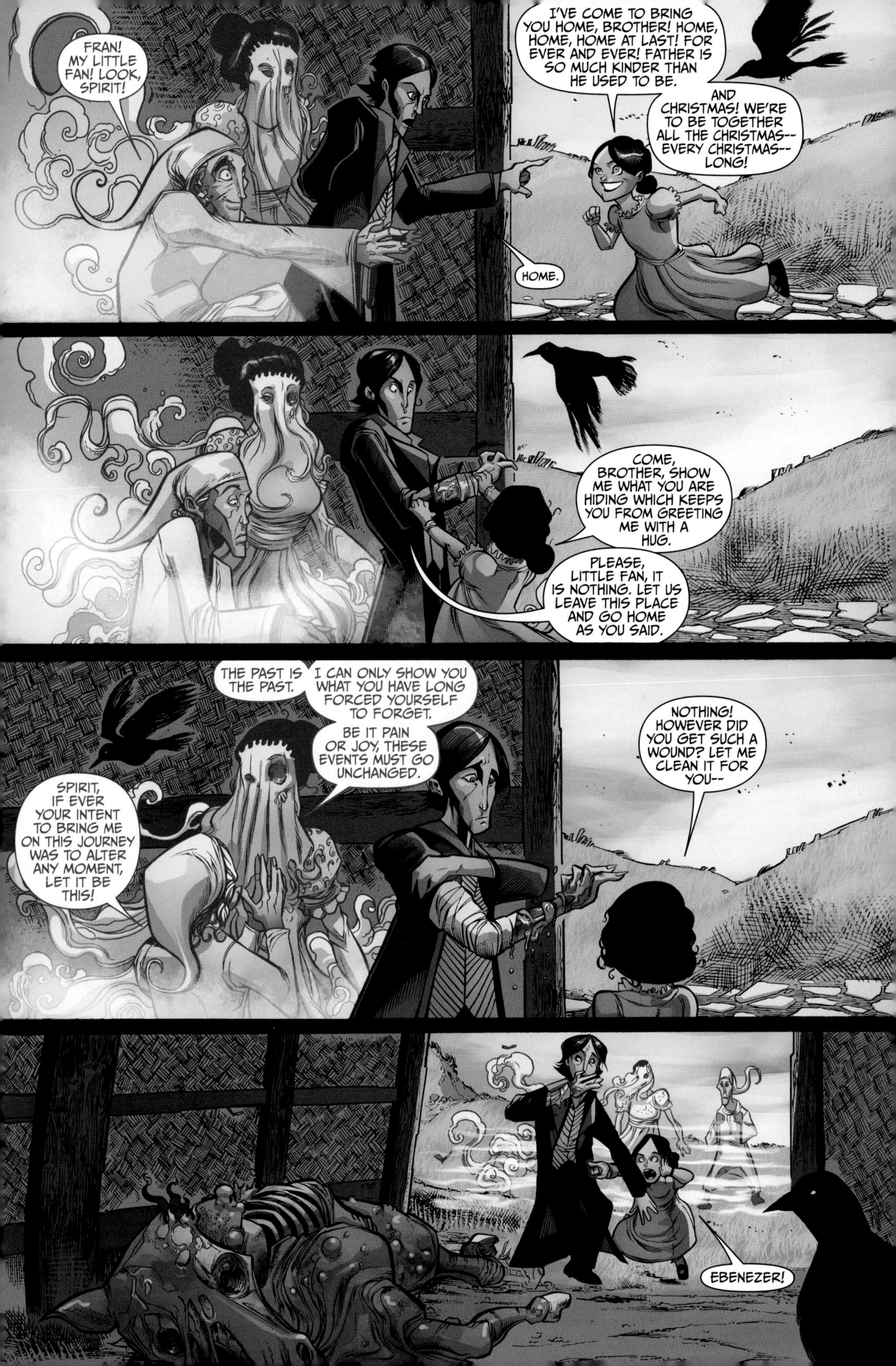
FRAN! MY LITTLE FAN! LOOK, SPIRIT!
I'VE COME TO BRING YOU HOME, BROTHER! HOME, HOME, HOME AT LAST! FOR EVER AND EVER! FATHER IS SO MUCH KINDER THAN HE USED TO BE.
AND CHRISTMAS! WE'RE TO BE TOGETHER ALL THE CHRISTMAS-- EVERY CHRISTMAS-- LONG!
HOME.
COME, BROTHER, SHOW ME WHAT YOU ARE HIDING WHICH KEEPS YOU FROM GREETING ME WITH A HUG.
PLEASE, LITTLE FAN, IT IS NOTHING. LET US LEAVE THIS PLACE AND GO HOME AS YOU SAID.
THE PAST IS THE PAST.
I CAN ONLY SHOW YOU WHAT YOU HAVE LONG FORCED YOURSELF TO FORGET.
BE IT PAIN OR JOY, THESE EVENTS MUST GO UNCHANGED.
SPIRIT, IF EVER YOUR INTENT TO BRING ME ON THIS JOURNEY WAS TO ALTER ANY MOMENT, LET IT BE THIS!
NOTHING! HOWEVER DID YOU GET SUCH A WOUND? LET ME CLEAN IT FOR YOU--
EBENEZER!

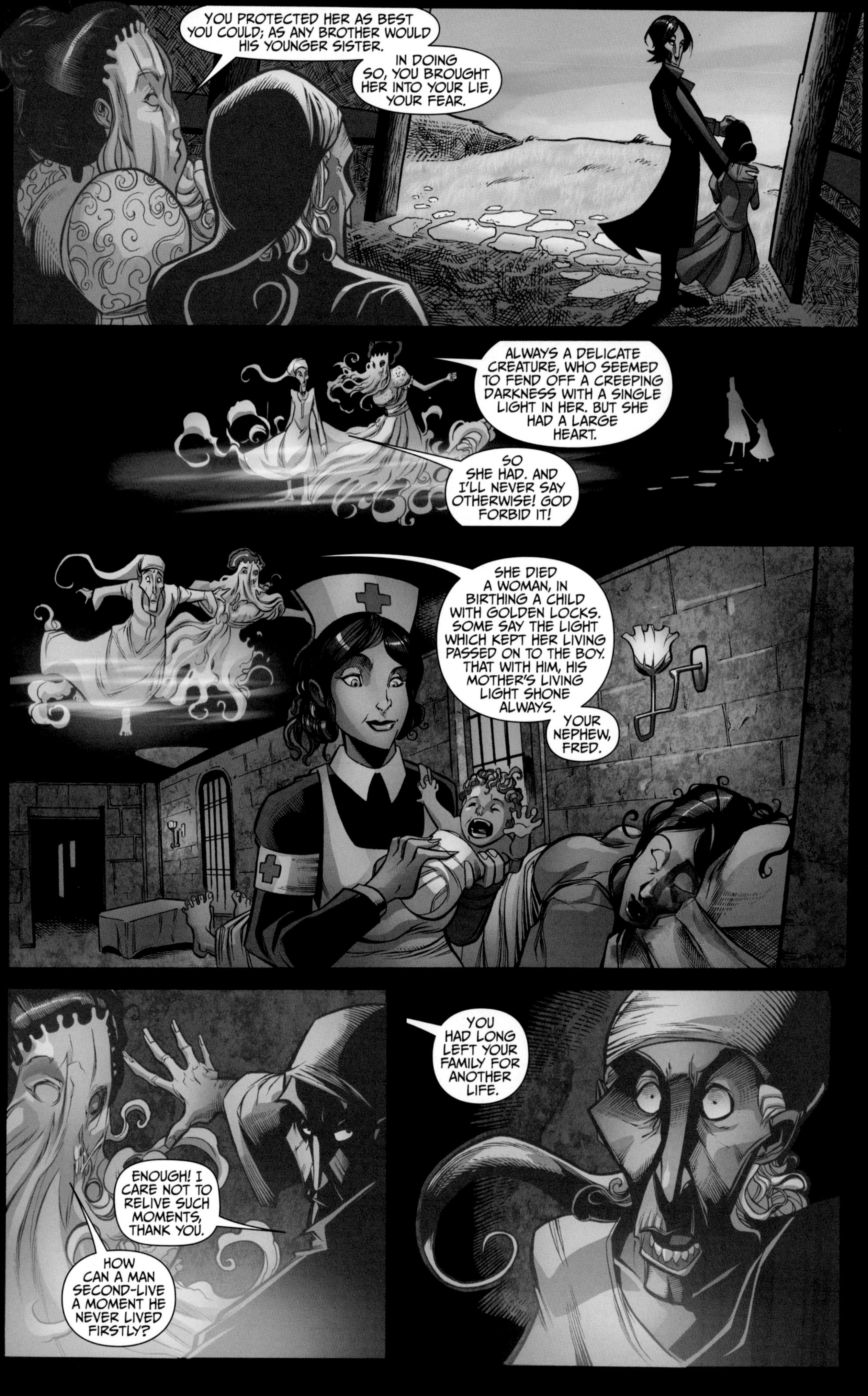
YOU PROTECTED HER AS BEST YOU COULD; AS ANY BROTHER WOULD HIS YOUNGER SISTER.
IN DOING SO, YOU BROUGHT HER INTO YOUR LIE, YOUR FEAR.
ALWAYS A DELICATE CREATURE, WHO SEEMED TO FEND OFF A CREEPING DARKNESS WITH A SINGLE LIGHT IN HER. BUT SHE HAD A LARGE HEART.
SO SHE HAD. AND I'LL NEVER SAY OTHERWISE! GOD FORBID IT!
SHE DIED A WOMAN, IN BIRTHING A CHILD WITH GOLDEN LOCKS. SOME SAY THE LIGHT WHICH KEPT HER LIVING PASSED ON TO THE BOY. THAT WITH HIM, HIS MOTHER'S LIVING LIGHT SHONE ALWAYS.
YOUR NEPHEW, FRED.
ENOUGH! I CARE NOT TO RELIVE SUCH MOMENTS, THANK YOU.
HOW CAN A MAN SECOND-LIVE A MOMENT HE NEVER LIVED FIRSTLY?
YOU HAD LONG LEFT YOUR FAMILY FOR ANOTHER LIFE.

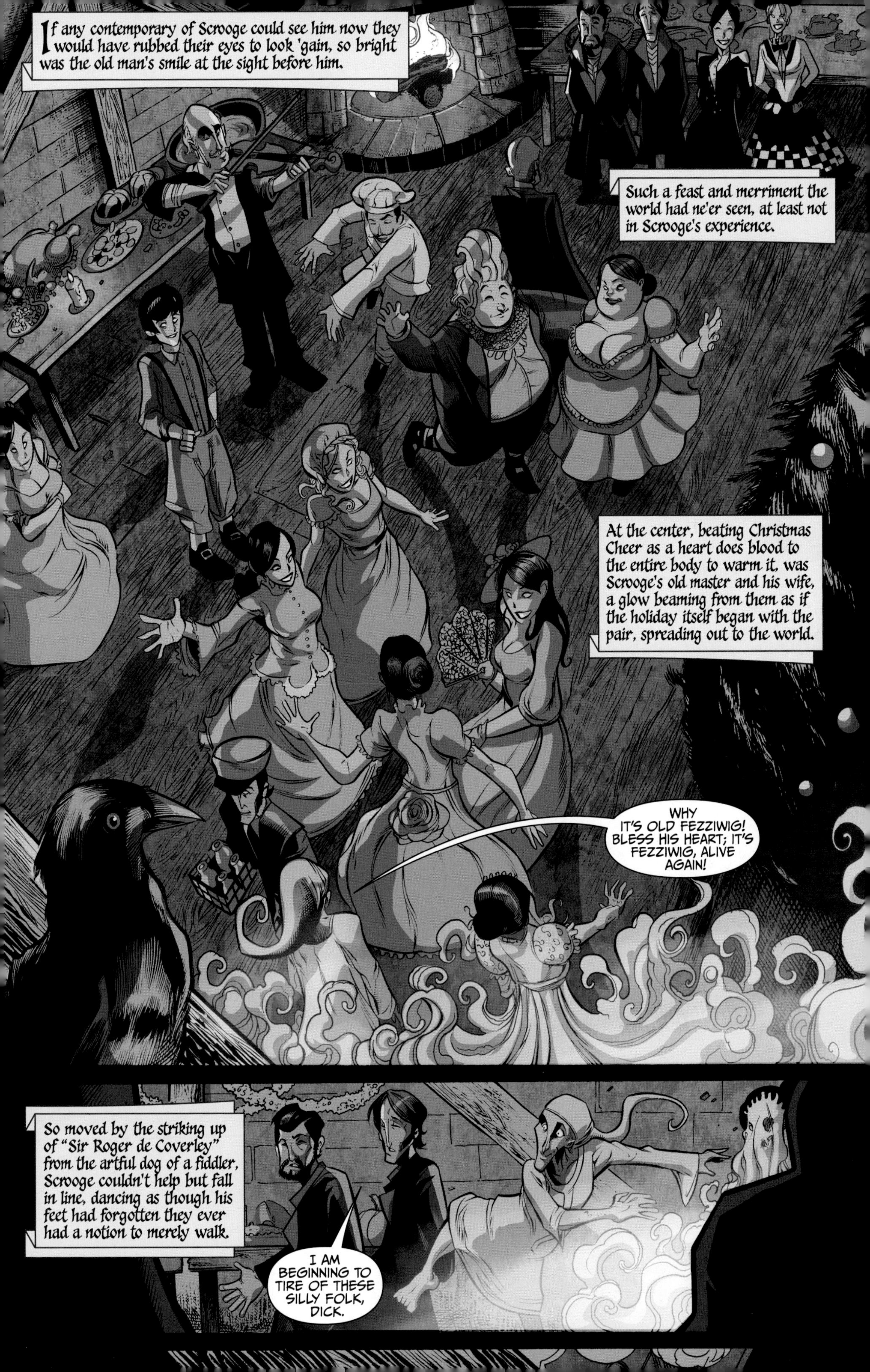
If any contemporary of Scrooge could see him now they would have rubbed their eyes to look 'gain, so bright was the old man's smile at the sight before him.
Such a feast and merriment the world had ne'er seen, at least not in Scrooge's experience.
At the center, beating Christmas Cheer as a heart does blood to the entire body to warm it, was Scrooge's old master and his wife, a glow beaming from them as if the holiday itself began with the pair, spreading out to the world.
WHY IT'S OLD FEZZIWIG! BLESS HIS HEART; IT'S FEZZIWIG, ALIVE AGAIN!
So moved by the striking up of "Sir Roger de Coverley" from the artful dog of a fiddler, Scrooge couldn't help but fall in line, dancing as though his feet had forgotten they ever had a notion to merely walk.
I AM BEGINNING TO TIRE OF THESE SILLY FOLK, DICK.

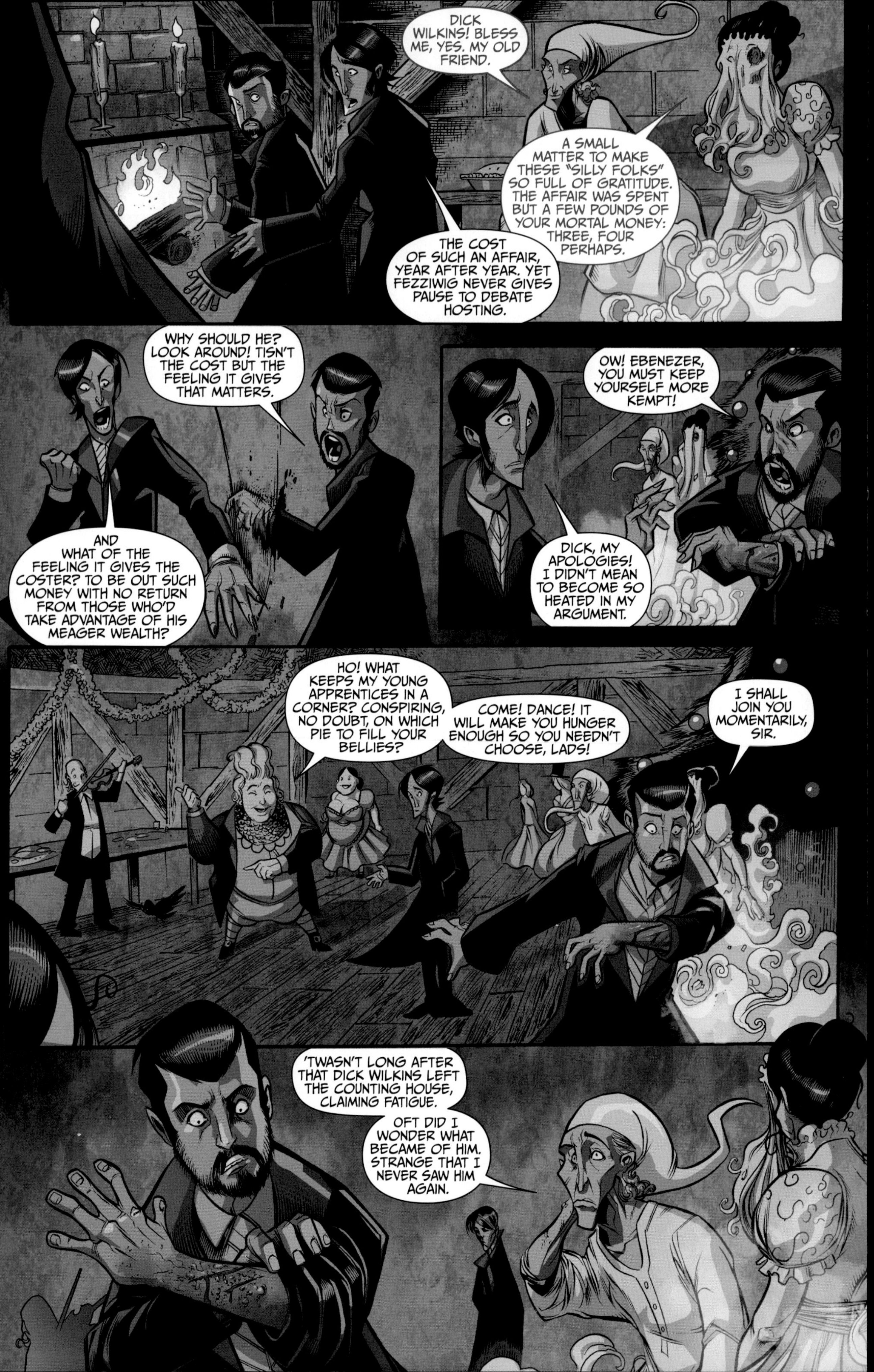
DICK WILKINS! BLESS ME, YES. MY OLD FRIEND.
THE COST OF SUCH AN AFFAIR, YEAR AFTER YEAR. YET FEZZIWIG NEVER GIVES PAUSE TO DEBATE HOSTING.
A SMALL MATTER TO MAKE THESE "SILLY FOLKS" SO FULL OF GRATITUDE. THE AFFAIR WAS SPENT BUT A FEW POUNDS OF YOUR MORTAL MONEY: THREE, FOUR PERHAPS.
WHY SHOULD HE? LOOK AROUND! TISN'T THE COST BUT THE FEELING IT GIVES THAT MATTERS.
AND WHAT OF THE FEELING IT GIVES THE COSTER? TO BE OUT SUCH MONEY WITH NO RETURN FROM THOSE WHO'D TAKE ADVANTAGE OF HIS MEAGER WEALTH?
OW! EBENEZER, YOU MUST KEEP YOURSELF MORE KEMPT!
DICK, MY APOLOGIES! I DIDN'T MEAN TO BECOME SO HEATED IN MY ARGUMENT.
HO! WHAT KEEPS MY YOUNG APPRENTICES IN A CORNER? CONSPIRING, NO DOUBT, ON WHICH PIE TO FILL YOUR BELLIES?
COME! DANCE! IT WILL MAKE YOU HUNGER ENOUGH SO YOU NEEDN'T CHOOSE, LADS!
I SHALL JOIN YOU MOMENTARILY, SIR.
'TWASN'T LONG AFTER THAT DICK WILKINS LEFT THE COUNTING HOUSE, CLAIMING FATIGUE.
OFT DID I WONDER WHAT BECAME OF HIM. STRANGE THAT I NEVER SAW HIM AGAIN.

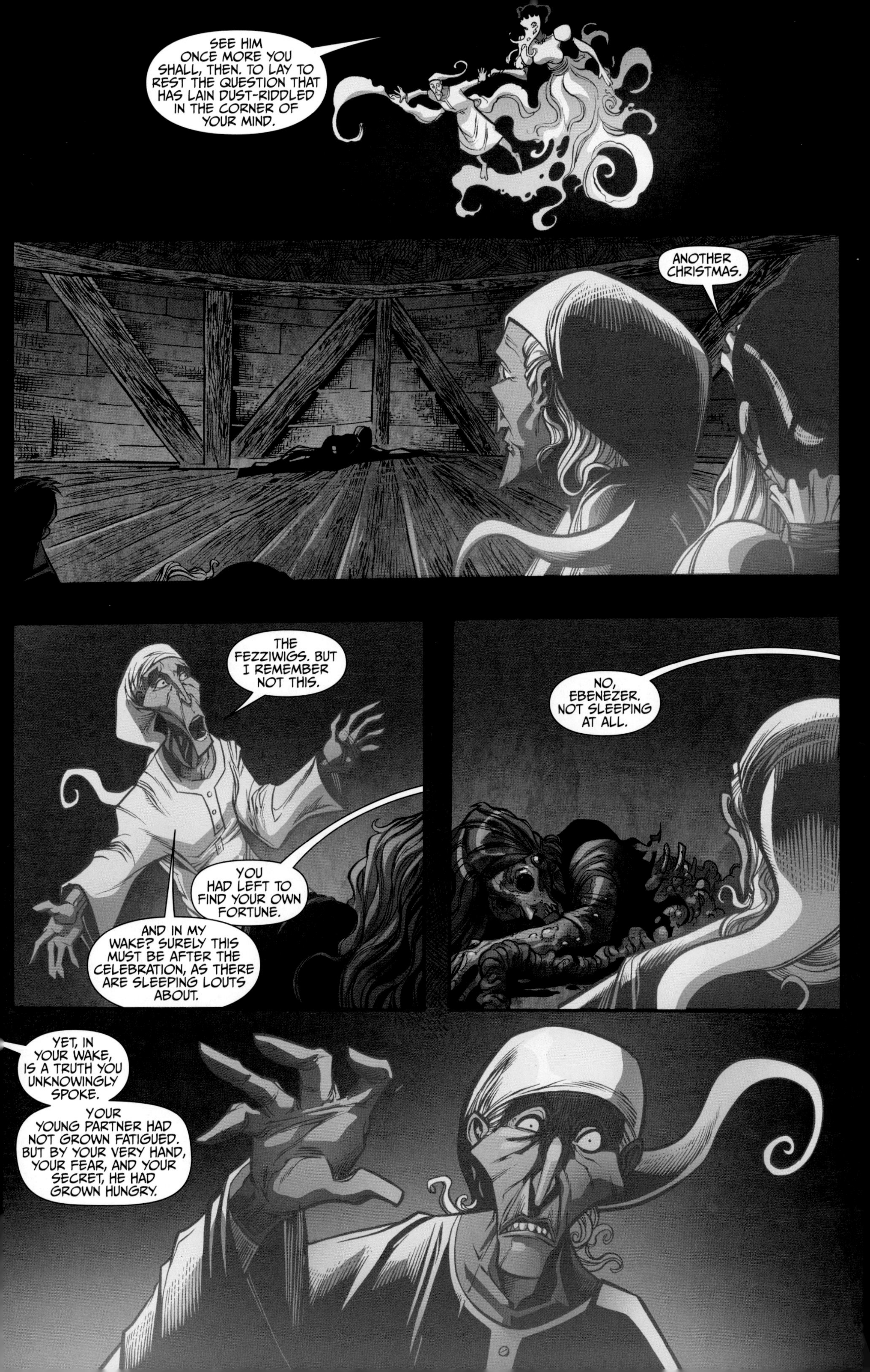
SEE HIM ONCE MORE YOU SHALL, THEN. TO LAY TO REST THE QUESTION THAT HAS LAIN DUST-RIDDLED IN THE CORNER OF YOUR MIND.
ANOTHER CHRISTMAS.
THE FEZZIWIGS. BUT I REMEMBER NOT THIS.
YOU HAD LEFT TO FIND YOUR OWN FORTUNE.
AND IN MY WAKE? SURELY THIS MUST BE AFTER THE CELEBRATION, AS THERE ARE SLEEPING LOUTS ABOUT.
NO, EBENEZER. NOT SLEEPING AT ALL.
YET, IN YOUR WAKE, IS A TRUTH YOU UNKNOWINGLY SPOKE.
YOUR YOUNG PARTNER HAD NOT GROWN FATIGUED. BUT BY YOUR VERY HAND, YOUR FEAR, AND YOUR SECRET, HE HAD GROWN HUNGRY.

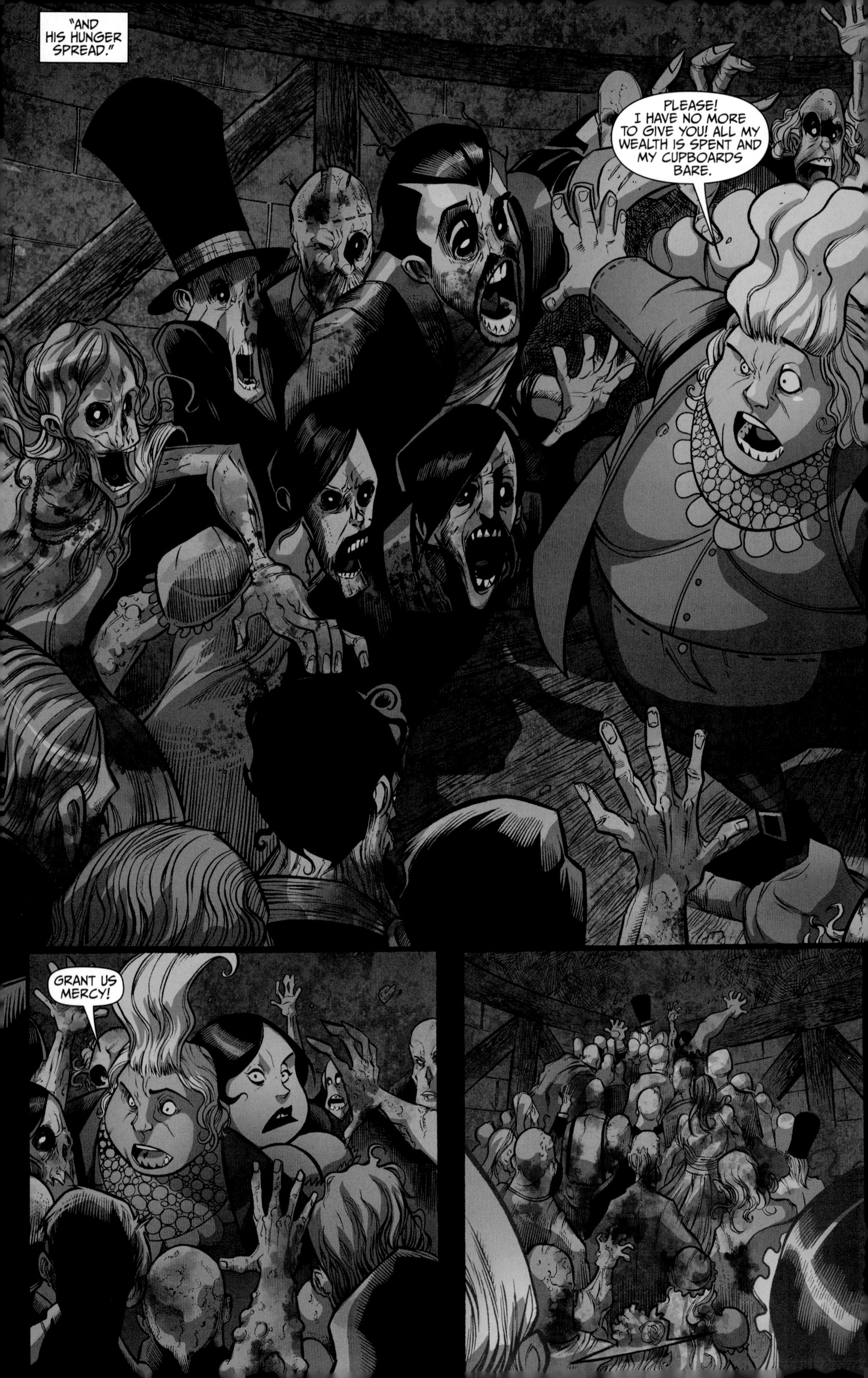
"AND HIS HUNGER SPREAD."
PLEASE! I HAVE NO MORE TO GIVE YOU! ALL MY WEALTH IS SPENT AND MY CUPBOARDS BARE.
GRANT US MERCY!

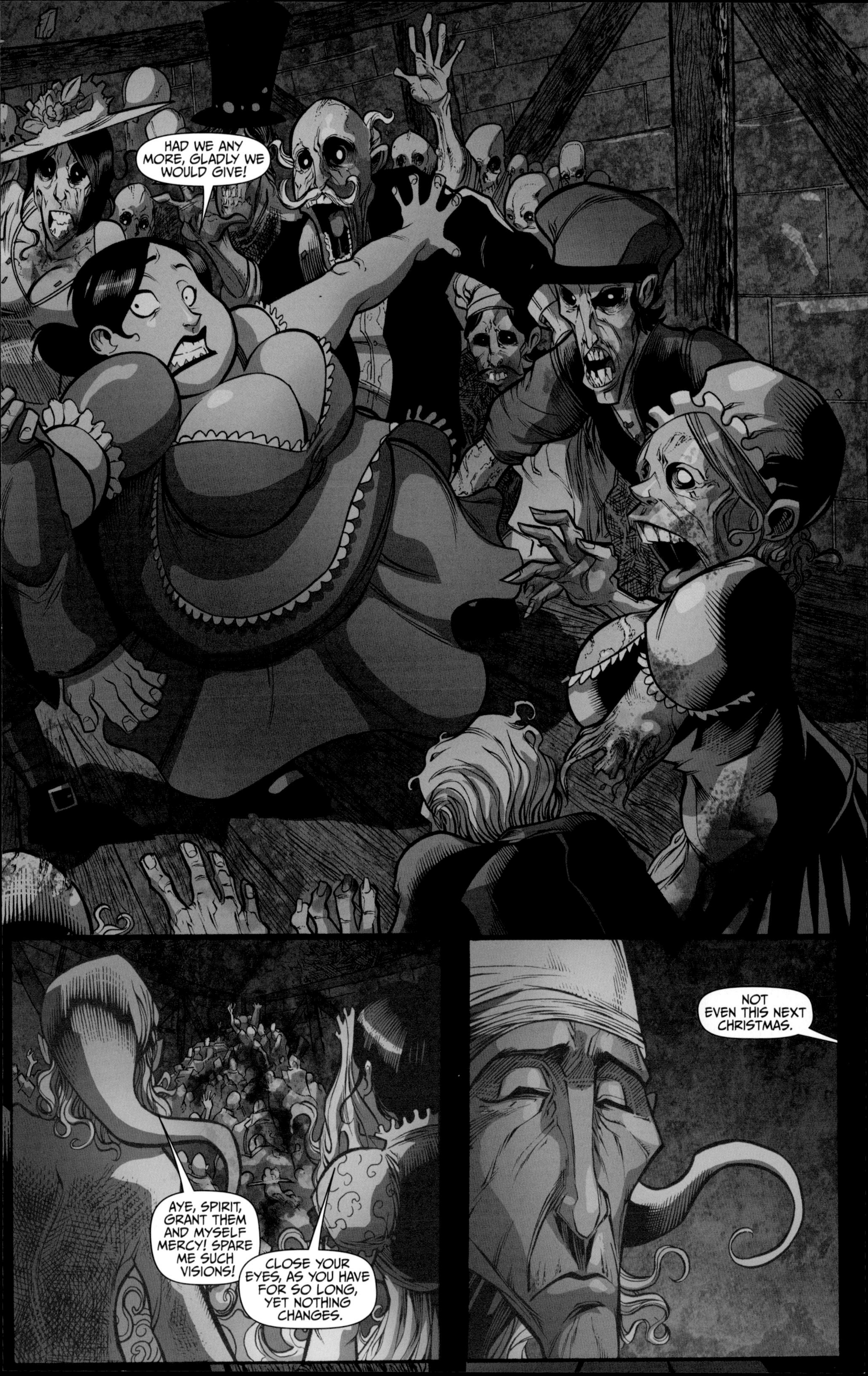
HAD WE ANY MORE, GLADLY WE WOULD GIVE!
AYE, SPIRIT, GRANT THEM AND MYSELF MERCY! SPARE ME SUCH VISIONS!
CLOSE YOUR EYES, AS YOU HAVE FOR SO LONG, YET NOTHING CHANGES.
NOT EVEN THIS NEXT CHRISTMAS.

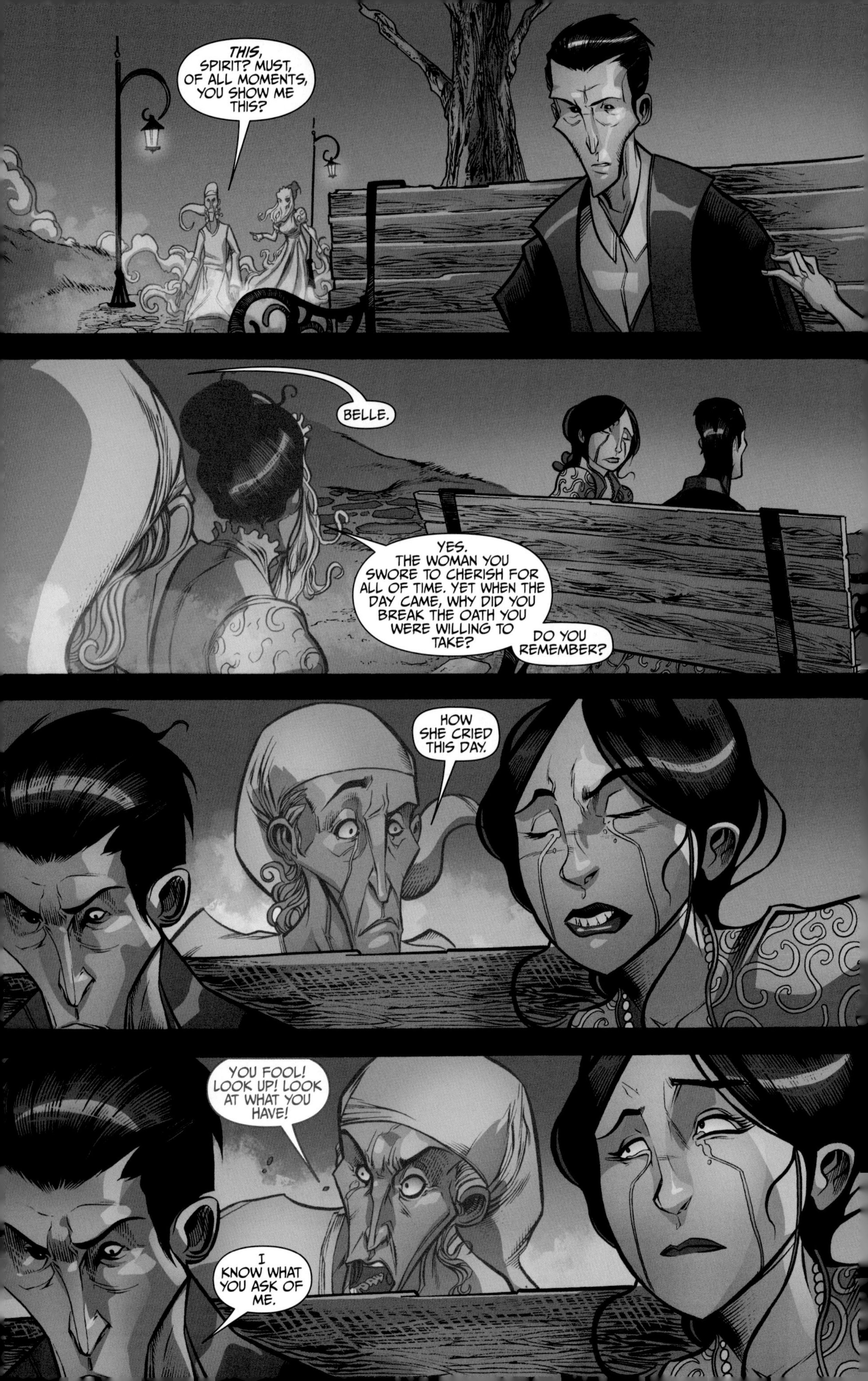
THIS, SPIRIT? MUST, OF ALL MOMENTS, YOU SHOW ME THIS?
BELLE.
YES. THE WOMAN YOU SWORE TO CHERISH FOR ALL OF TIME. YET WHEN THE DAY CAME, WHY DID YOU BREAK THE OATH YOU WERE WILLING TO TAKE?
DO YOU REMEMBER?
HOW SHE CRIED THIS DAY.
YOU FOOL! LOOK UP! LOOK AT WHAT YOU HAVE!
I KNOW WHAT YOU ASK OF ME.

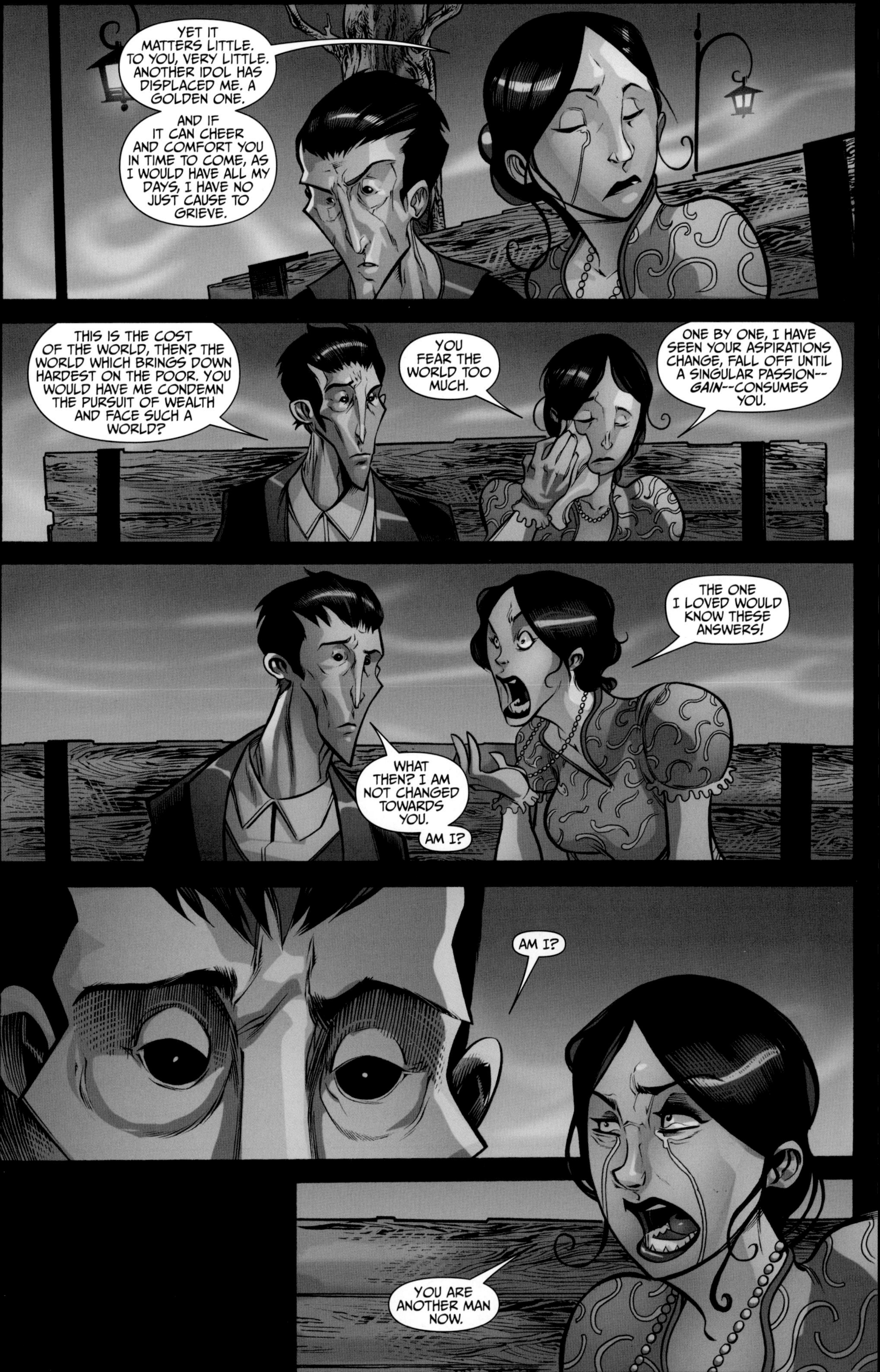
YET IT MATTERS LITTLE. TO YOU, VERY LITTLE. ANOTHER IDOL HAS DISPLACED ME. A GOLDEN ONE.
AND IF IT CAN CHEER AND COMFORT YOU IN TIME TO COME, AS I WOULD HAVE ALL MY DAYS, I HAVE NO JUST CAUSE TO GRIEVE.
THIS IS THE COST OF THE WORLD, THEN? THE WORLD WHICH BRINGS DOWN HARDEST ON THE POOR. YOU WOULD HAVE ME CONDEMN THE PURSUIT OF WEALTH AND FACE SUCH A WORLD?
YOU FEAR THE WORLD TOO MUCH.
ONE BY ONE, I HAVE SEEN YOUR ASPIRATIONS CHANGE, FALL OFF UNTIL A SINGULAR PASSION-- *GAIN*--CONSUMES YOU.
WHAT THEN? I AM NOT CHANGED TOWARDS YOU.
AM I?
THE ONE I LOVED WOULD KNOW THESE ANSWERS!
AM I?
YOU ARE ANOTHER MAN NOW.

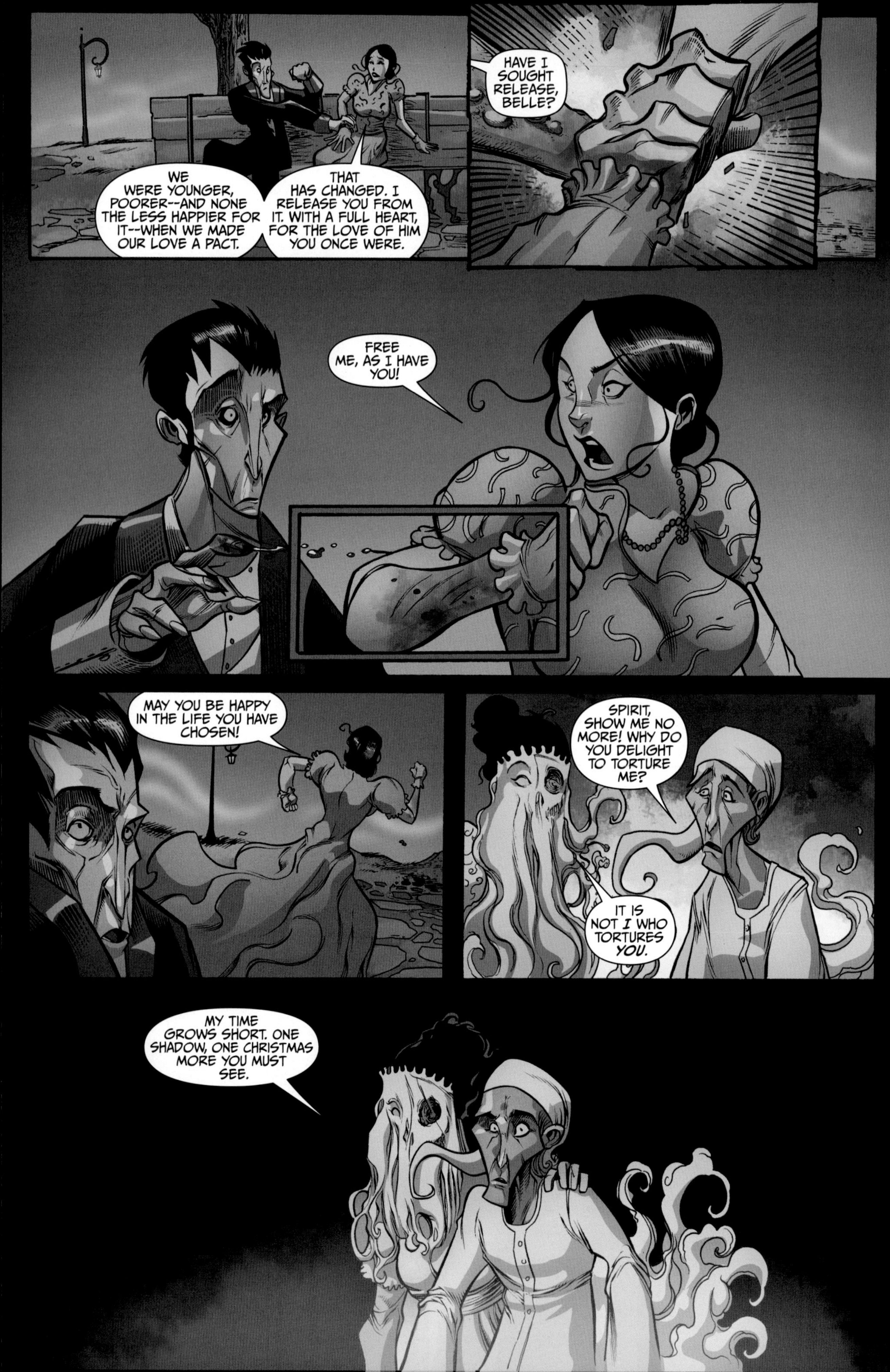
WE WERE YOUNGER, POORER--AND NONE THE LESS HAPPIER FOR IT--WHEN WE MADE OUR LOVE A PACT.
THAT HAS CHANGED. I RELEASE YOU FROM IT. WITH A FULL HEART, FOR THE LOVE OF HIM YOU ONCE WERE.
HAVE I SOUGHT RELEASE, BELLE?
FREE ME, AS I HAVE YOU!
MAY YOU BE HAPPY IN THE LIFE YOU HAVE CHOSEN!
SPIRIT, SHOW ME NO MORE! WHY DO YOU DELIGHT TO TORTURE ME?
IT IS NOT *I* WHO TORTURES *YOU*.
MY TIME GROWS SHORT. ONE SHADOW, ONE CHRISTMAS MORE YOU MUST SEE.

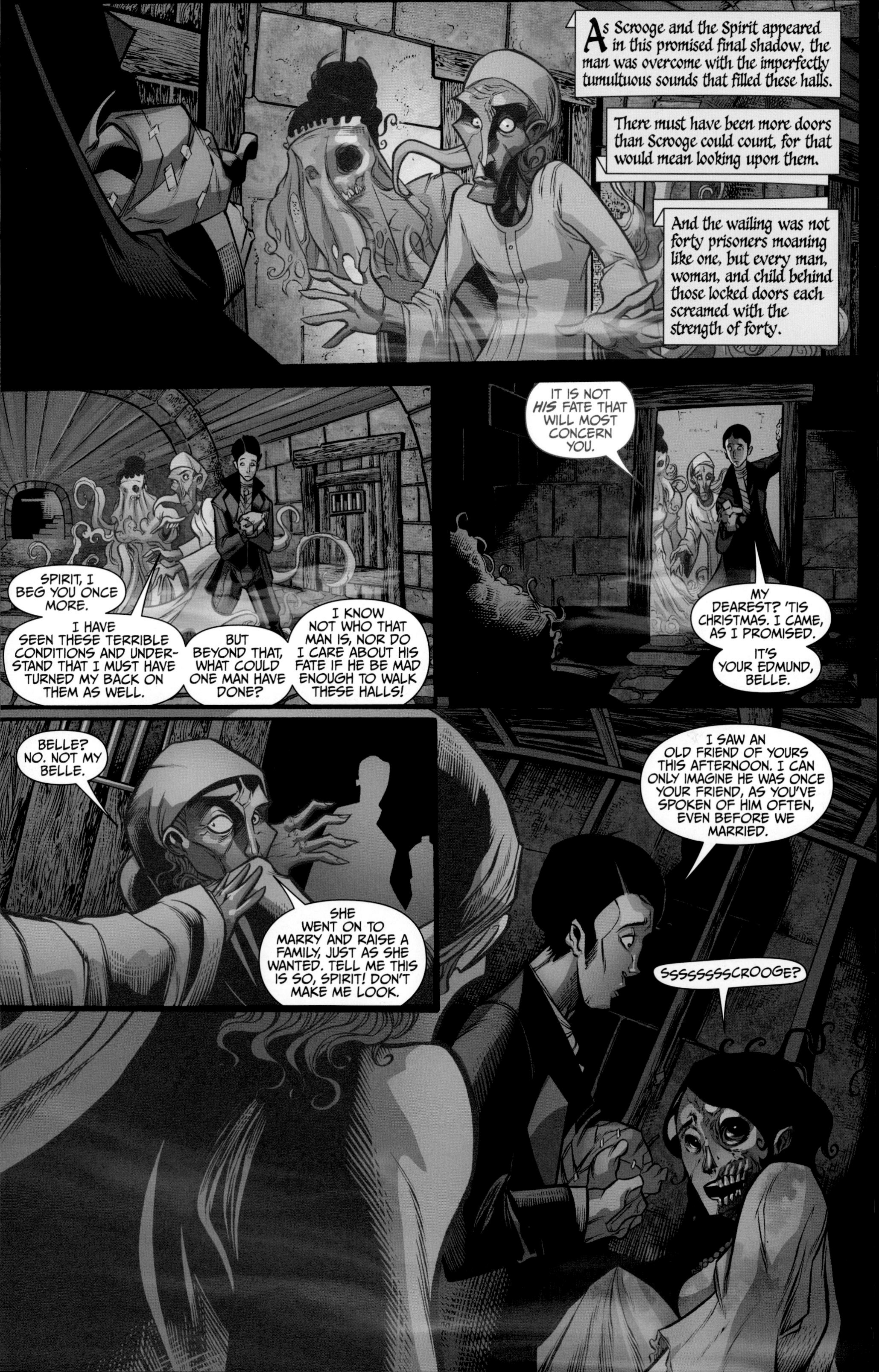
As Scrooge and the Spirit appeared in this promised final shadow, the man was overcome with the imperfectly tumultuous sounds that filled these halls.
There must have been more doors than Scrooge could count, for that would mean looking upon them.
And the wailing was not forty prisoners moaning like one, but every man, woman, and child behind those locked doors each screamed with the strength of forty.
SPIRIT, I BEG YOU ONCE MORE.
I HAVE SEEN THESE TERRIBLE CONDITIONS AND UNDERSTAND THAT I MUST HAVE TURNED MY BACK ON THEM AS WELL.
BUT BEYOND THAT, WHAT COULD ONE MAN HAVE DONE?
I KNOW NOT WHO THAT MAN IS, NOR DO I CARE ABOUT HIS FATE IF HE BE MAD ENOUGH TO WALK THESE HALLS!
IT IS NOT HIS FATE THAT WILL MOST CONCERN YOU.
MY DEAREST? 'TIS CHRISTMAS. I CAME, AS I PROMISED.
IT'S YOUR EDMUND, BELLE.
BELLE? NO. NOT MY BELLE.
SHE WENT ON TO MARRY AND RAISE A FAMILY, JUST AS SHE WANTED. TELL ME THIS IS SO, SPIRIT! DON'T MAKE ME LOOK.
I SAW AN OLD FRIEND OF YOURS THIS AFTERNOON. I CAN ONLY IMAGINE HE WAS ONCE YOUR FRIEND, AS YOU'VE SPOKEN OF HIM OFTEN, EVEN BEFORE WE MARRIED.
SSSSSSSSCROOGE?

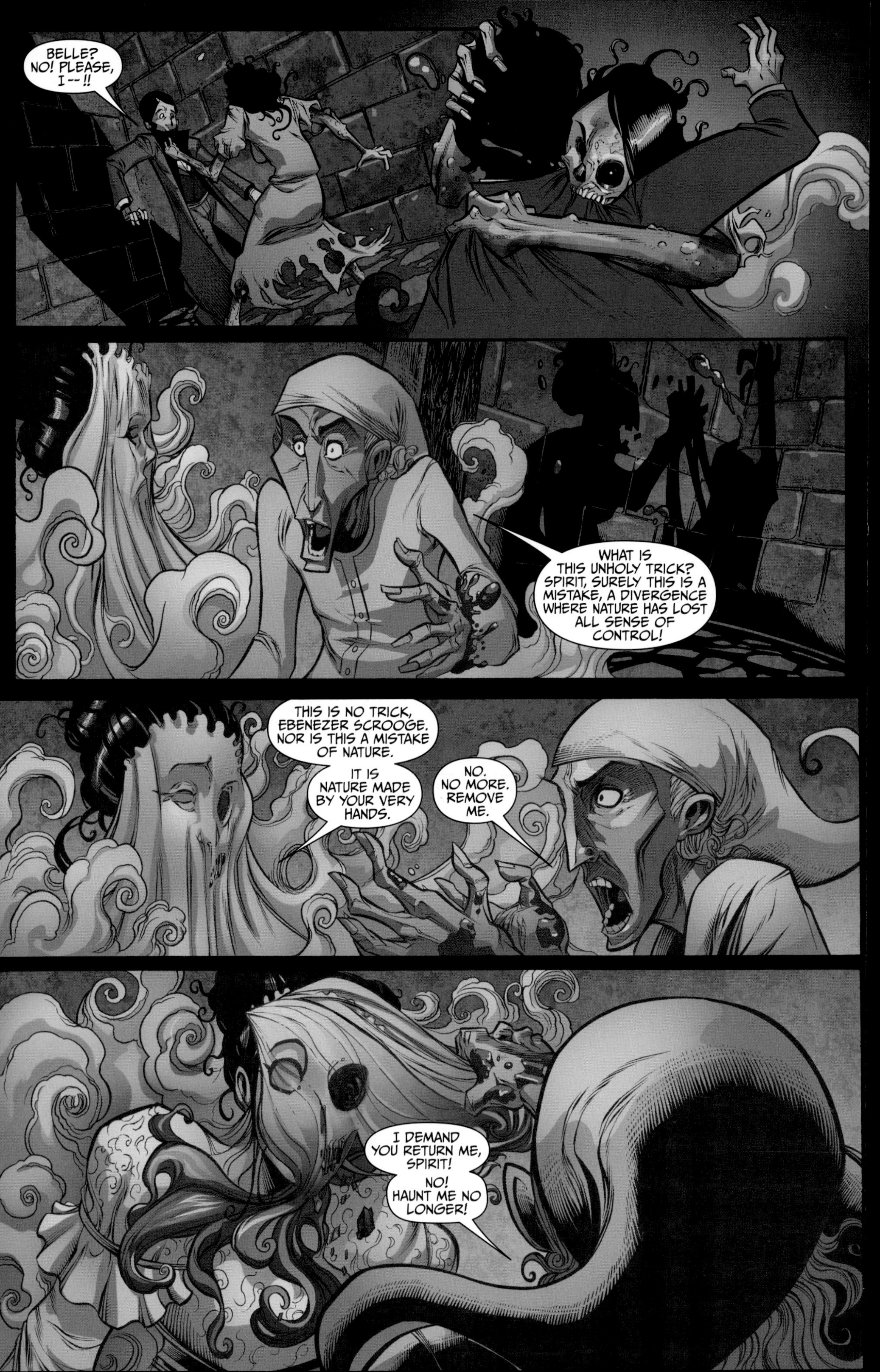
BELLE? NO! PLEASE, I--!!
WHAT IS THIS UNHOLY TRICK? SPIRIT, SURELY THIS IS A MISTAKE, A DIVERGENCE WHERE NATURE HAS LOST ALL SENSE OF CONTROL!
THIS IS NO TRICK, EBENEZER SCROOGE. NOR IS THIS A MISTAKE OF NATURE.
IT IS NATURE MADE BY YOUR VERY HANDS.
NO. NO MORE. REMOVE ME.
I DEMAND YOU RETURN ME, SPIRIT!
NO! HAUNT ME NO LONGER!

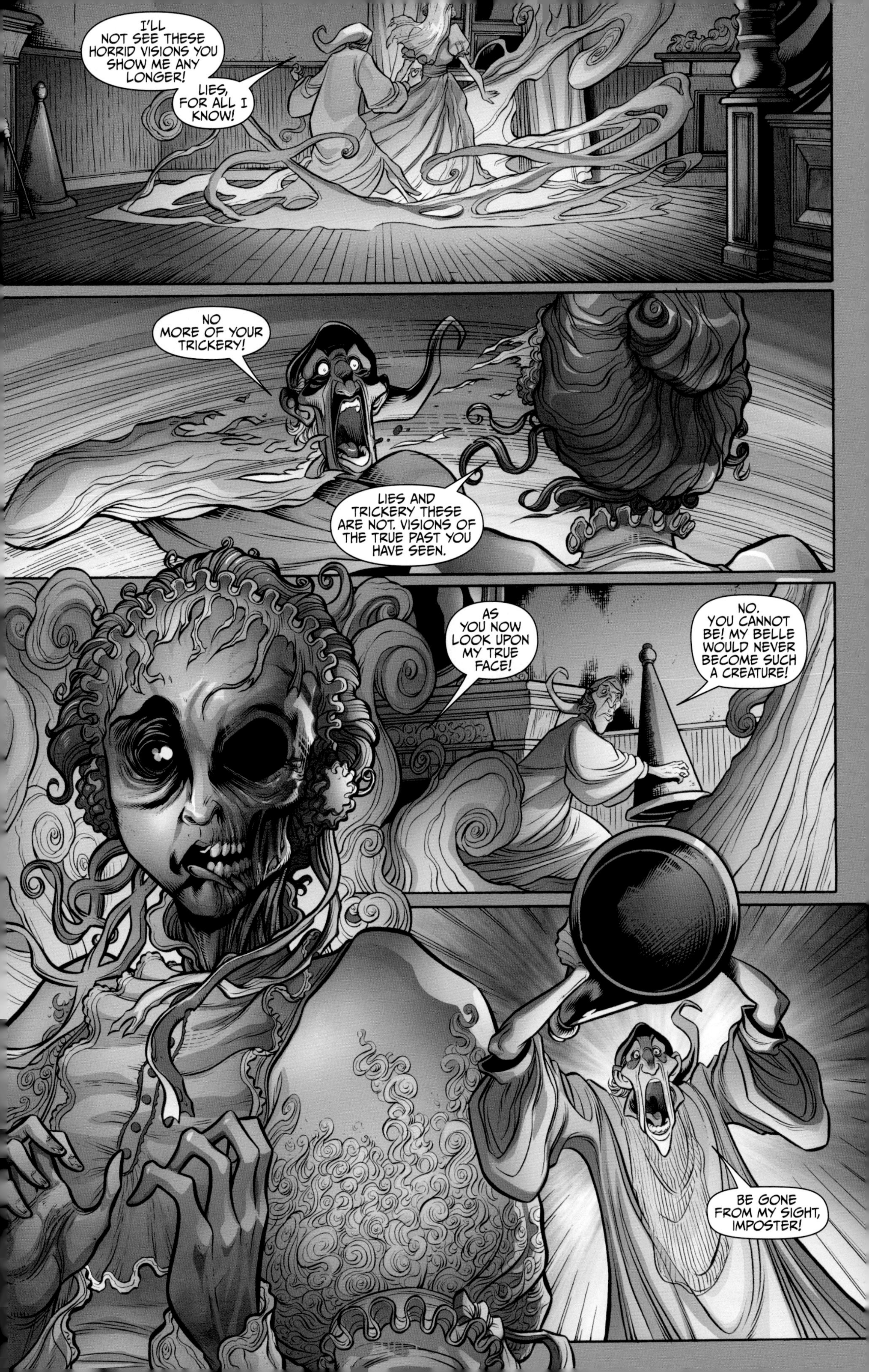
I'LL NOT SEE THESE HORRID VISIONS YOU SHOW ME ANY LONGER!
LIES, FOR ALL I KNOW!
NO MORE OF YOUR TRICKERY!
LIES AND TRICKERY THESE ARE NOT. VISIONS OF THE TRUE PAST YOU HAVE SEEN.
AS YOU NOW LOOK UPON MY TRUE FACE!
NO. YOU CANNOT BE! MY BELLE WOULD NEVER BECOME SUCH A CREATURE!
BE GONE FROM MY SIGHT, IMPOSTER!

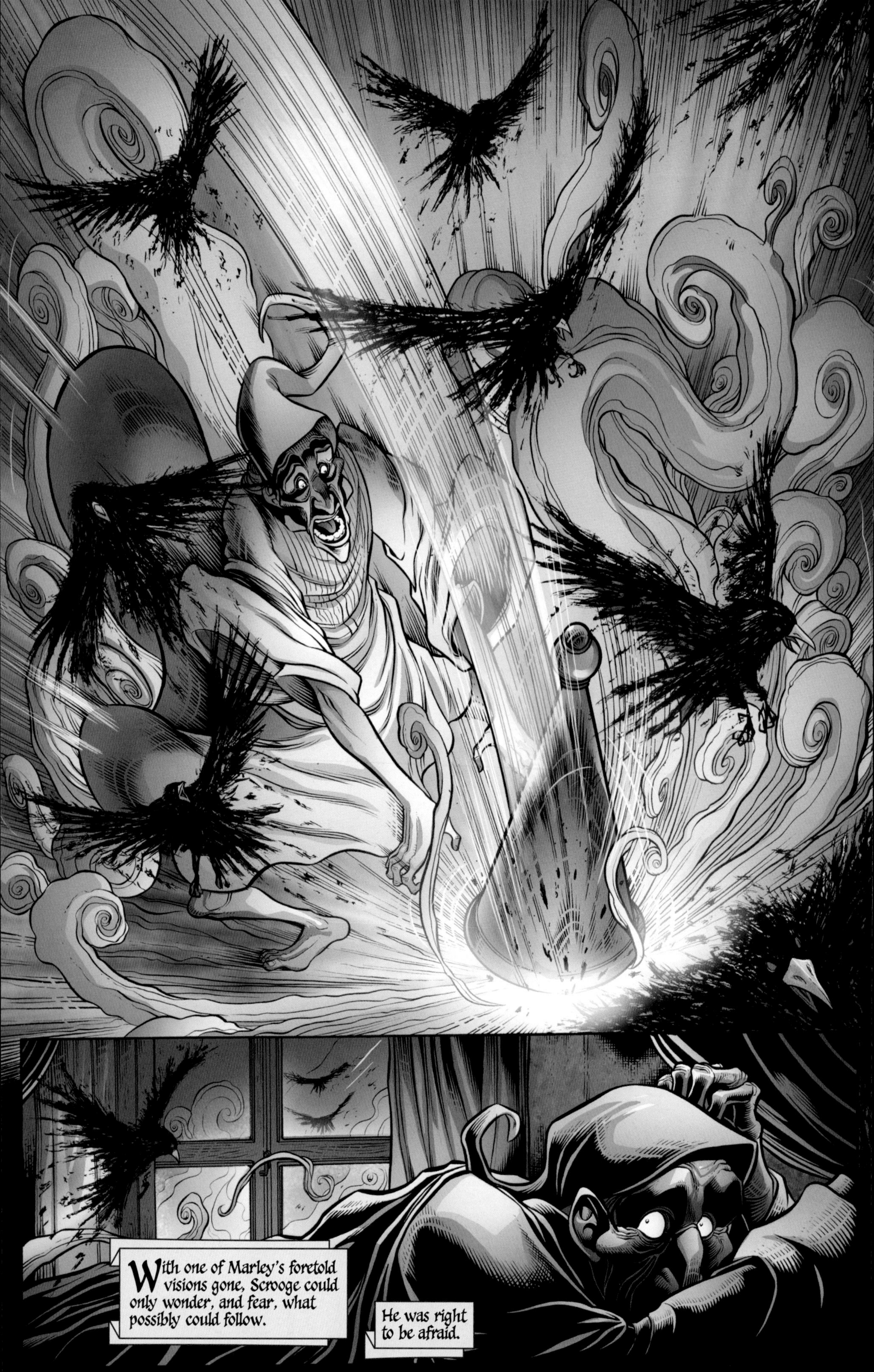
With one of Marley's foretold visions gone, Scrooge could only wonder, and fear, what possibly could follow.
He was right to be afraid.

STAVE 3:

A Christmas Feast for the Presently Hungry Dead

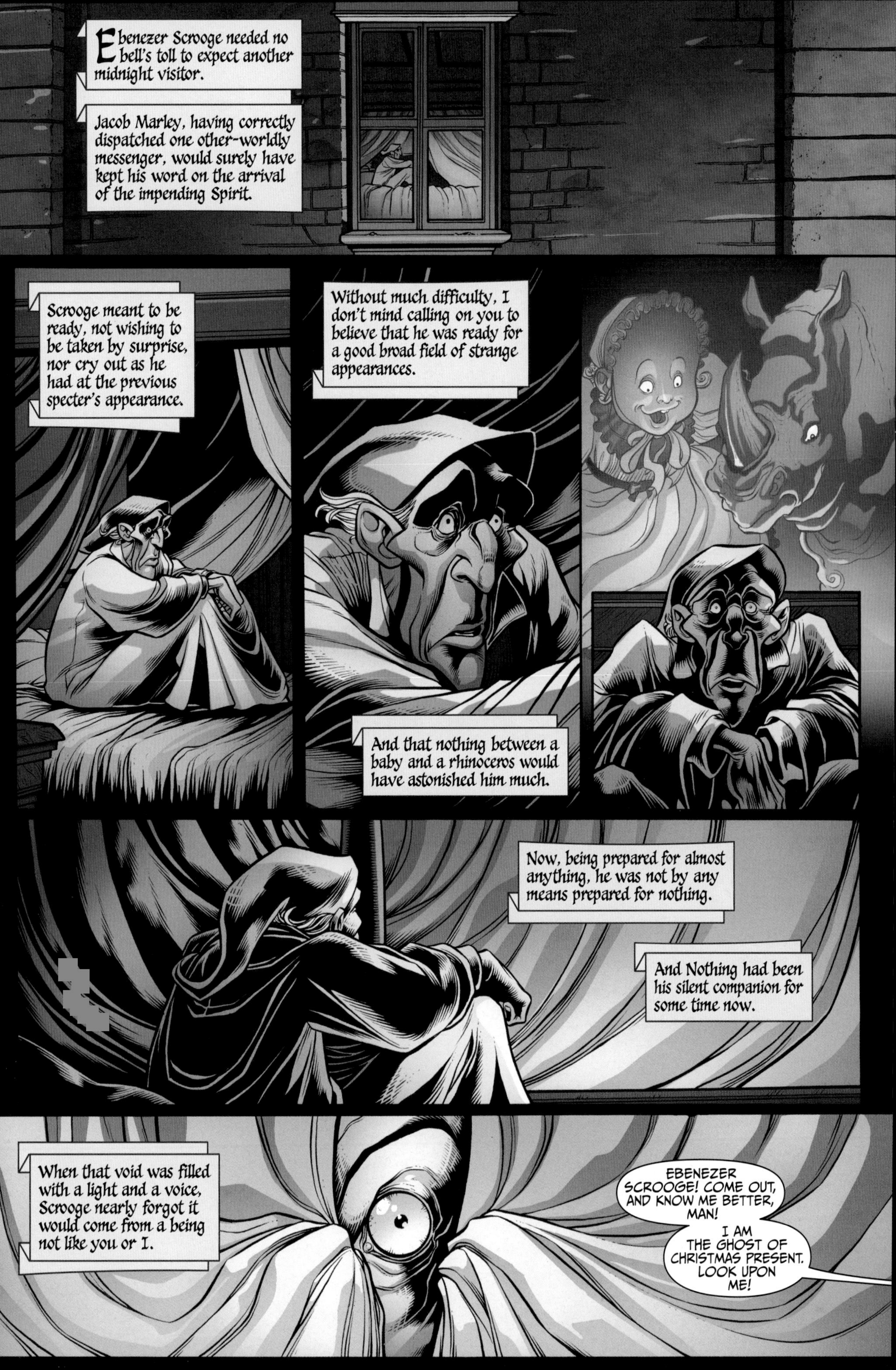
Ebenezer Scrooge needed no bell's toll to expect another midnight visitor.
Jacob Marley, having correctly dispatched one other-worldly messenger, would surely have kept his word on the arrival of the impending Spirit.
Scrooge meant to be ready, not wishing to be taken by surprise, nor cry out as he had at the previous specter's appearance.
Without much difficulty, I don't mind calling on you to believe that he was ready for a good broad field of strange appearances.
And that nothing between a baby and a rhinoceros would have astonished him much.
Now, being prepared for almost anything, he was not by any means prepared for nothing.
And Nothing had been his silent companion for some time now.
When that void was filled with a light and a voice, Scrooge nearly forgot it would come from a being not like you or I.
EBENEZER SCROOGE! COME OUT, AND KNOW ME BETTER, MAN!
I AM THE GHOST OF CHRISTMAS PRESENT. LOOK UPON ME!

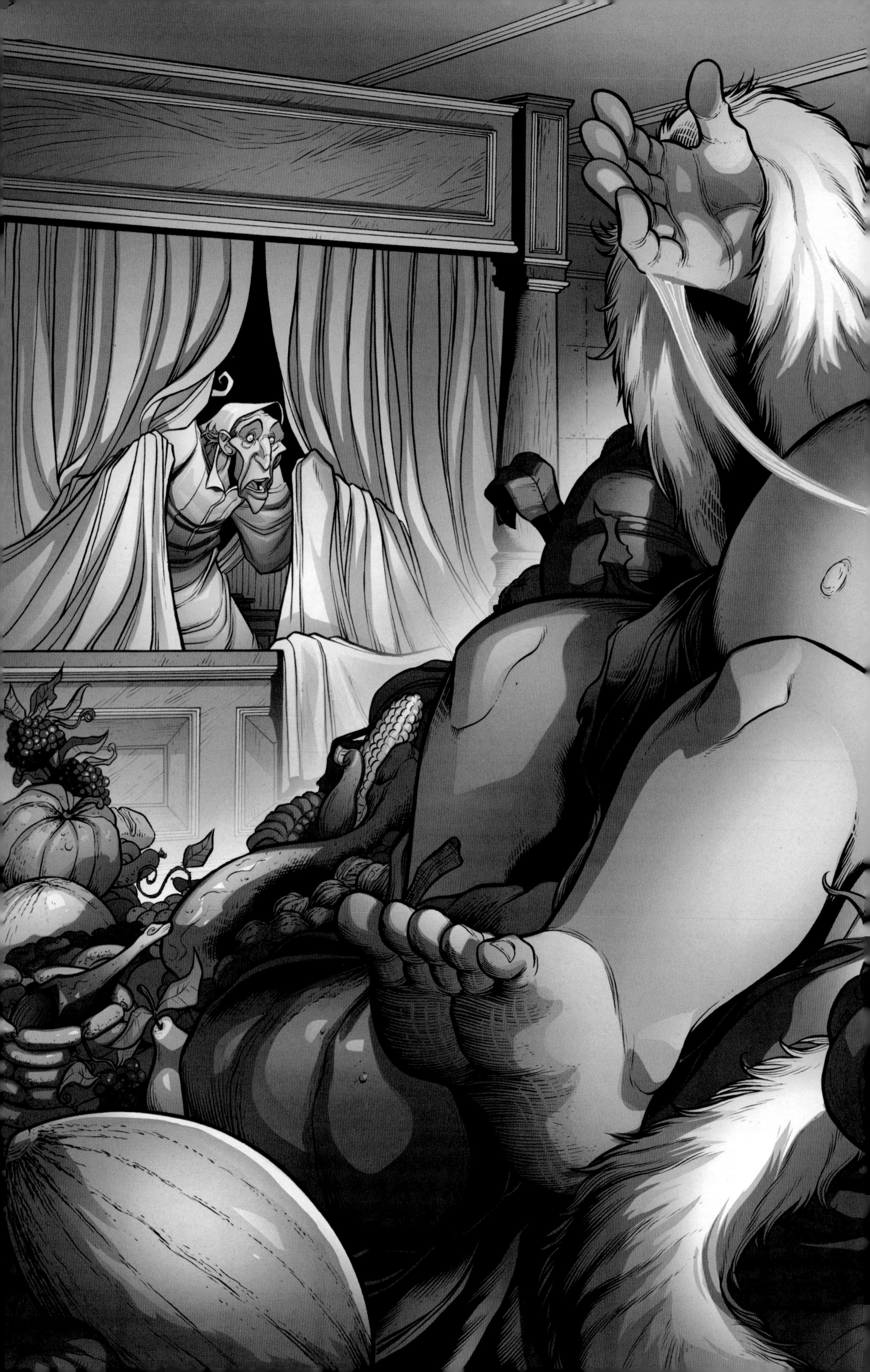

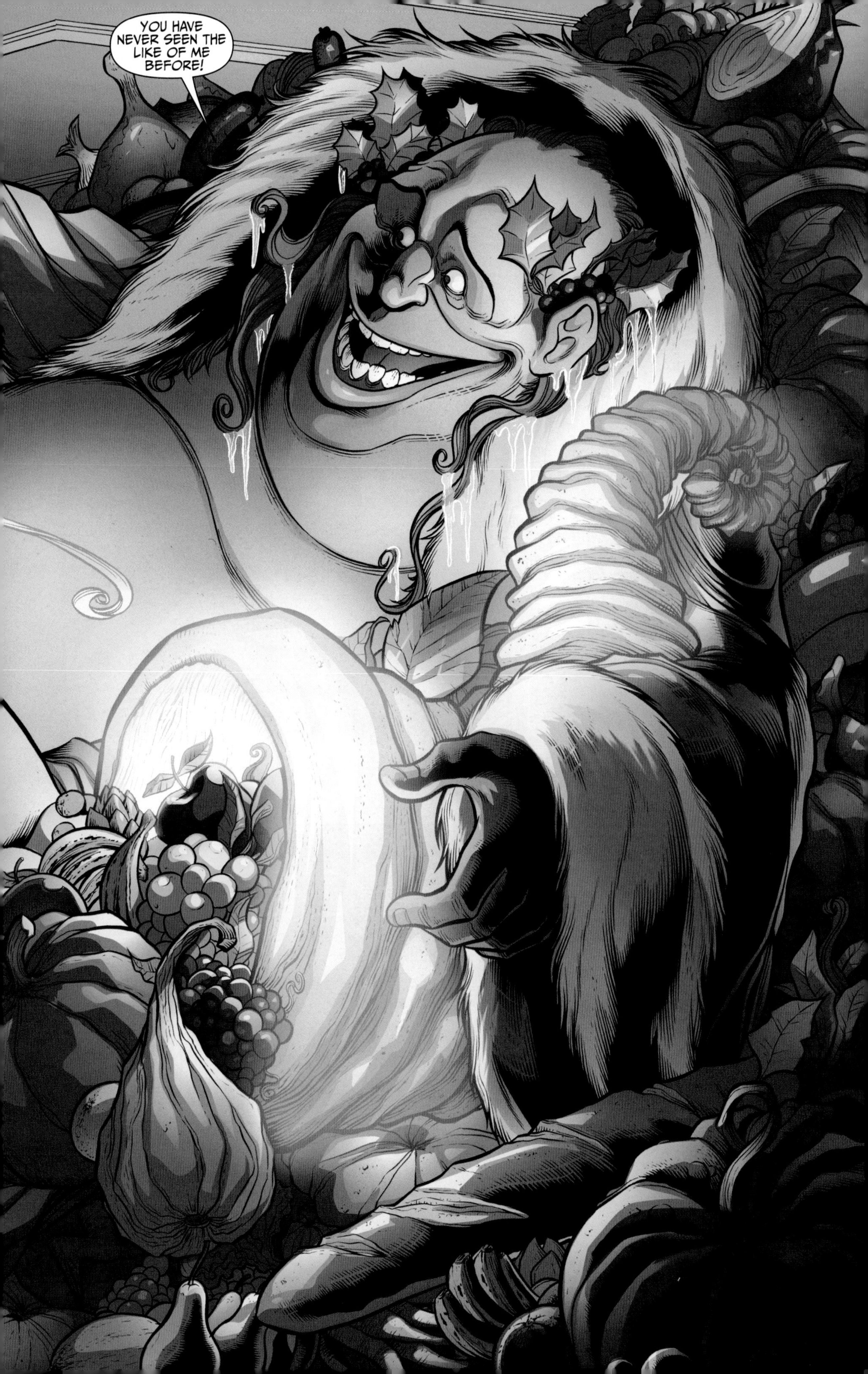
YOU HAVE NEVER SEEN THE LIKE OF ME BEFORE!

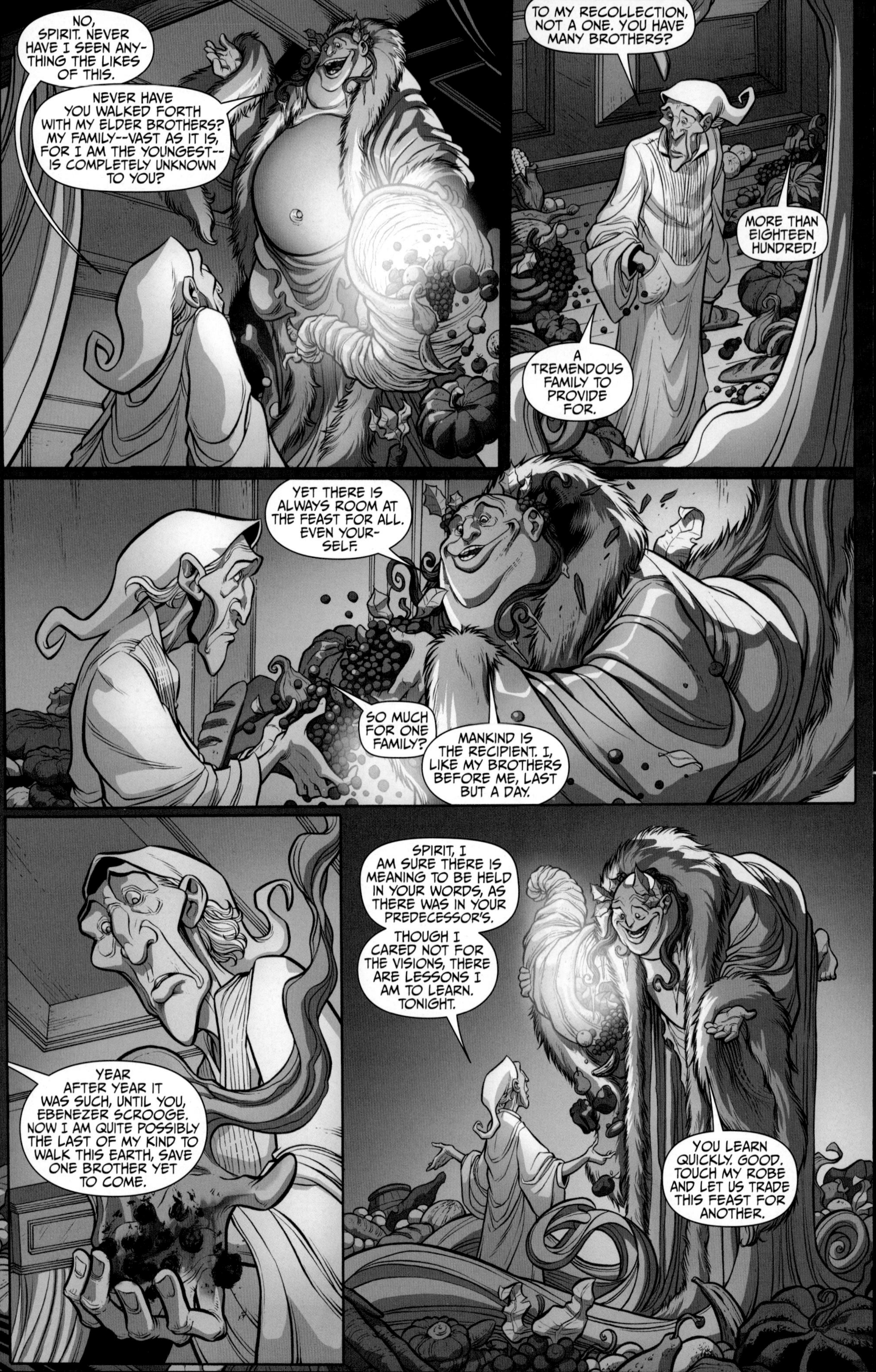
NO, SPIRIT. NEVER HAVE I SEEN ANYTHING THE LIKES OF THIS.
NEVER HAVE YOU WALKED FORTH WITH MY ELDER BROTHERS? MY FAMILY--VAST AS IT IS, FOR I AM THE YOUNGEST--IS COMPLETELY UNKNOWN TO YOU?
TO MY RECOLLECTION, NOT A ONE. YOU HAVE MANY BROTHERS?
MORE THAN EIGHTEEN HUNDRED!
A TREMENDOUS FAMILY TO PROVIDE FOR.
YET THERE IS ALWAYS ROOM AT THE FEAST FOR ALL. EVEN YOURSELF.
SO MUCH FOR ONE FAMILY?
MANKIND IS THE RECIPIENT. I, LIKE MY BROTHERS BEFORE ME, LAST BUT A DAY.
YEAR AFTER YEAR IT WAS SUCH, UNTIL YOU, EBENEZER SCROOGE. NOW I AM QUITE POSSIBLY THE LAST OF MY KIND TO WALK THIS EARTH, SAVE ONE BROTHER YET TO COME.
SPIRIT, I AM SURE THERE IS MEANING TO BE HELD IN YOUR WORDS, AS THERE WAS IN YOUR PREDECESSOR'S.
THOUGH I CARED NOT FOR THE VISIONS, THERE ARE LESSONS I AM TO LEARN. TONIGHT.
YOU LEARN QUICKLY. GOOD. TOUCH MY ROBE AND LET US TRADE THIS FEAST FOR ANOTHER.

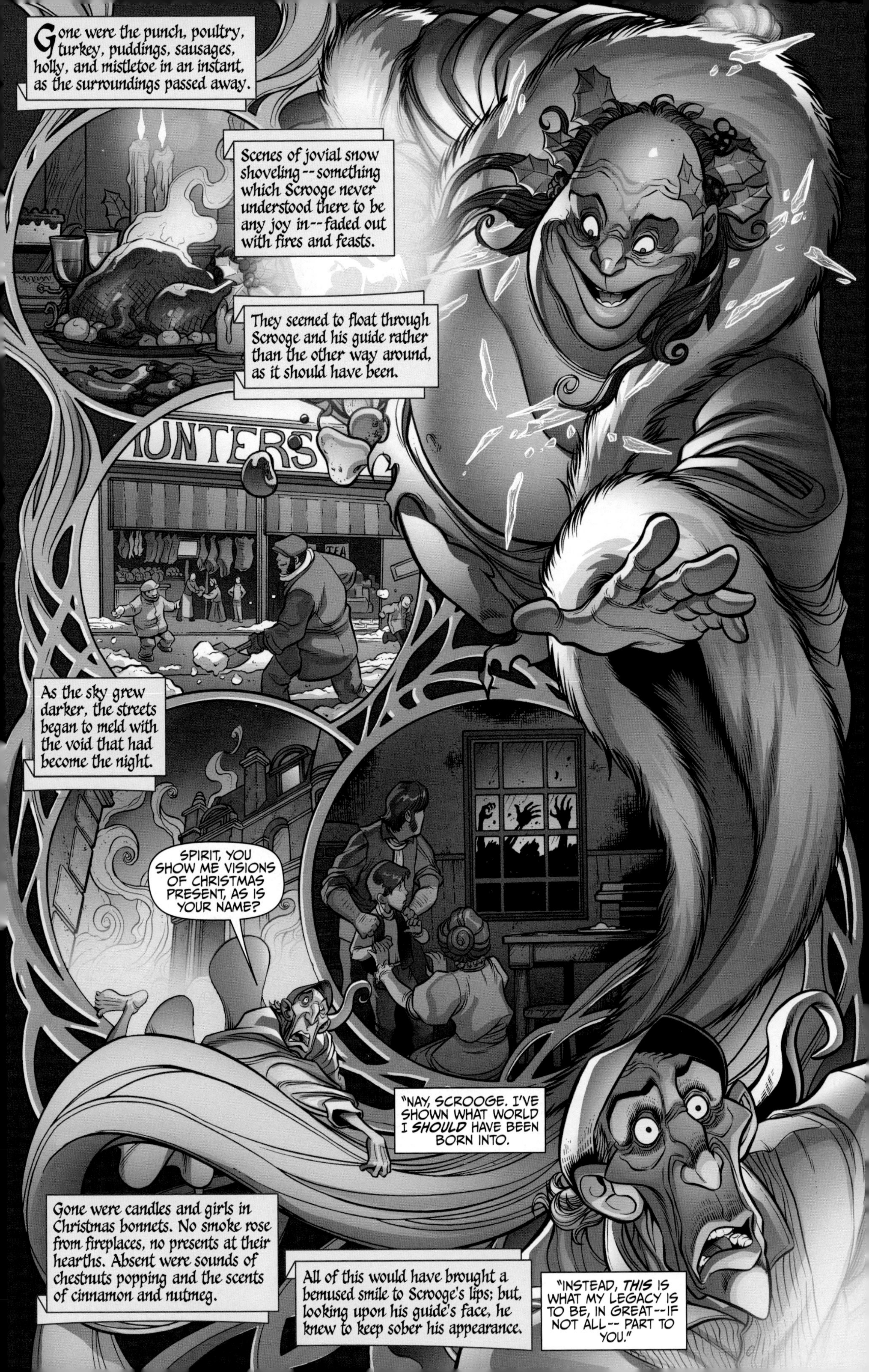
Gone were the punch, poultry, turkey, puddings, sausages, holly, and mistletoe in an instant, as the surroundings passed away.
Scenes of jovial snow shoveling--something which Scrooge never understood there to be any joy in--faded out with fires and feasts.
They seemed to float through Scrooge and his guide rather than the other way around, as it should have been.
UNTERS
TEA
As the sky grew darker, the streets began to meld with the void that had become the night.
SPIRIT, YOU SHOW ME VISIONS OF CHRISTMAS PRESENT, AS IS YOUR NAME?
"NAY, SCROOGE. I'VE SHOWN WHAT WORLD I *SHOULD* HAVE BEEN BORN INTO.
Gone were candles and girls in Christmas bonnets. No smoke rose from fireplaces, no presents at their hearths. Absent were sounds of chestnuts popping and the scents of cinnamon and nutmeg.
All of this would have brought a bemused smile to Scrooge's lips; but, looking upon his guide's face, he knew to keep sober his appearance.
"INSTEAD, *THIS* IS WHAT MY LEGACY IS TO BE, IN GREAT--IF NOT ALL-- PART TO YOU."

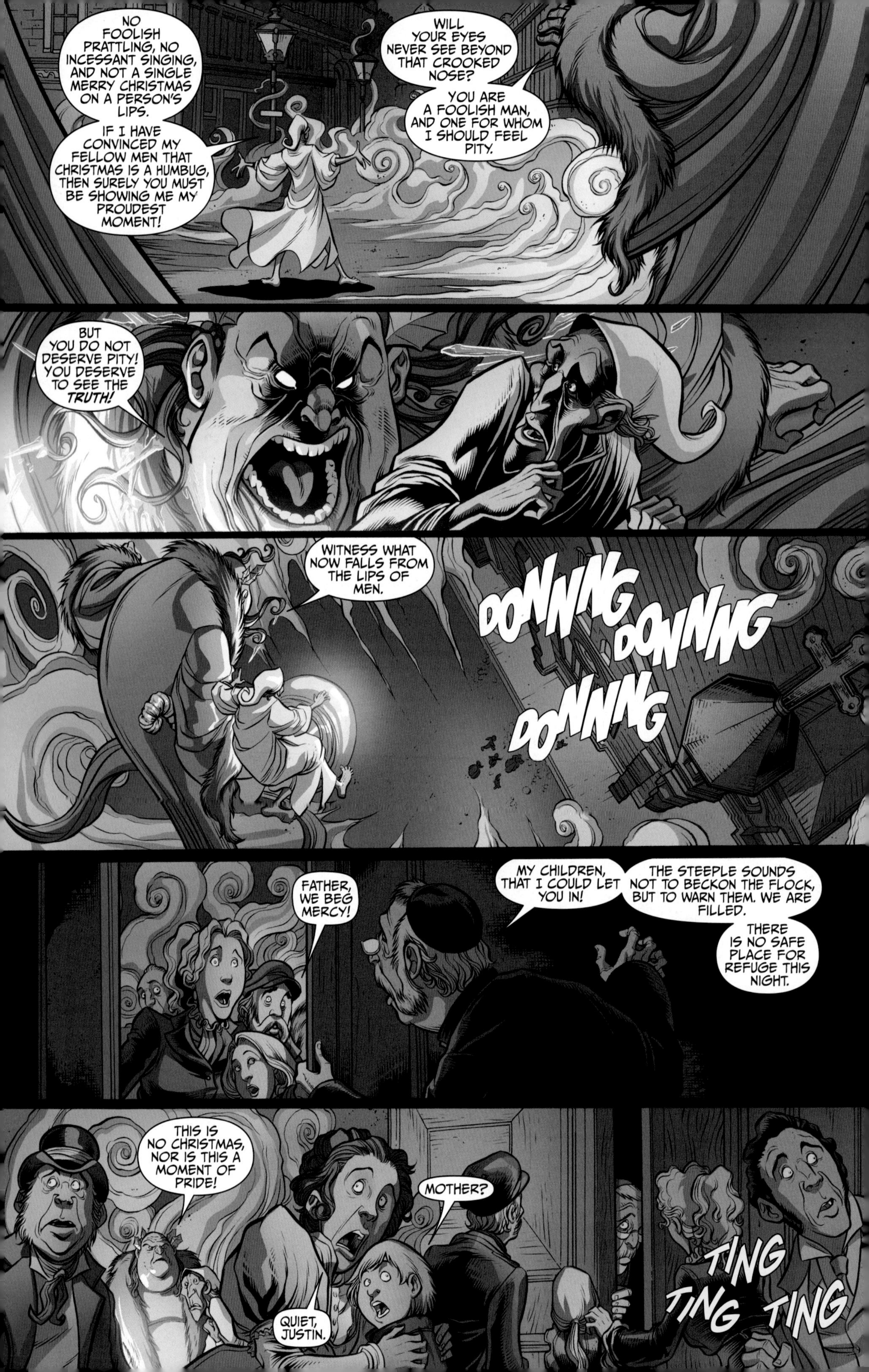
NO FOOLISH PRATTLING, NO INCESSANT SINGING, AND NOT A SINGLE MERRY CHRISTMAS ON A PERSON'S LIPS.
IF I HAVE CONVINCED MY FELLOW MEN THAT CHRISTMAS IS A HUMBUG, THEN SURELY YOU MUST BE SHOWING ME MY PROUDEST MOMENT!
WILL YOUR EYES NEVER SEE BEYOND THAT CROOKED NOSE?
YOU ARE A FOOLISH MAN, AND ONE FOR WHOM I SHOULD FEEL PITY.
BUT YOU DO NOT DESERVE PITY! YOU DESERVE TO SEE THE *TRUTH!*
WITNESS WHAT NOW FALLS FROM THE LIPS OF MEN.
DONNNG DONNNG DONNNG
FATHER, WE BEG MERCY!
MY CHILDREN, THAT I COULD LET YOU IN!
THE STEEPLE SOUNDS NOT TO BECKON THE FLOCK, BUT TO WARN THEM. WE ARE FILLED.
THERE IS NO SAFE PLACE FOR REFUGE THIS NIGHT.
THIS IS NO CHRISTMAS, NOR IS THIS A MOMENT OF PRIDE!
MOTHER?
QUIET, JUSTIN.
TING TING TING

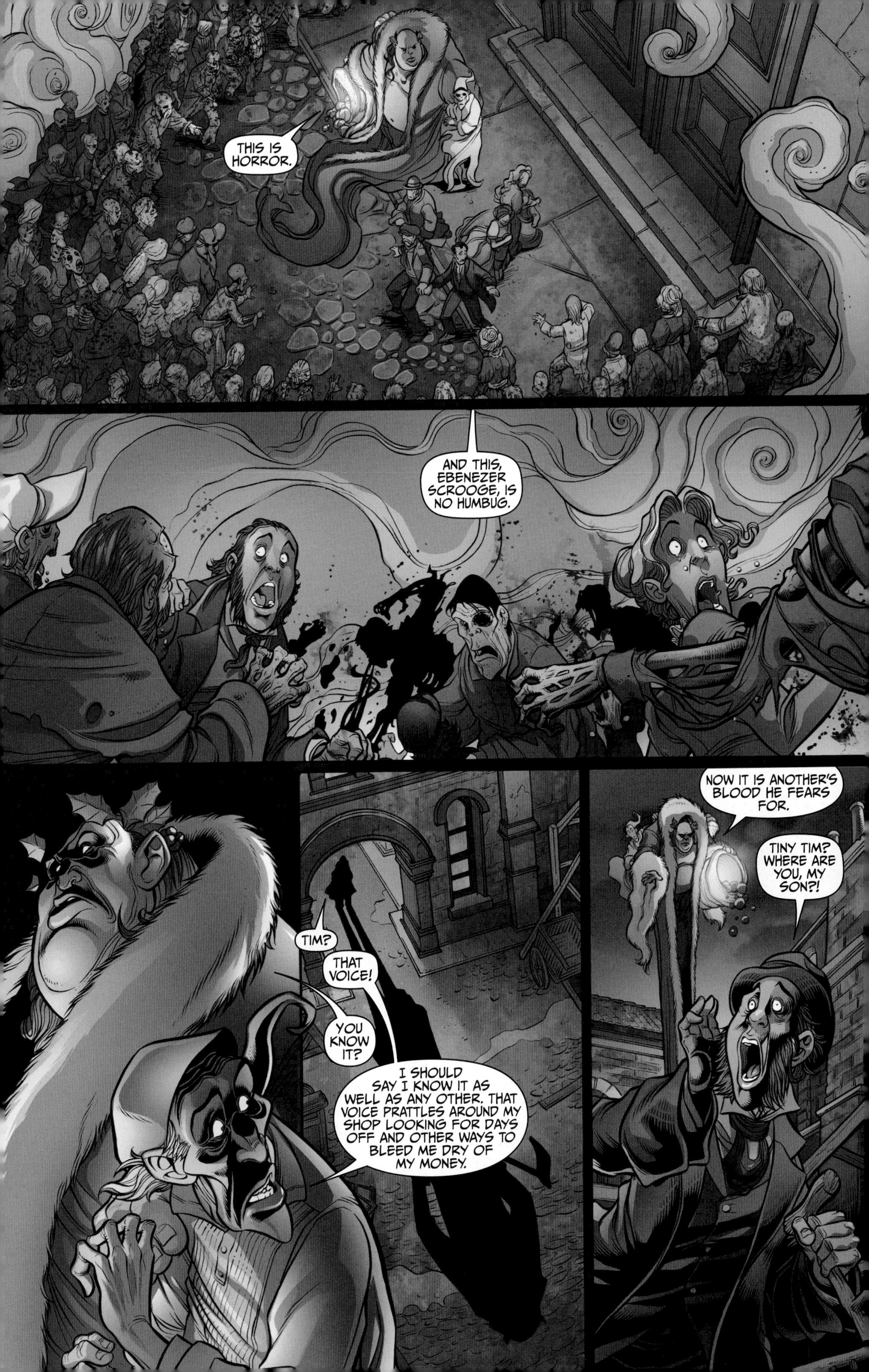
THIS IS HORROR.
AND THIS, EBENEZER SCROOGE, IS NO HUMBUG.
TIM?
THAT VOICE!
YOU KNOW IT?
I SHOULD SAY I KNOW IT AS WELL AS ANY OTHER. THAT VOICE PRATTLES AROUND MY SHOP LOOKING FOR DAYS OFF AND OTHER WAYS TO BLEED ME DRY OF MY MONEY.
NOW IT IS ANOTHER'S BLOOD HE FEARS FOR.
TINY TIM? WHERE ARE YOU, MY SON?!

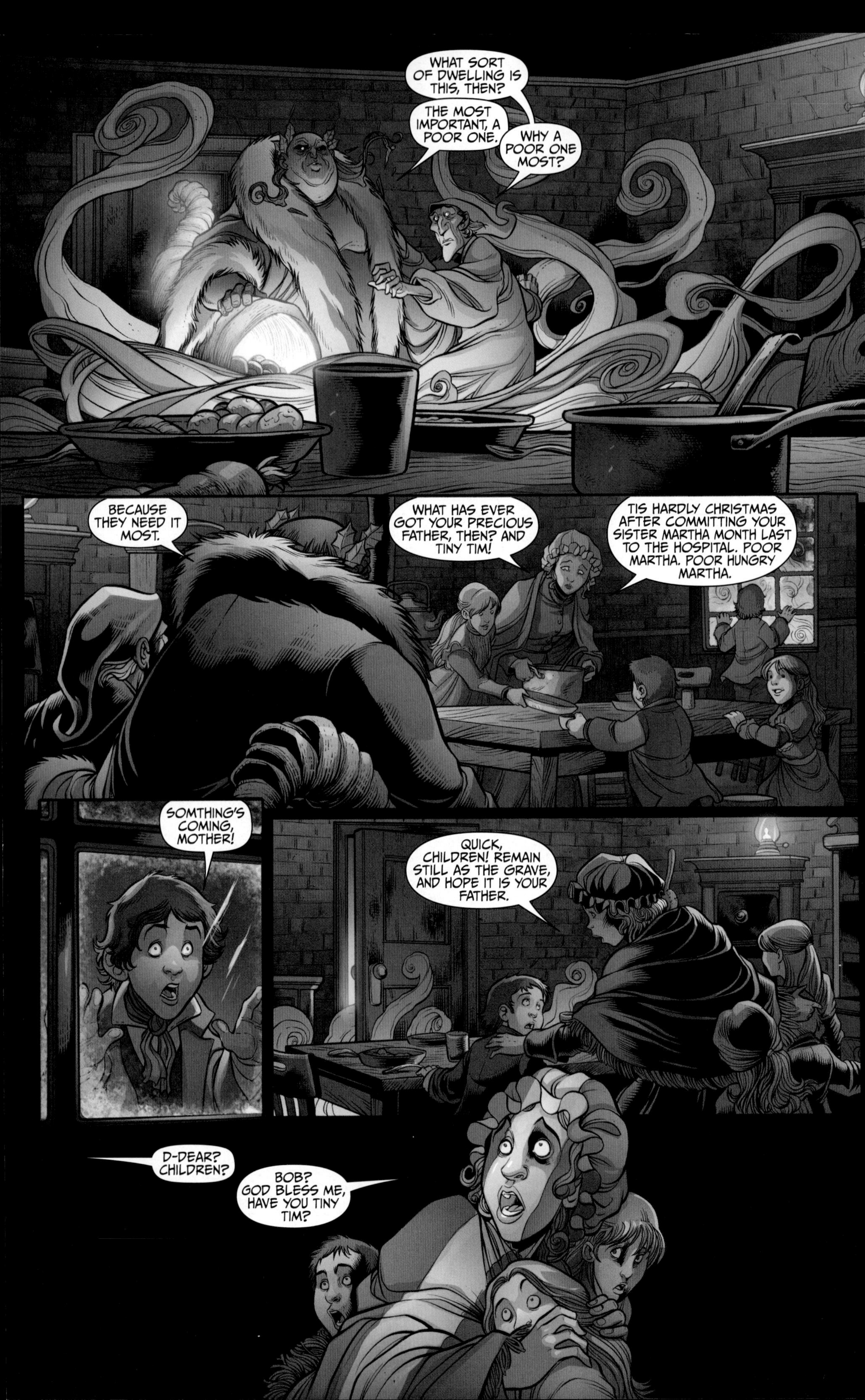
WHAT SORT OF DWELLING IS THIS, THEN?
THE MOST IMPORTANT, A POOR ONE.
WHY A POOR ONE MOST?
BECAUSE THEY NEED IT MOST.
WHAT HAS EVER GOT YOUR PRECIOUS FATHER, THEN? AND TINY TIM!
TIS HARDLY CHRISTMAS AFTER COMMITTING YOUR SISTER MARTHA MONTH LAST TO THE HOSPITAL. POOR MARTHA. POOR HUNGRY MARTHA.
SOMTHING'S COMING, MOTHER!
QUICK, CHILDREN! REMAIN STILL AS THE GRAVE, AND HOPE IT IS YOUR FATHER.
D-DEAR? CHILDREN?
BOB? GOD BLESS ME, HAVE YOU TINY TIM?

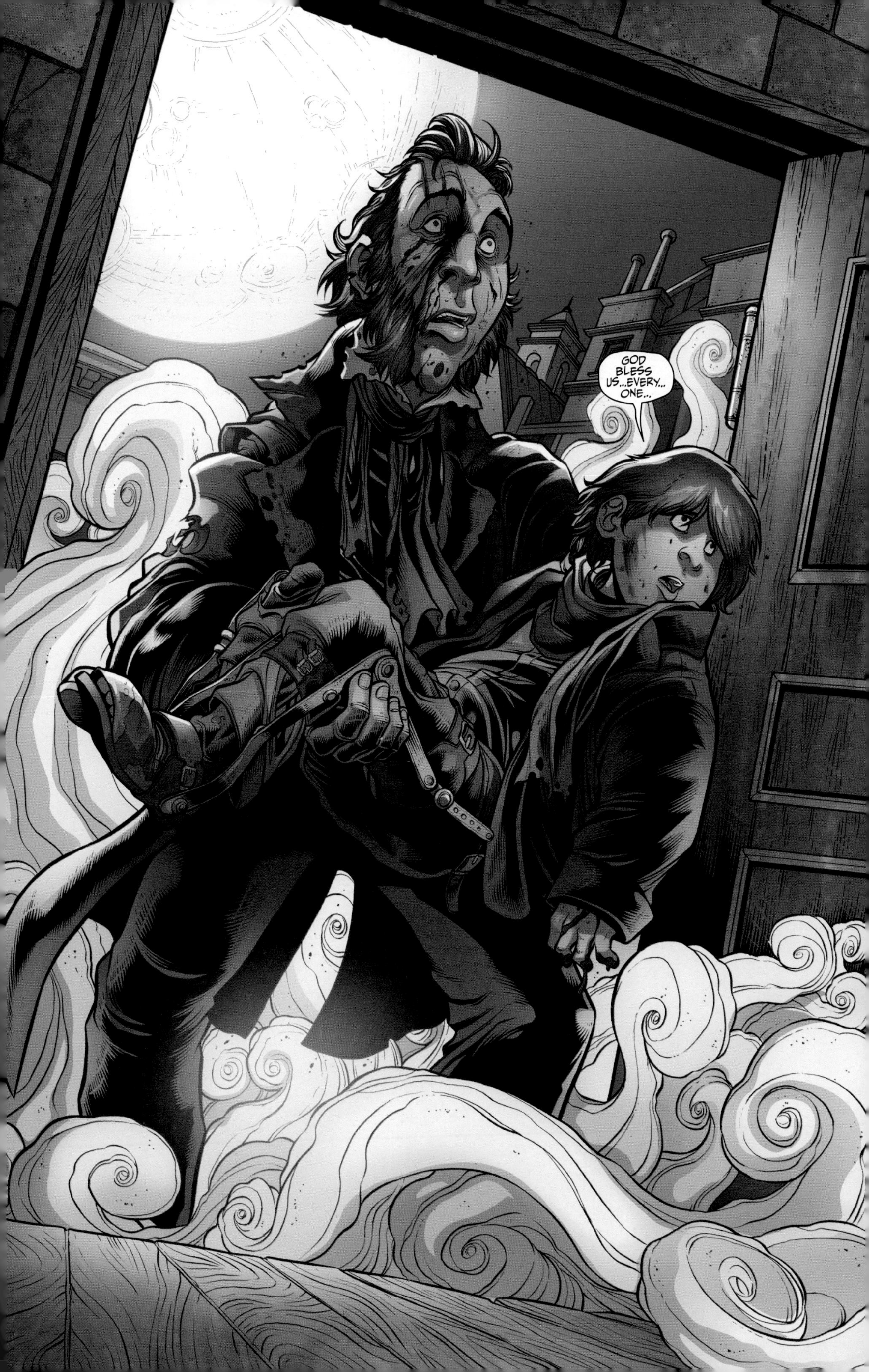
GOD BLESS US...EVERY... ONE...

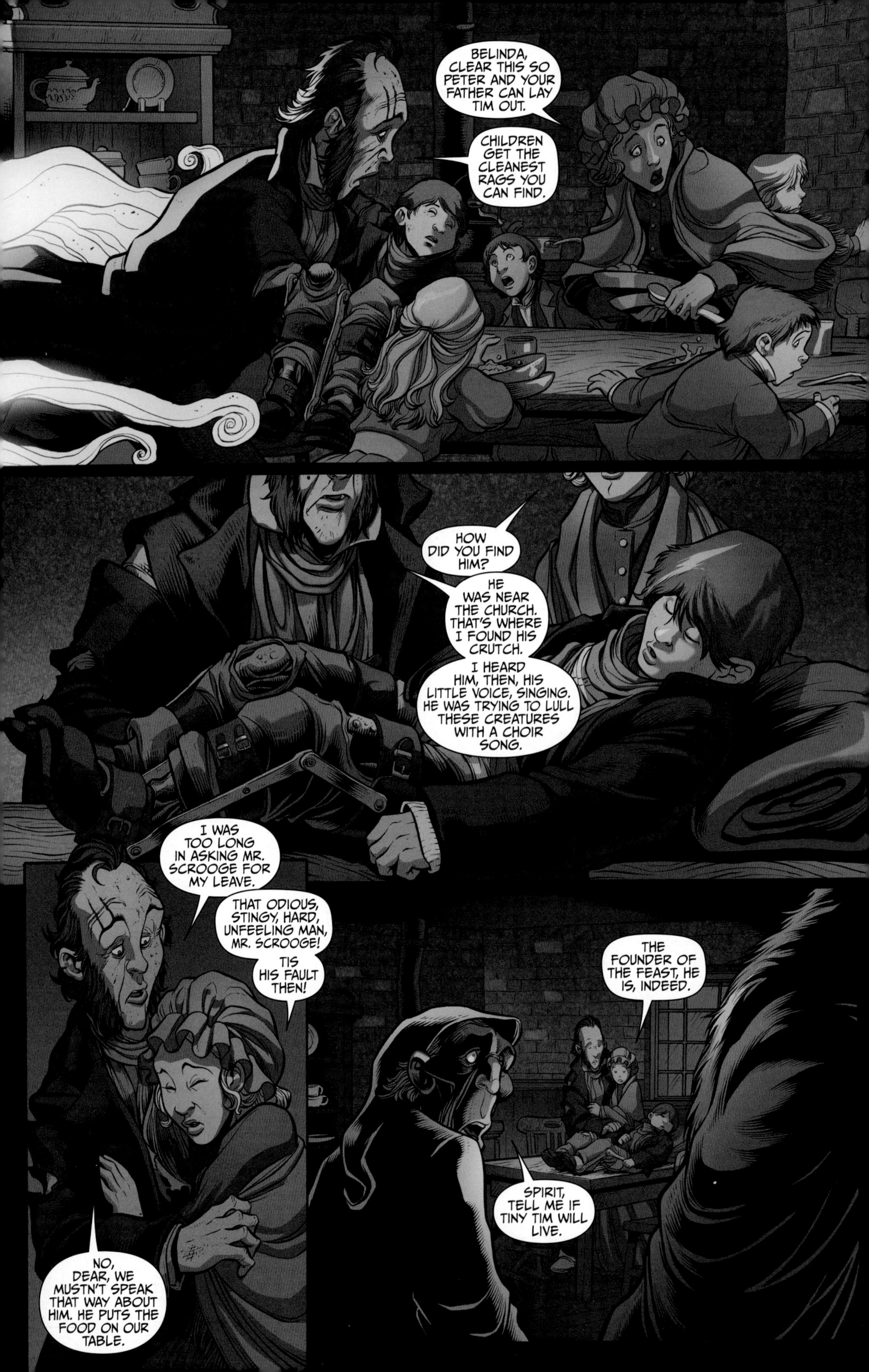
BELINDA, CLEAR THIS SO PETER AND YOUR FATHER CAN LAY TIM OUT.
CHILDREN GET THE CLEANEST RAGS YOU CAN FIND.
HOW DID YOU FIND HIM?
HE WAS NEAR THE CHURCH. THAT'S WHERE I FOUND HIS CRUTCH.
I HEARD HIM, THEN, HIS LITTLE VOICE, SINGING. HE WAS TRYING TO LULL THESE CREATURES WITH A CHOIR SONG.
I WAS TOO LONG IN ASKING MR. SCROOGE FOR MY LEAVE.
THAT ODIOUS, STINGY, HARD, UNFEELING MAN, MR. SCROOGE!
TIS HIS FAULT THEN!
NO, DEAR, WE MUSTN'T SPEAK THAT WAY ABOUT HIM. HE PUTS THE FOOD ON OUR TABLE.
THE FOUNDER OF THE FEAST, HE IS, INDEED.
SPIRIT, TELL ME IF TINY TIM WILL LIVE.

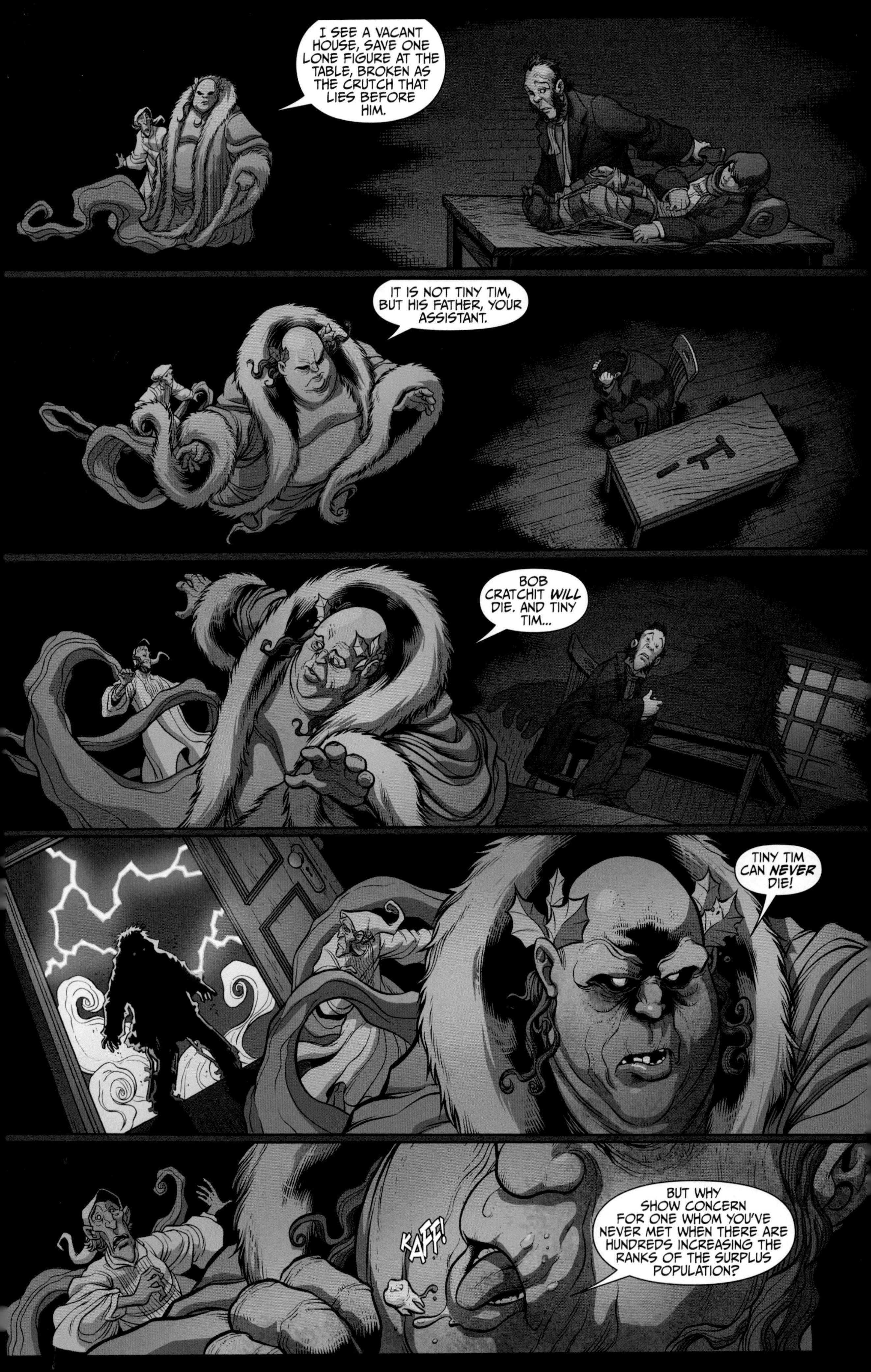
I SEE A VACANT HOUSE, SAVE ONE LONE FIGURE AT THE TABLE, BROKEN AS THE CRUTCH THAT LIES BEFORE HIM.
IT IS NOT TINY TIM, BUT HIS FATHER, YOUR ASSISTANT.
BOB CRATCHIT *WILL* DIE. AND TINY TIM...
TINY TIM CAN *NEVER* DIE!
KAFF!
BUT WHY SHOW CONCERN FOR ONE WHOM YOU'VE NEVER MET WHEN THERE ARE HUNDREDS INCREASING THE RANKS OF THE SURPLUS POPULATION?

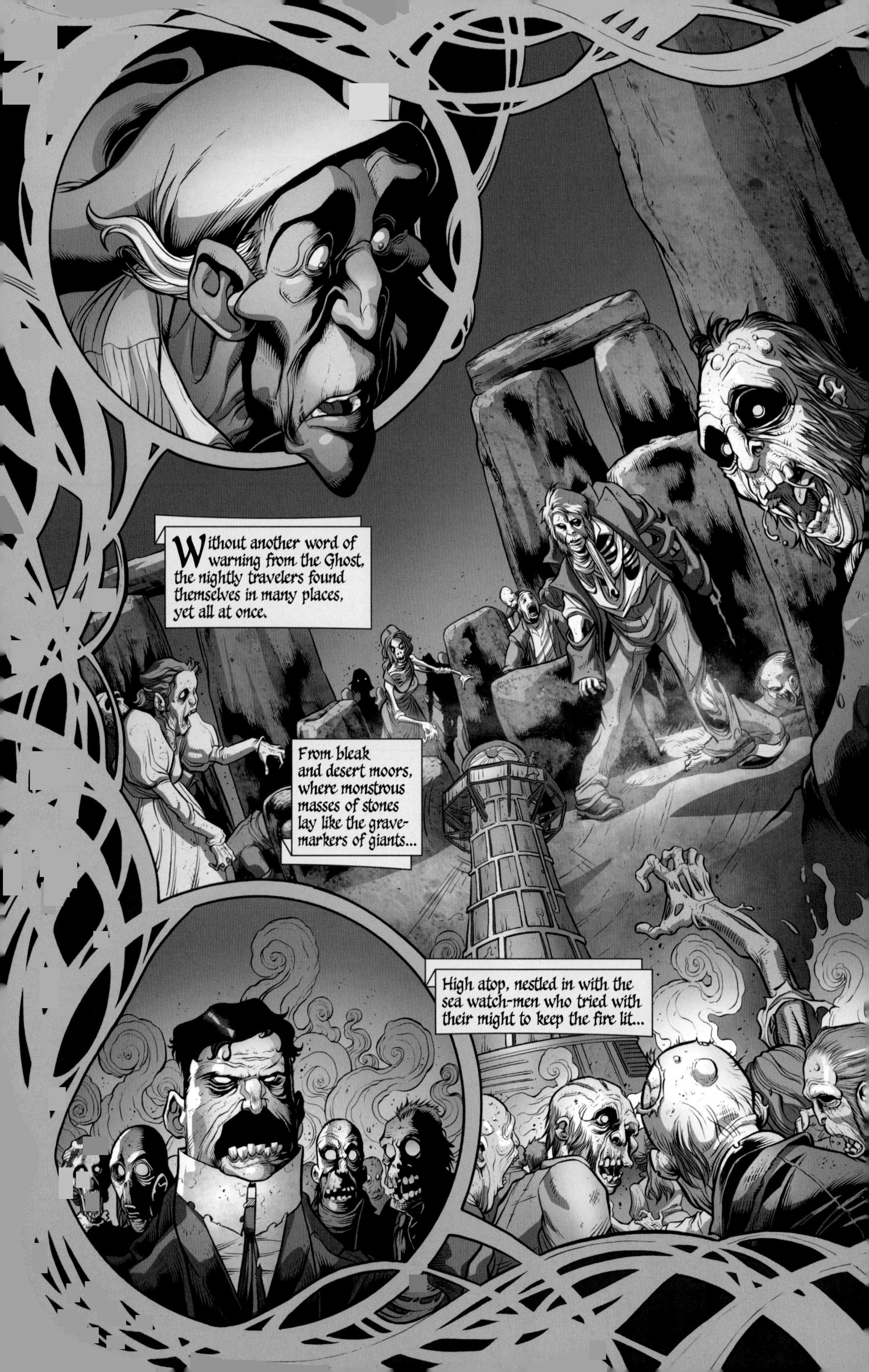
Without another word of warning from the Ghost, the nightly travelers found themselves in many places, yet all at once.
From bleak and desert moors, where monstrous masses of stones lay like the grave-markers of giants...
High atop, nestled in with the sea watch-men who tried with their might to keep the fire lit...

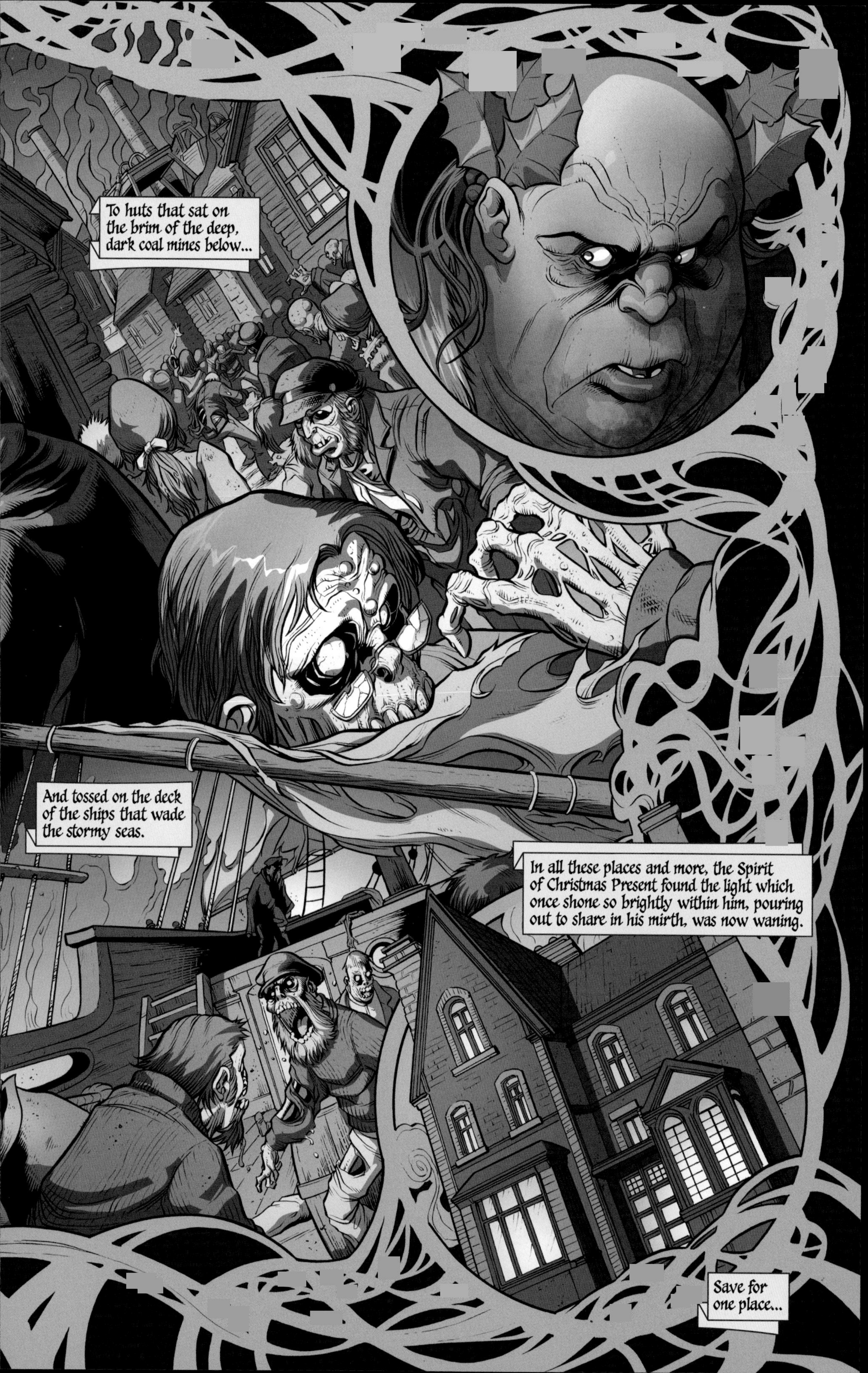

To huts that sat on the brim of the deep, dark coal mines below...
And tossed on the deck of the ships that wade the stormy seas.
In all these places and more, the Spirit of Christmas Present found the light which once shone so brightly within him, pouring out to share in his mirth, was now waning.
Save for one place...

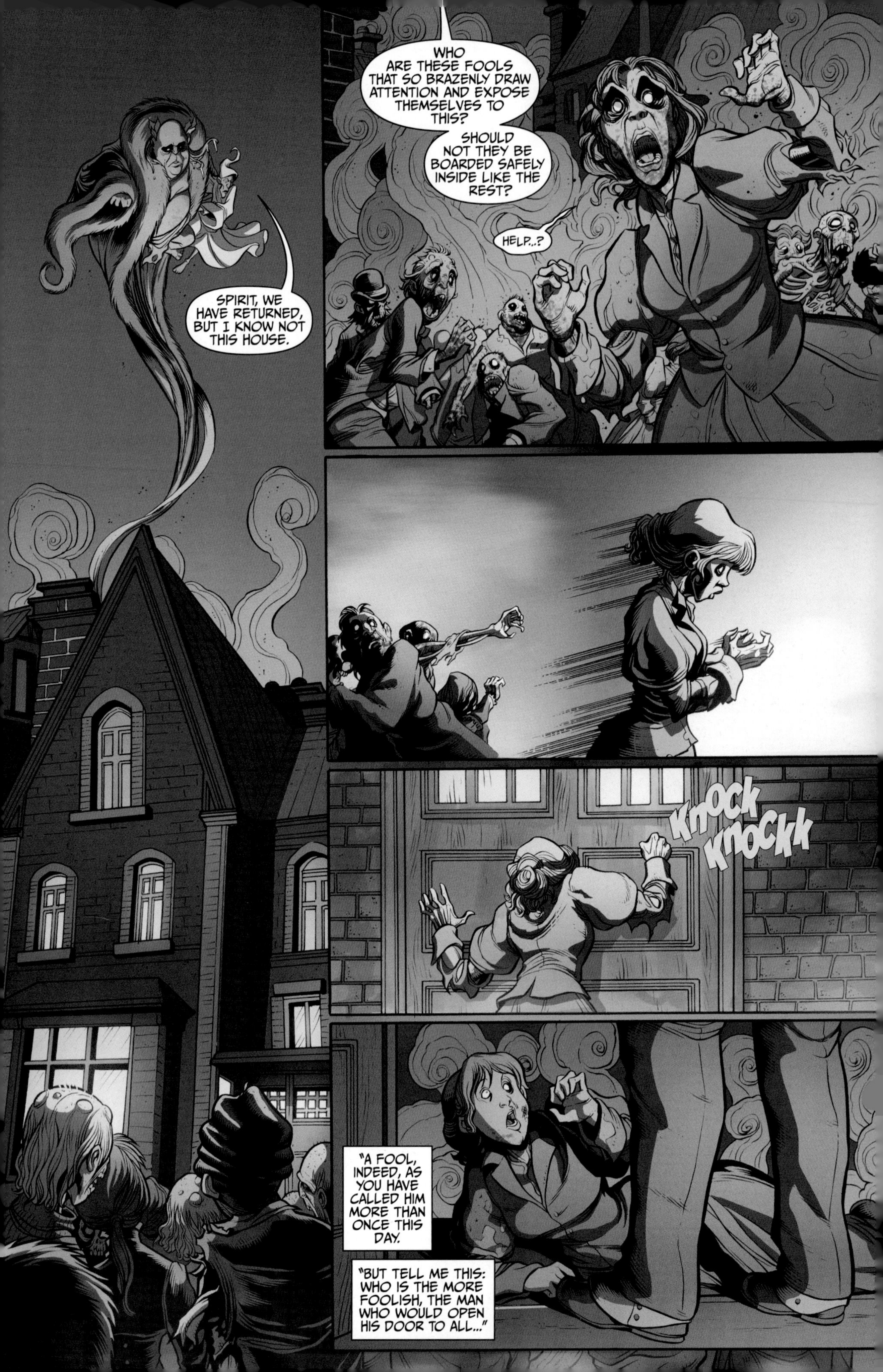
SPIRIT, WE HAVE RETURNED, BUT I KNOW NOT THIS HOUSE.
WHO ARE THESE FOOLS THAT SO BRAZENLY DRAW ATTENTION AND EXPOSE THEMSELVES TO THIS?
SHOULD NOT THEY BE BOARDED SAFELY INSIDE LIKE THE REST?
HELP...?
KNOCK KNOCKK
"A FOOL, INDEED, AS YOU HAVE CALLED HIM MORE THAN ONCE THIS DAY.
"BUT TELL ME THIS: WHO IS THE MORE FOOLISH, THE MAN WHO WOULD OPEN HIS DOOR TO ALL..."

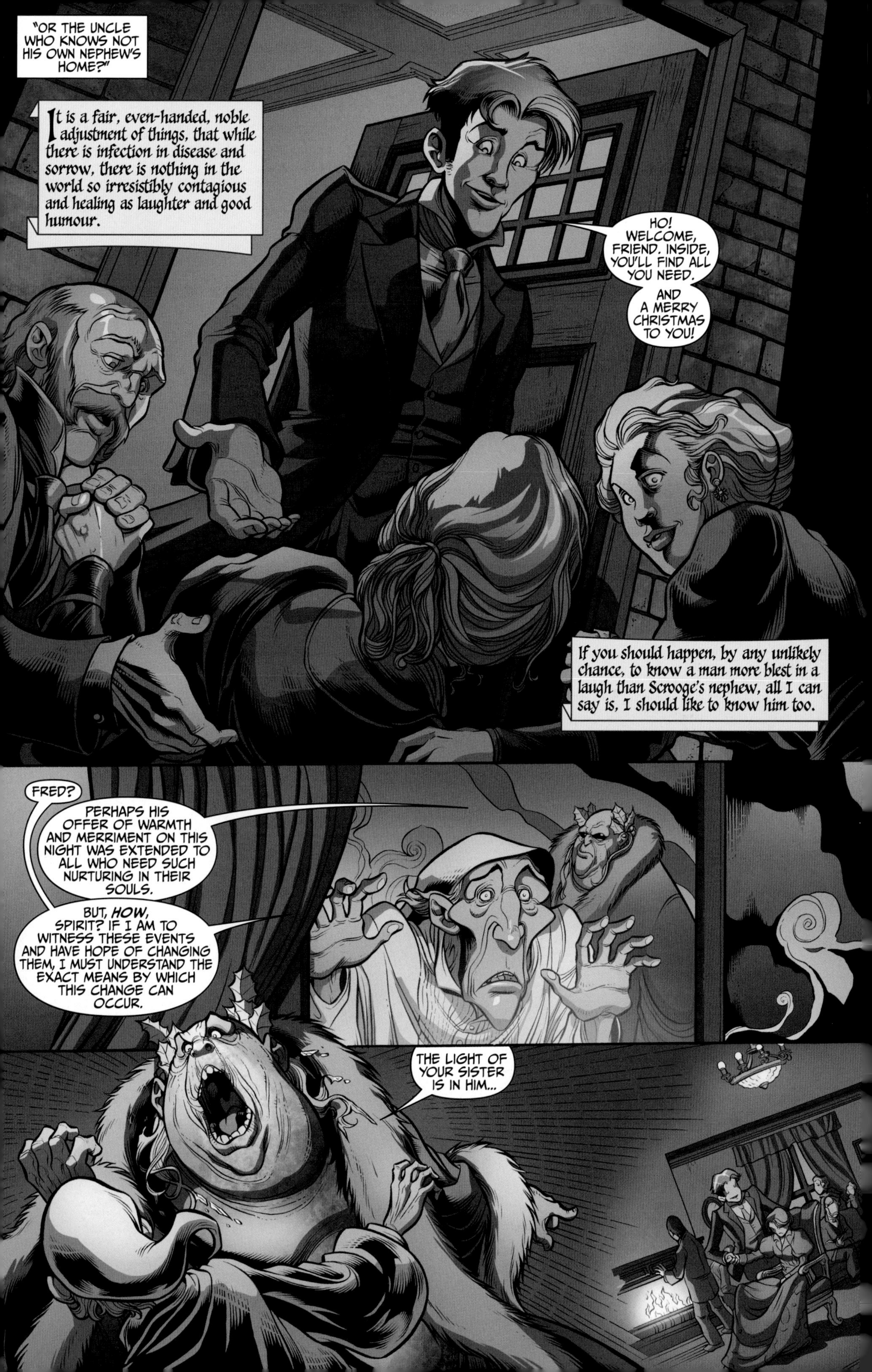
"OR THE UNCLE WHO KNOWS NOT HIS OWN NEPHEW'S HOME?"
It is a fair, even-handed, noble adjustment of things, that while there is infection in disease and sorrow, there is nothing in the world so irresistibly contagious and healing as laughter and good humour.
HO! WELCOME, FRIEND. INSIDE, YOU'LL FIND ALL YOU NEED.
AND A MERRY CHRISTMAS TO YOU!
If you should happen, by any unlikely chance, to know a man more blest in a laugh than Scrooge's nephew, all I can say is, I should like to know him too.
FRED?
PERHAPS HIS OFFER OF WARMTH AND MERRIMENT ON THIS NIGHT WAS EXTENDED TO ALL WHO NEED SUCH NURTURING IN THEIR SOULS.
BUT, *HOW*, SPIRIT? IF I AM TO WITNESS THESE EVENTS AND HAVE HOPE OF CHANGING THEM, I MUST UNDERSTAND THE EXACT MEANS BY WHICH THIS CHANGE CAN OCCUR.
THE LIGHT OF YOUR SISTER IS IN HIM...

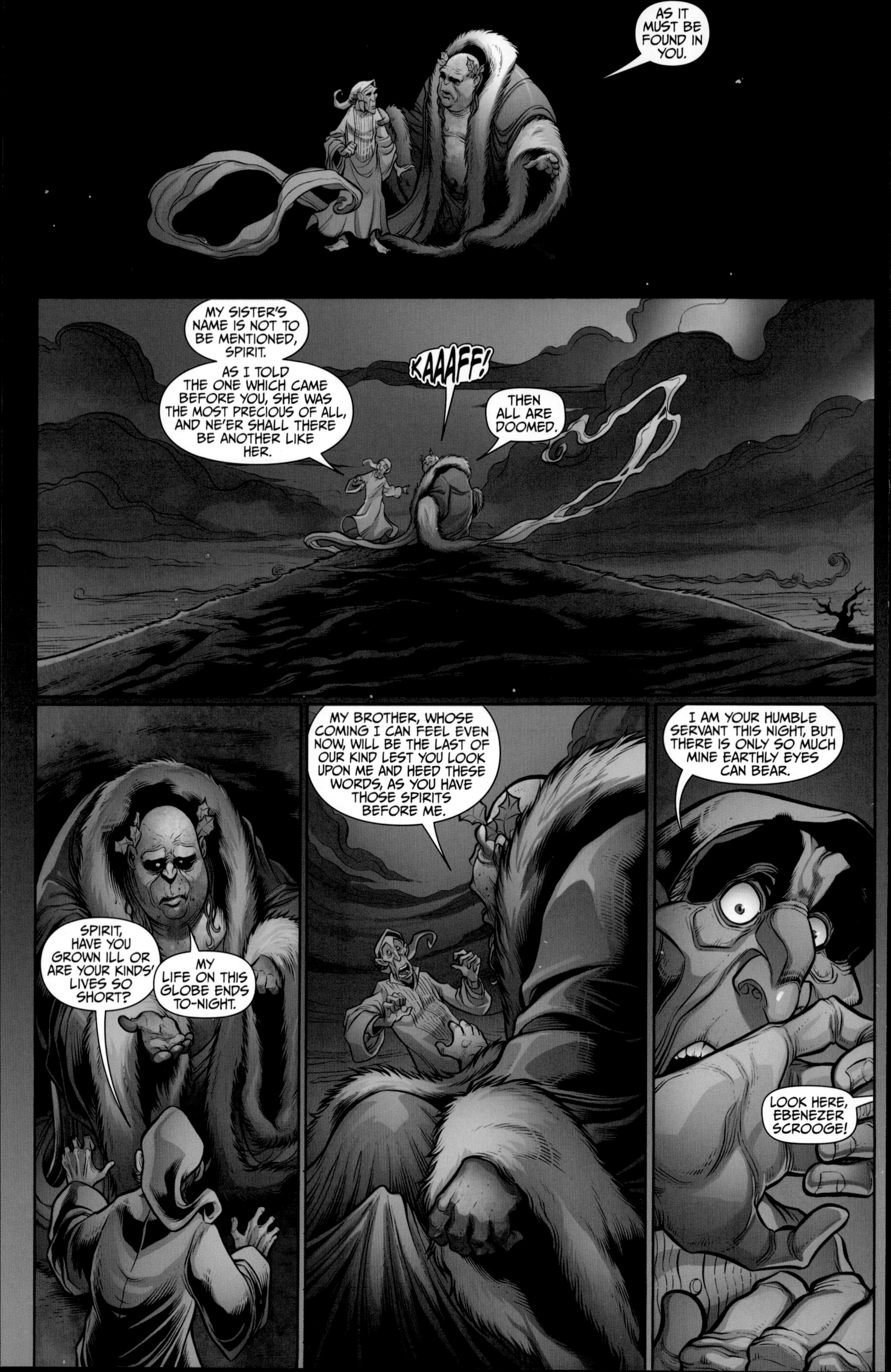
AS IT MUST BE FOUND IN YOU.
MY SISTER'S NAME IS NOT TO BE MENTIONED, SPIRIT.
AS I TOLD THE ONE WHICH CAME BEFORE YOU, SHE WAS THE MOST PRECIOUS OF ALL, AND NE'ER SHALL THERE BE ANOTHER LIKE HER.
KAAAFF!
THEN ALL ARE DOOMED.
SPIRIT, HAVE YOU GROWN ILL OR ARE YOUR KINDS' LIVES SO SHORT?
MY LIFE ON THIS GLOBE ENDS TO-NIGHT.
MY BROTHER, WHOSE COMING I CAN FEEL EVEN NOW, WILL BE THE LAST OF OUR KIND LEST YOU LOOK UPON ME AND HEED THESE WORDS, AS YOU HAVE THOSE SPIRITS BEFORE ME.
I AM YOUR HUMBLE SERVANT THIS NIGHT, BUT THERE IS ONLY SO MUCH MINE EARTHLY EYES CAN BEAR.
LOOK HERE, EBENEZER SCROOGE!

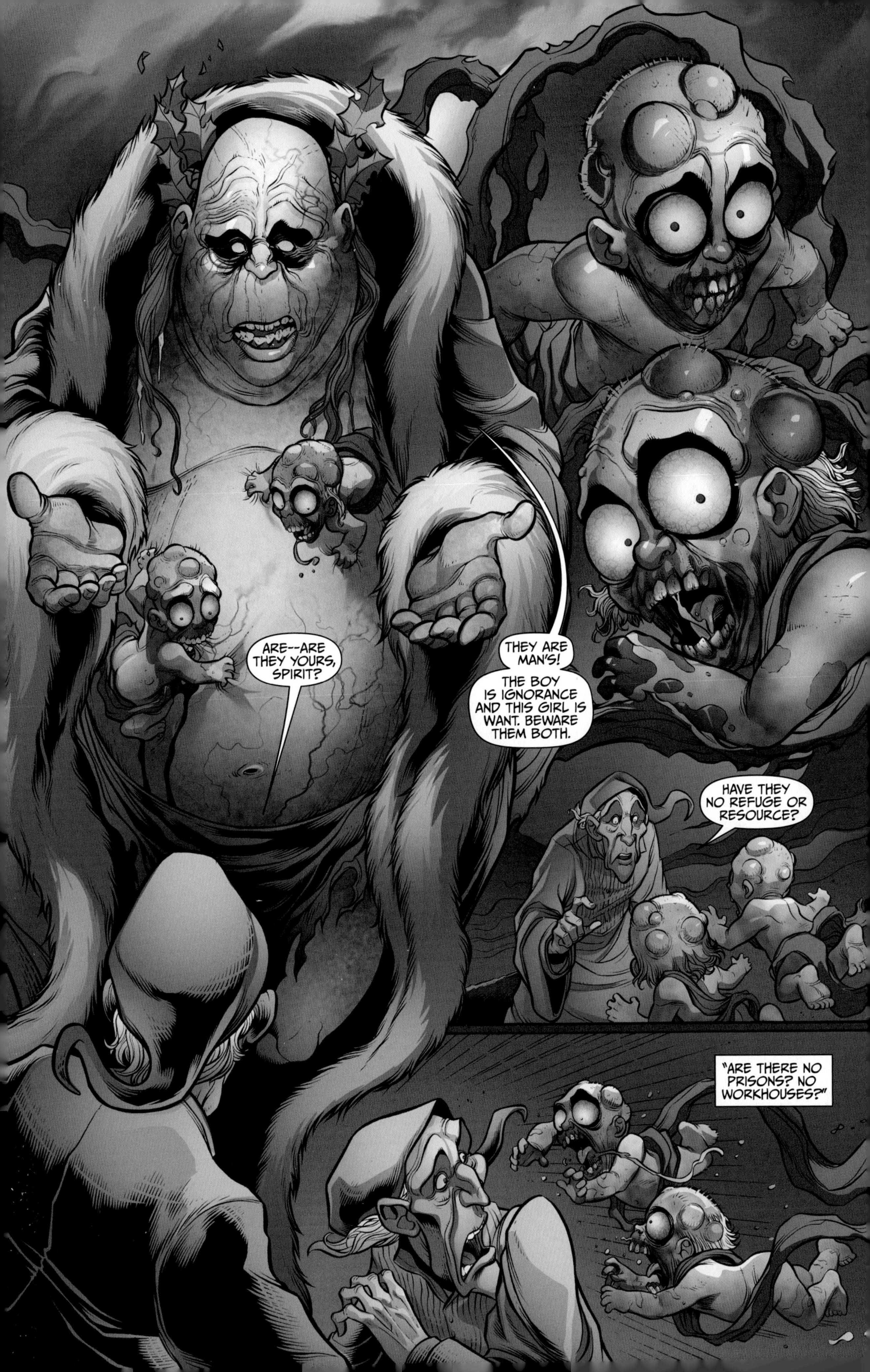
ARE--ARE THEY YOURS, SPIRIT?
THEY ARE MAN'S!
THE BOY IS IGNORANCE AND THIS GIRL IS WANT. BEWARE THEM BOTH.
HAVE THEY NO REFUGE OR RESOURCE?
"ARE THERE NO PRISONS? NO WORKHOUSES?"

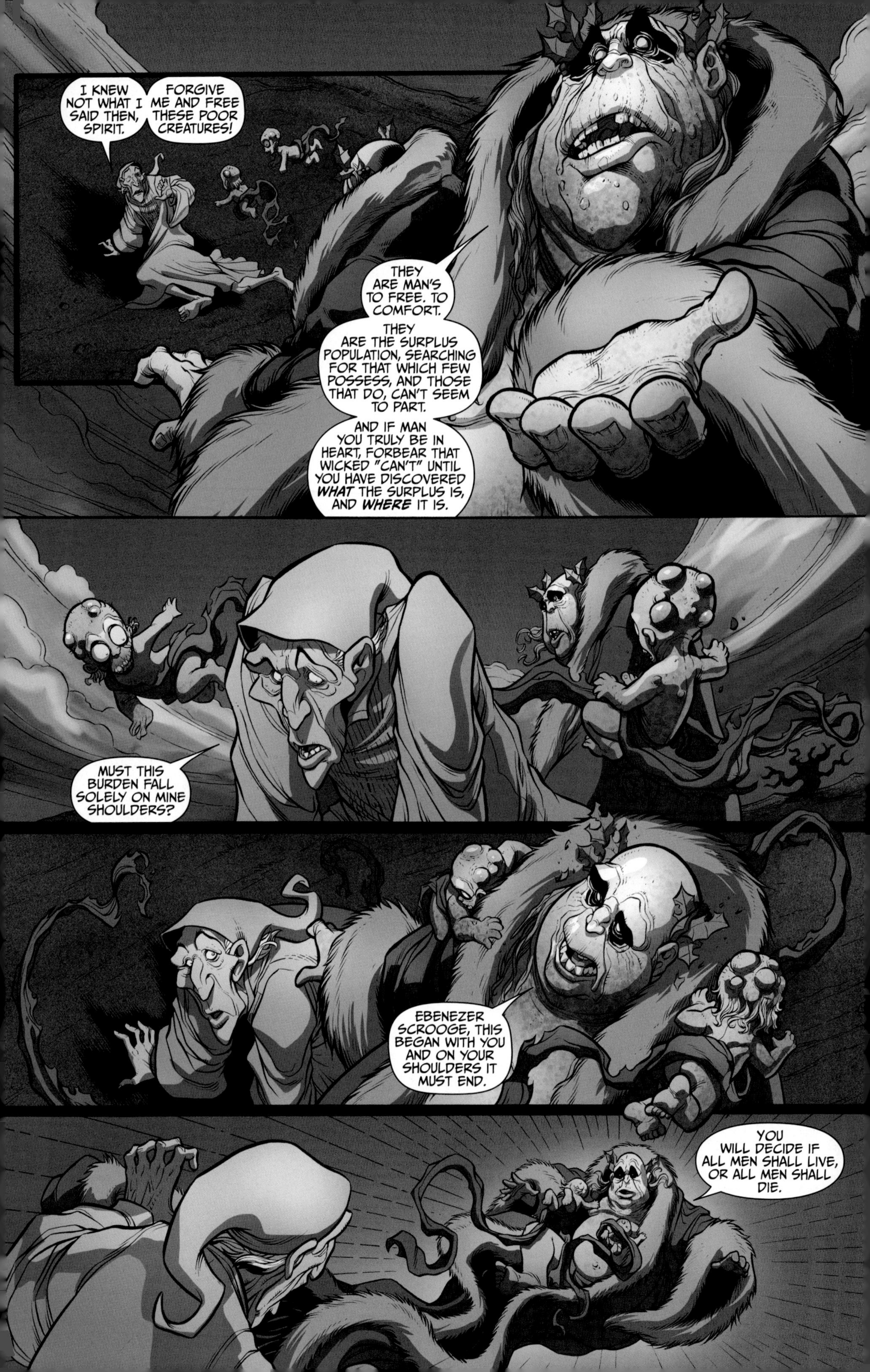
I KNEW NOT WHAT I SAID THEN, SPIRIT.
FORGIVE ME AND FREE THESE POOR CREATURES!
THEY ARE MAN'S TO FREE. TO COMFORT.
THEY ARE THE SURPLUS POPULATION, SEARCHING FOR THAT WHICH FEW POSSESS, AND THOSE THAT DO, CAN'T SEEM TO PART.
AND IF MAN YOU TRULY BE IN HEART, FORBEAR THAT WICKED "CAN'T" UNTIL YOU HAVE DISCOVERED *WHAT* THE SURPLUS IS, AND *WHERE* IT IS.
MUST THIS BURDEN FALL SOLELY ON MINE SHOULDERS?
EBENEZER SCROOGE, THIS BEGAN WITH YOU AND ON YOUR SHOULDERS IT MUST END.
YOU WILL DECIDE IF ALL MEN SHALL LIVE, OR ALL MEN SHALL DIE.

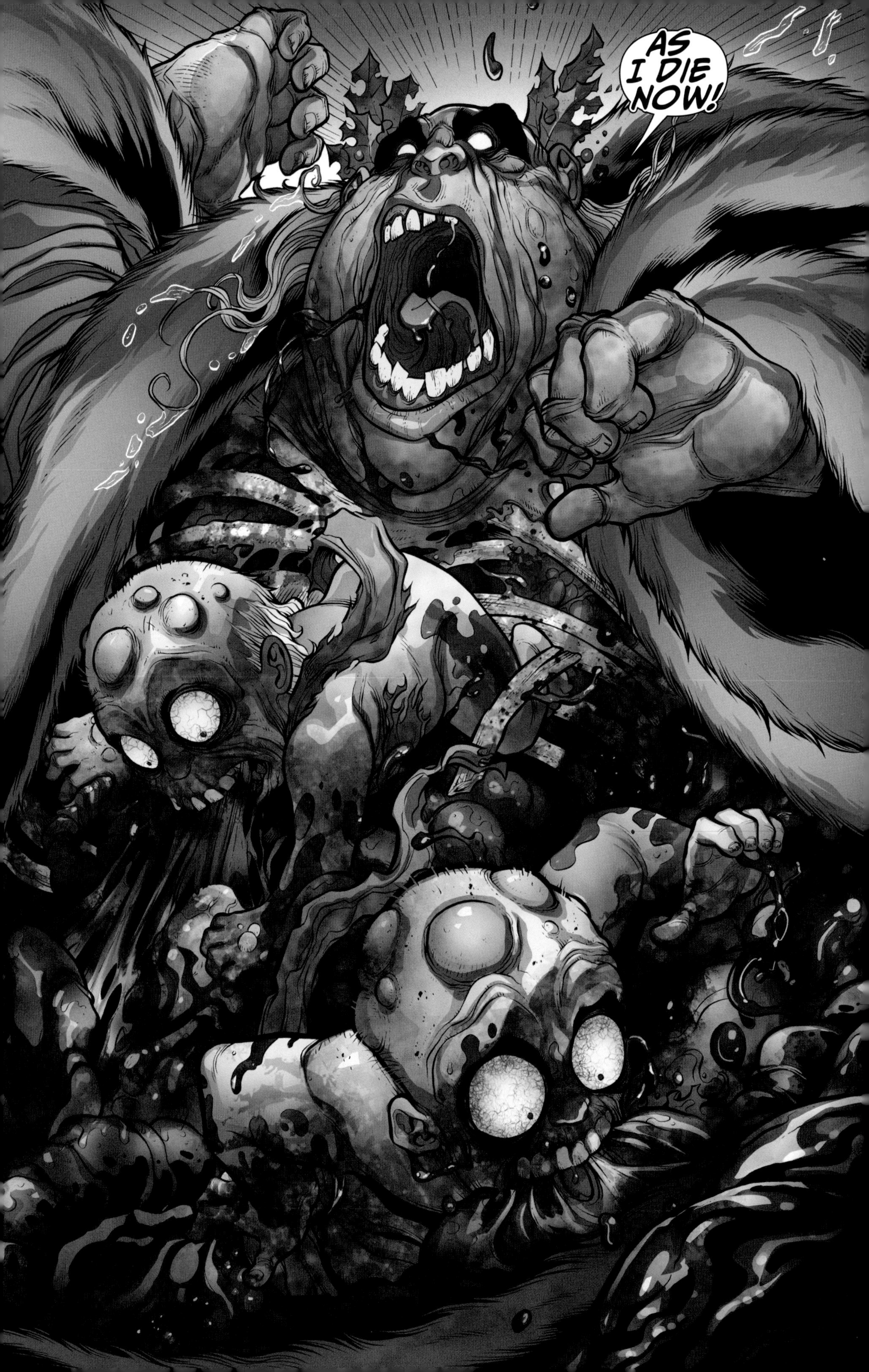
AS I DIE NOW!

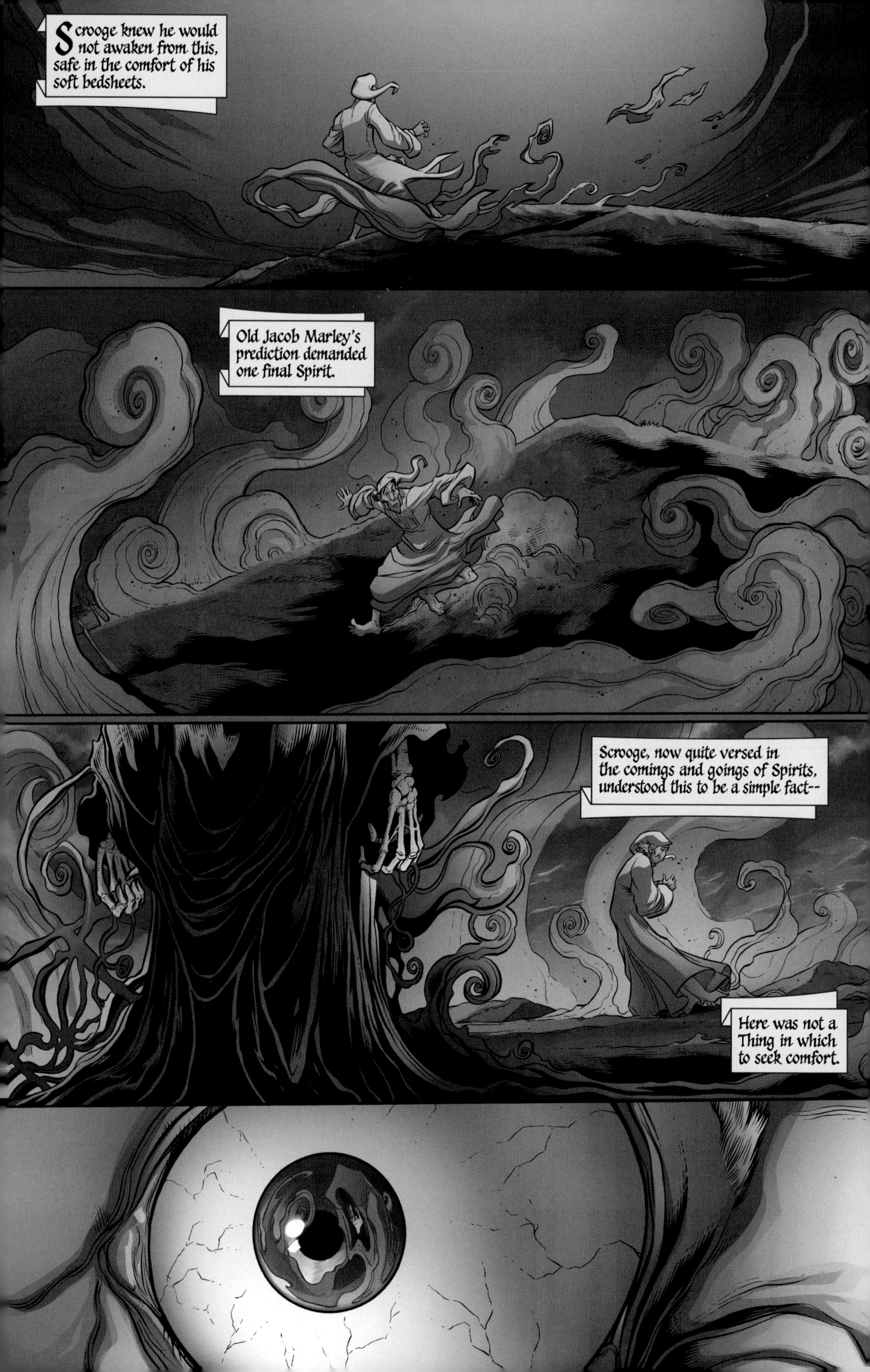
Scrooge knew he would not awaken from this, safe in the comfort of his soft bedsheets.
Old Jacob Marley's prediction demanded one final Spirit.
Scrooge, now quite versed in the comings and goings of Spirits, understood this to be a simple fact--
Here was not a Thing in which to seek comfort.

STAVE 4:

The Last Christmas
of Ebenezer Scrooge

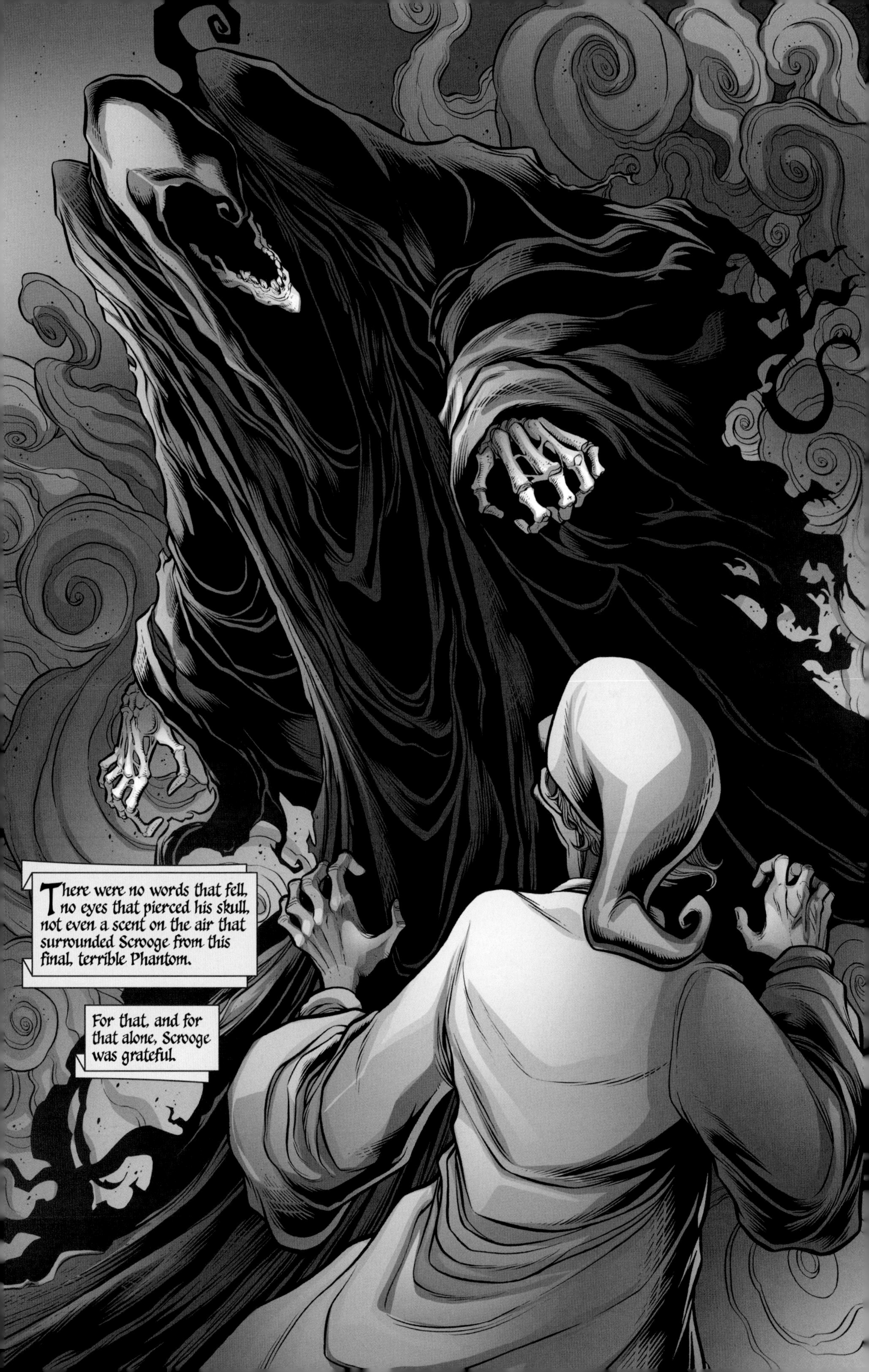
There were no words that fell, no eyes that pierced his skull, not even a scent on the air that surrounded Scrooge from this final, terrible Phantom.
For that, and for that alone, Scrooge was grateful.

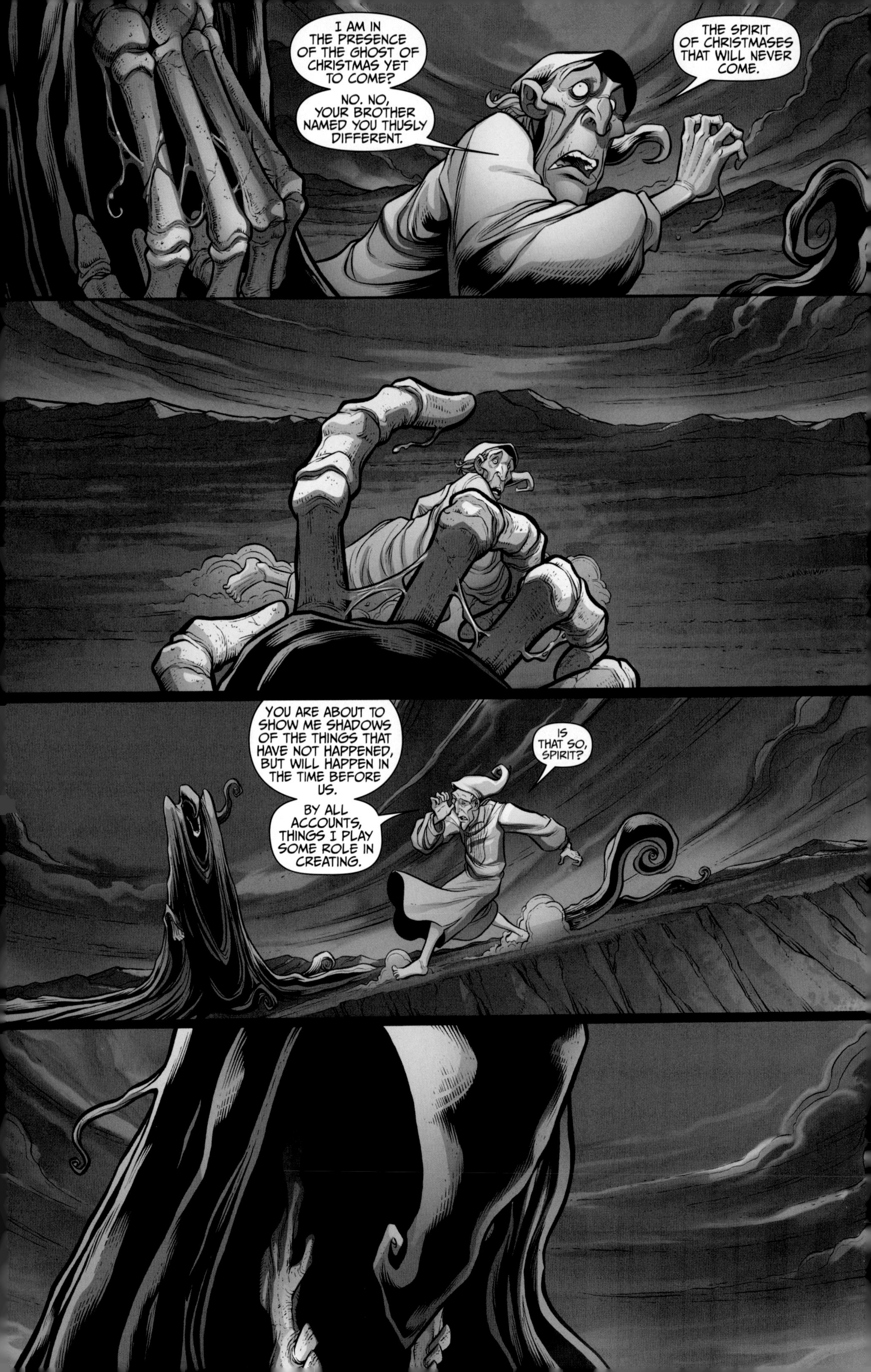
I AM IN THE PRESENCE OF THE GHOST OF CHRISTMAS YET TO COME?
NO. NO, YOUR BROTHER NAMED YOU THUSLY DIFFERENT.
THE SPIRIT OF CHRISTMASES THAT WILL NEVER COME.
YOU ARE ABOUT TO SHOW ME SHADOWS OF THE THINGS THAT HAVE NOT HAPPENED, BUT WILL HAPPEN IN THE TIME BEFORE US.
BY ALL ACCOUNTS, THINGS I PLAY SOME ROLE IN CREATING.
IS THAT SO, SPIRIT?

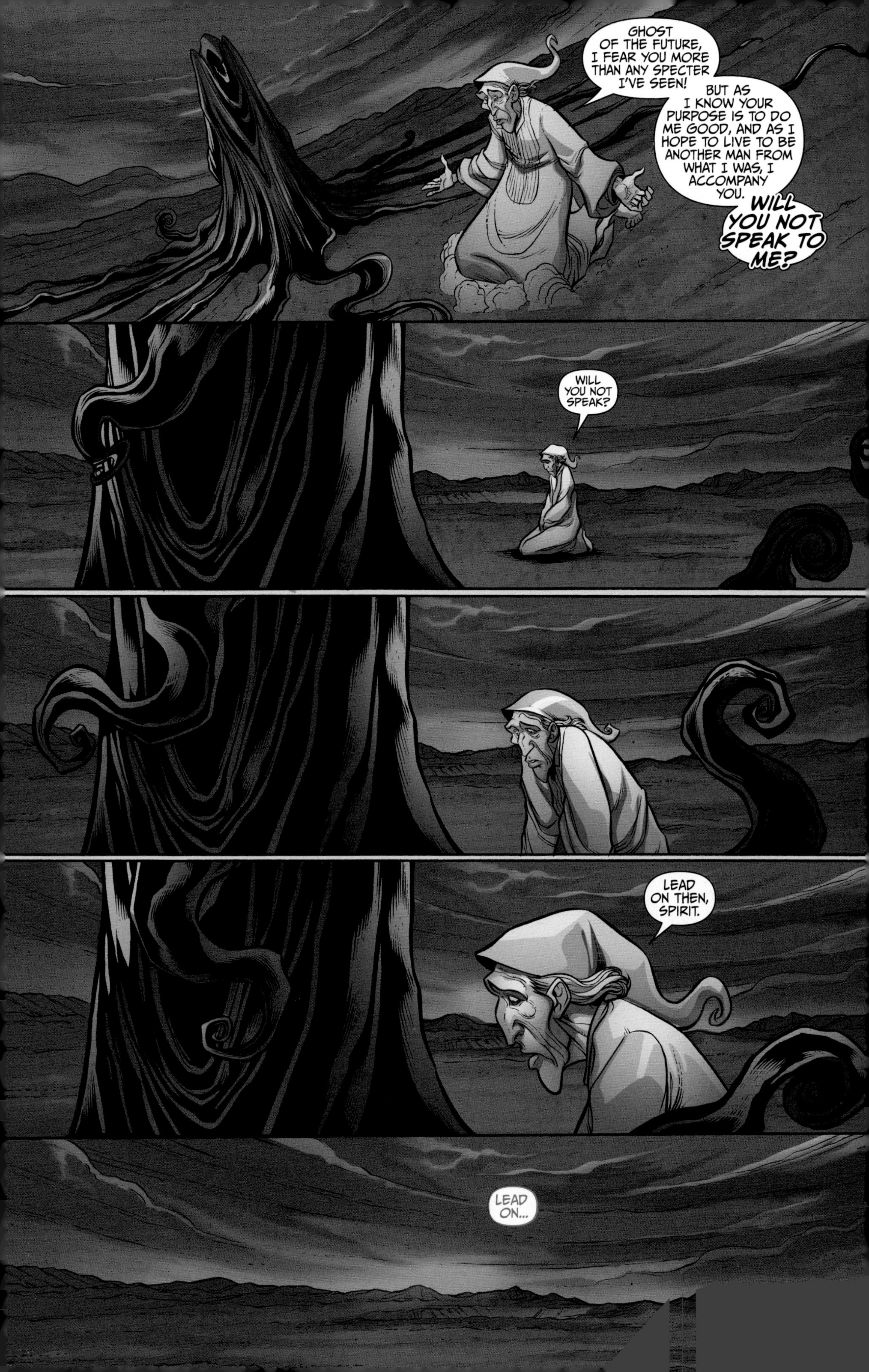
GHOST OF THE FUTURE, I FEAR YOU MORE THAN ANY SPECTER I'VE SEEN!
BUT AS I KNOW YOUR PURPOSE IS TO DO ME GOOD, AND AS I HOPE TO LIVE TO BE ANOTHER MAN FROM WHAT I WAS, I ACCOMPANY YOU.
WILL YOU NOT SPEAK TO ME?
WILL YOU NOT SPEAK?
LEAD ON THEN, SPIRIT.
LEAD ON...

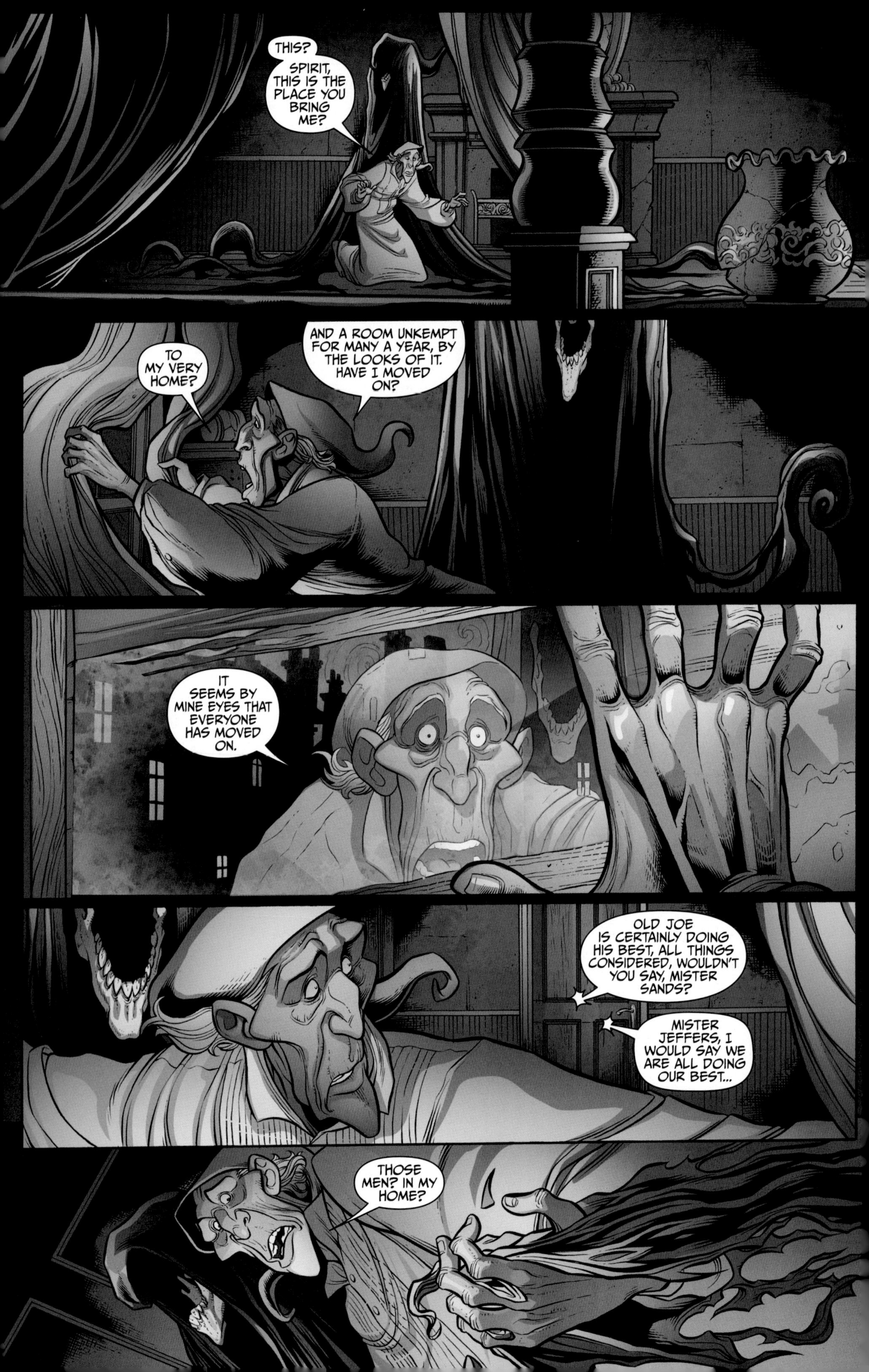
THIS?
SPIRIT, THIS IS THE PLACE YOU BRING ME?
TO MY VERY HOME?
AND A ROOM UNKEMPT FOR MANY A YEAR, BY THE LOOKS OF IT. HAVE I MOVED ON?
IT SEEMS BY MINE EYES THAT EVERYONE HAS MOVED ON.
OLD JOE IS CERTAINLY DOING HIS BEST, ALL THINGS CONSIDERED, WOULDN'T YOU SAY, MISTER SANDS?
MISTER JEFFERS, I WOULD SAY WE ARE ALL DOING OUR BEST...
THOSE MEN? IN MY HOME?

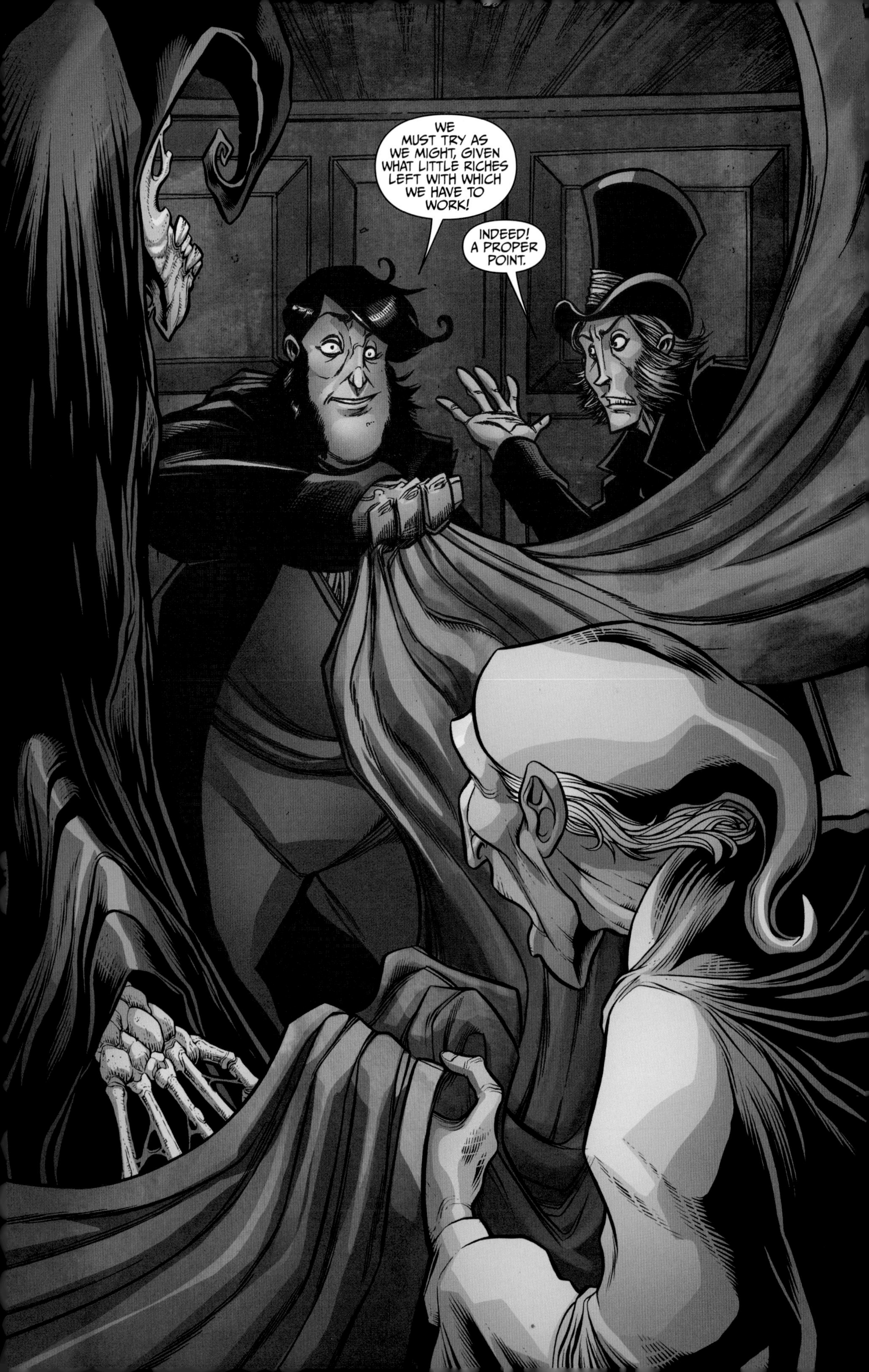
WE MUST TRY AS WE MIGHT, GIVEN WHAT LITTLE RICHES LEFT WITH WHICH WE HAVE TO WORK!
INDEED! A PROPER POINT.

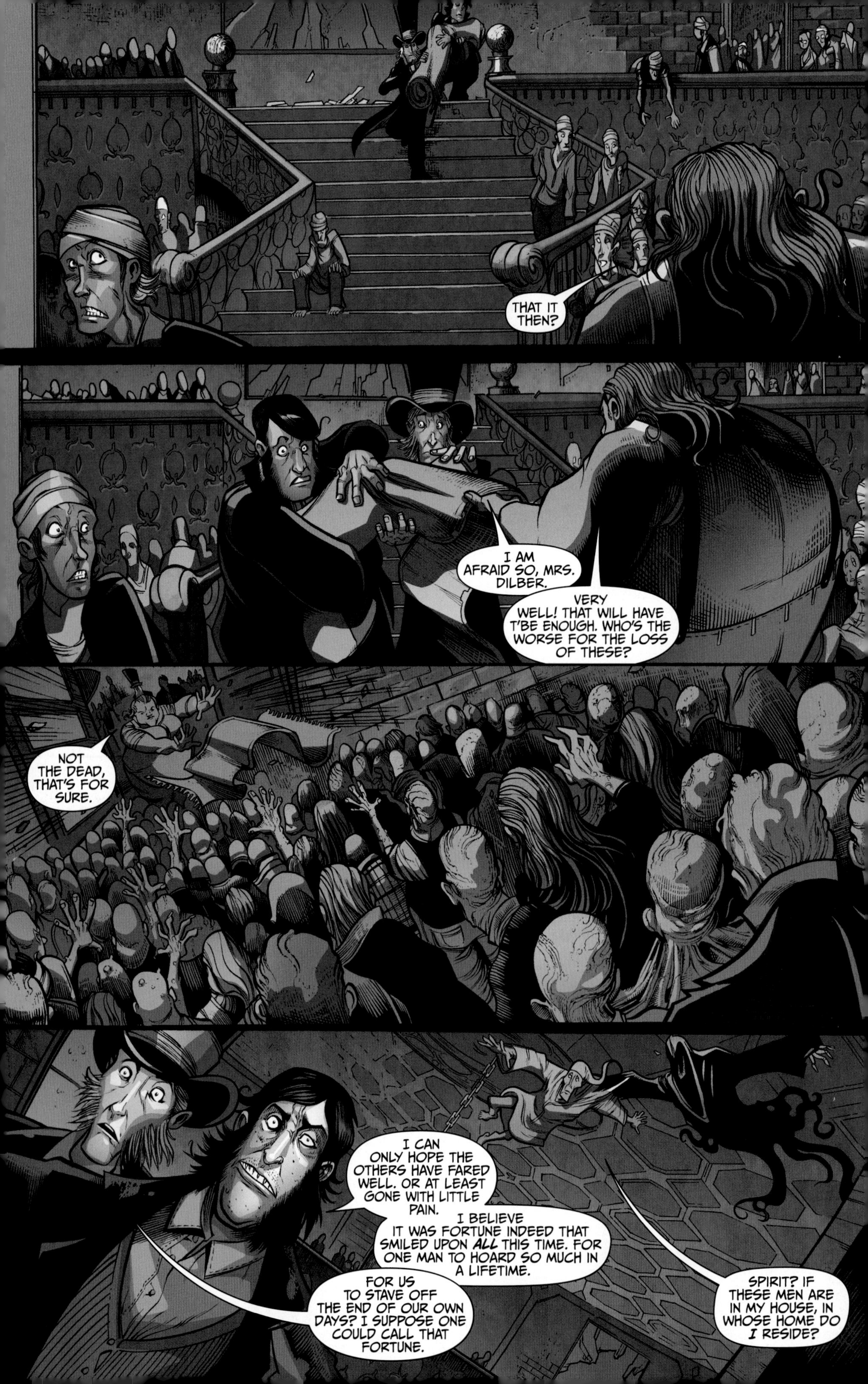
THAT IT THEN?
I AM AFRAID SO, MRS. DILBER.
VERY WELL! THAT WILL HAVE T'BE ENOUGH. WHO'S THE WORSE FOR THE LOSS OF THESE?
NOT THE DEAD, THAT'S FOR SURE.
I CAN ONLY HOPE THE OTHERS HAVE FARED WELL. OR AT LEAST GONE WITH LITTLE PAIN.
I BELIEVE IT WAS FORTUNE INDEED THAT SMILED UPON ALL THIS TIME. FOR ONE MAN TO HOARD SO MUCH IN A LIFETIME.
FOR US TO STAVE OFF THE END OF OUR OWN DAYS? I SUPPOSE ONE COULD CALL THAT FORTUNE.
SPIRIT? IF THESE MEN ARE IN MY HOUSE, IN WHOSE HOME DO I RESIDE?

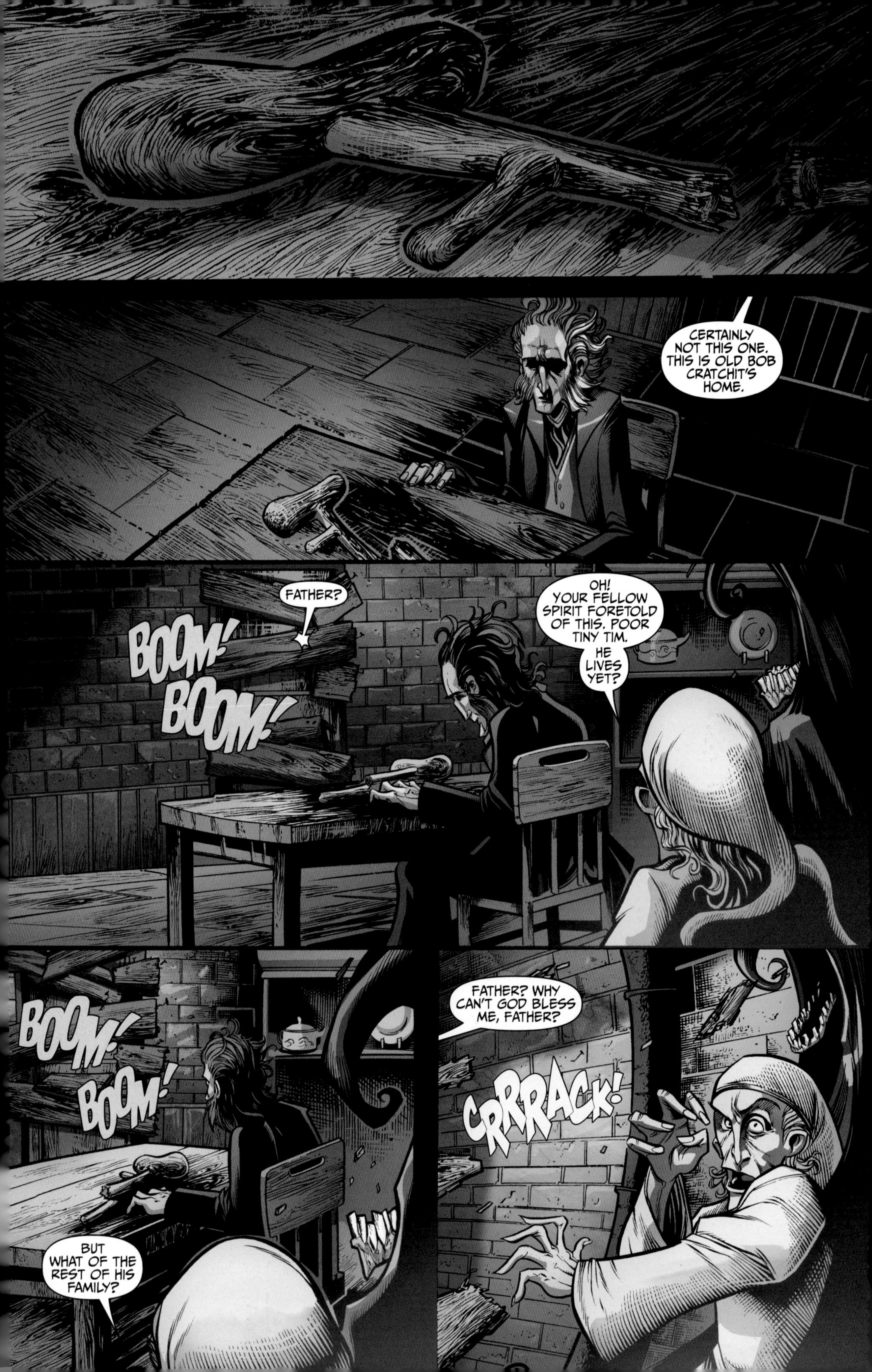
CERTAINLY NOT THIS ONE. THIS IS OLD BOB CRATCHIT'S HOME.
FATHER?
BOOM! BOOM!
OH! YOUR FELLOW SPIRIT FORETOLD OF THIS. POOR TINY TIM.
HE LIVES YET?
BOOM! BOOM!
BUT WHAT OF THE REST OF HIS FAMILY?
FATHER? WHY CAN'T GOD BLESS ME, FATHER?
CRRRACK!

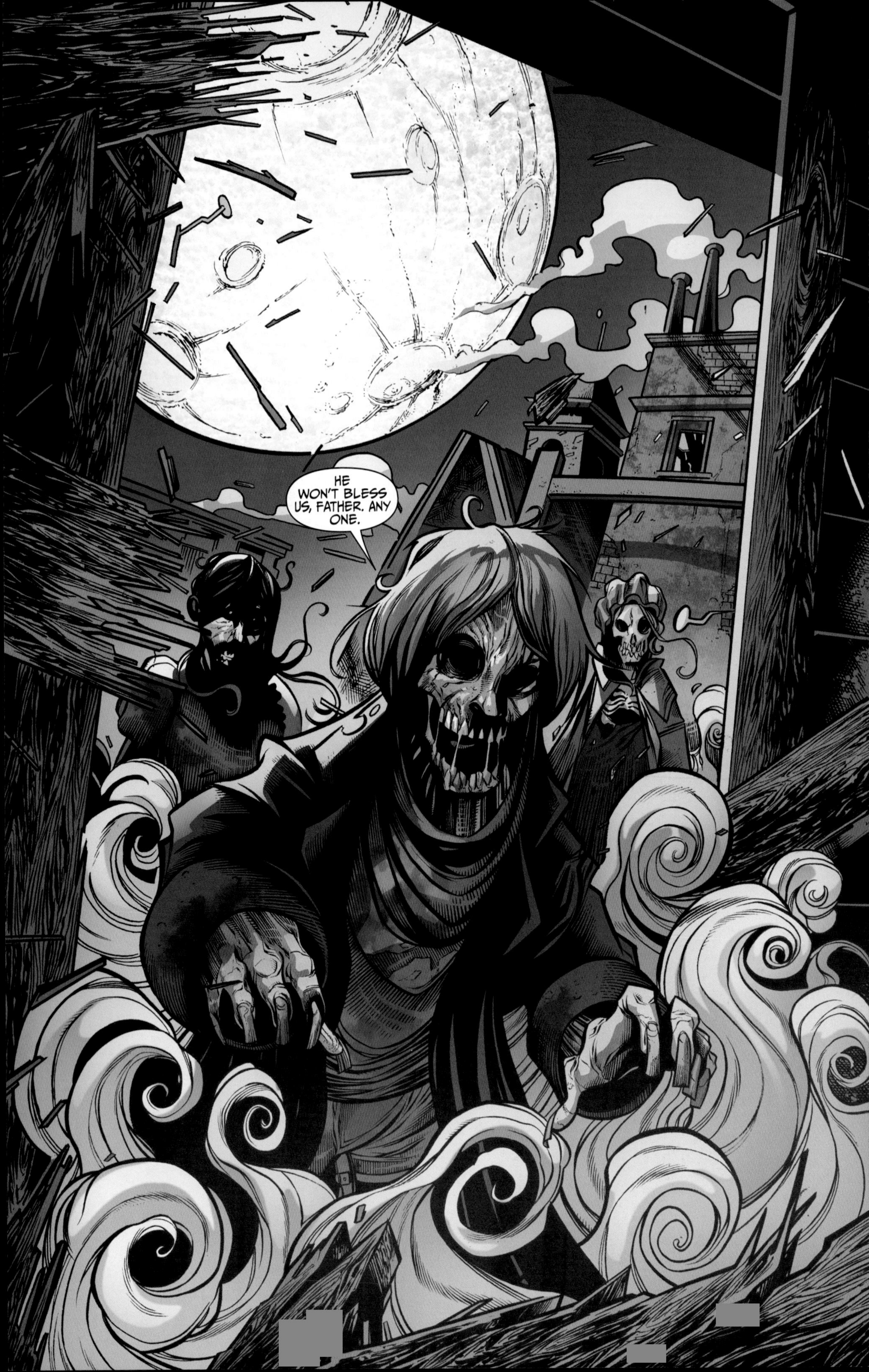
HE WON'T BLESS US, FATHER. ANY ONE.

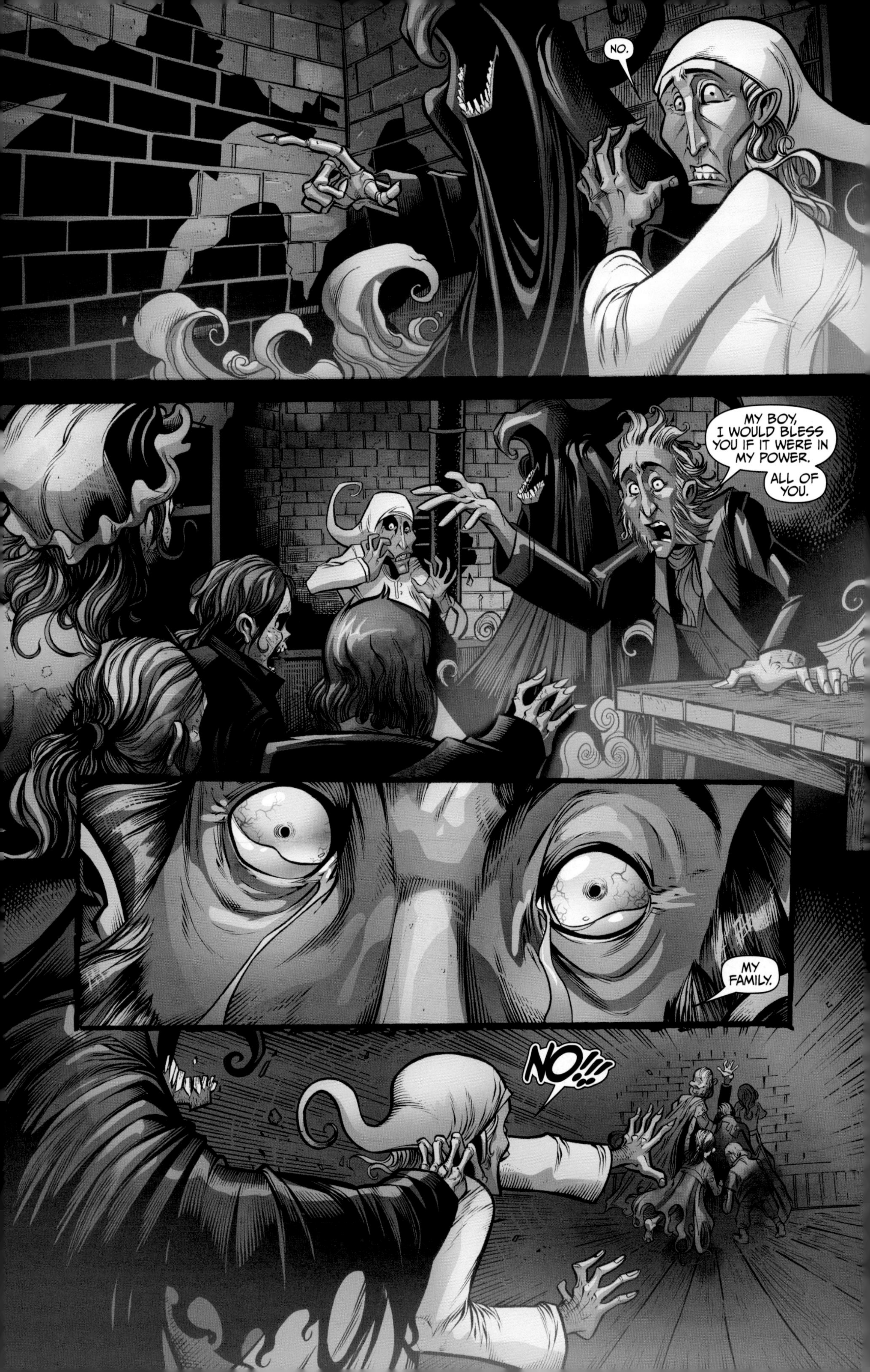
NO.
MY BOY, I WOULD BLESS YOU IF IT WERE IN MY POWER.
ALL OF YOU.
MY FAMILY.
NO!!!

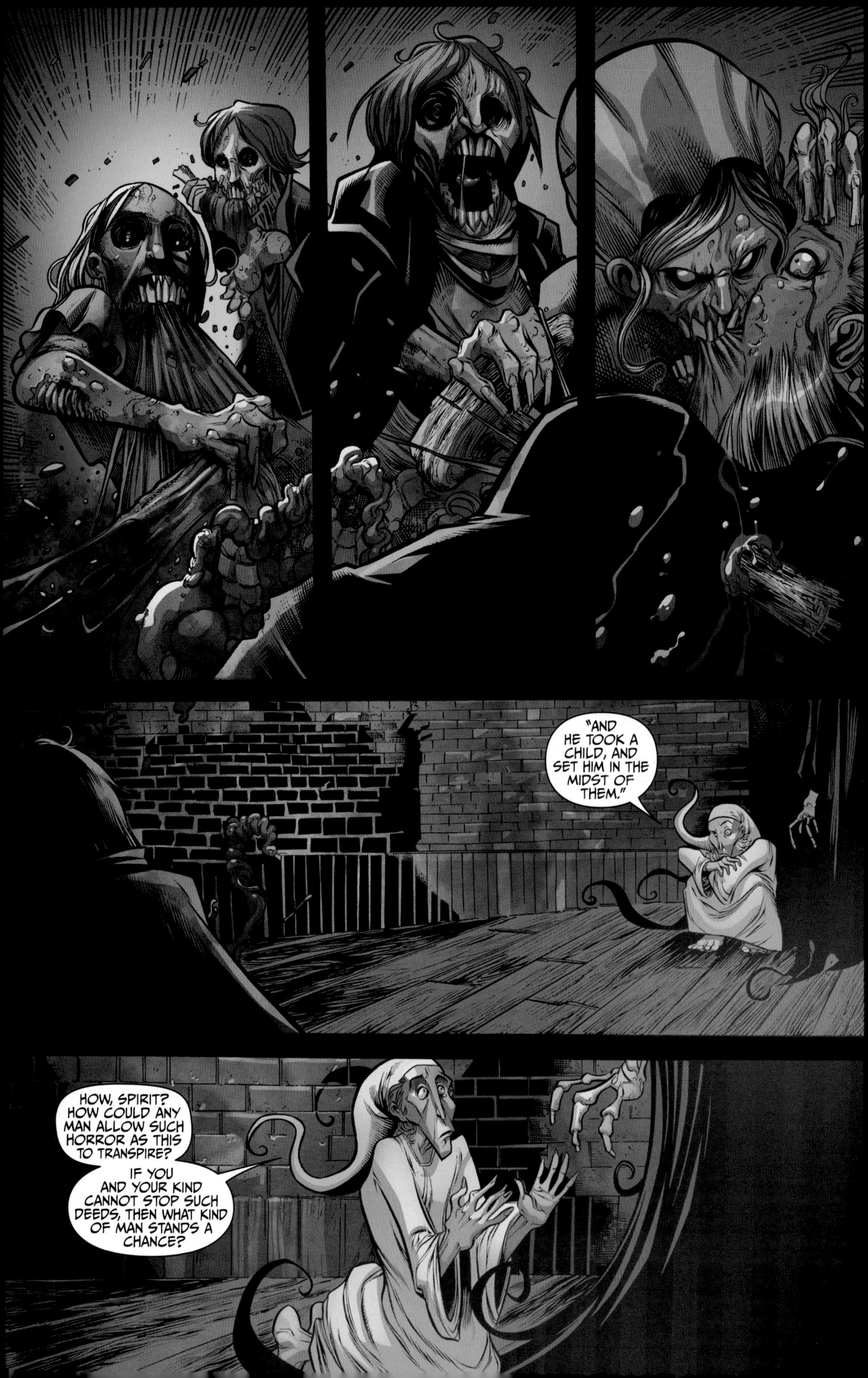
"AND HE TOOK A CHILD, AND SET HIM IN THE MIDST OF THEM."
HOW, SPIRIT? HOW COULD ANY MAN ALLOW SUCH HORROR AS THIS TO TRANSPIRE?
IF YOU AND YOUR KIND CANNOT STOP SUCH DEEDS, THEN WHAT KIND OF MAN STANDS A CHANCE?

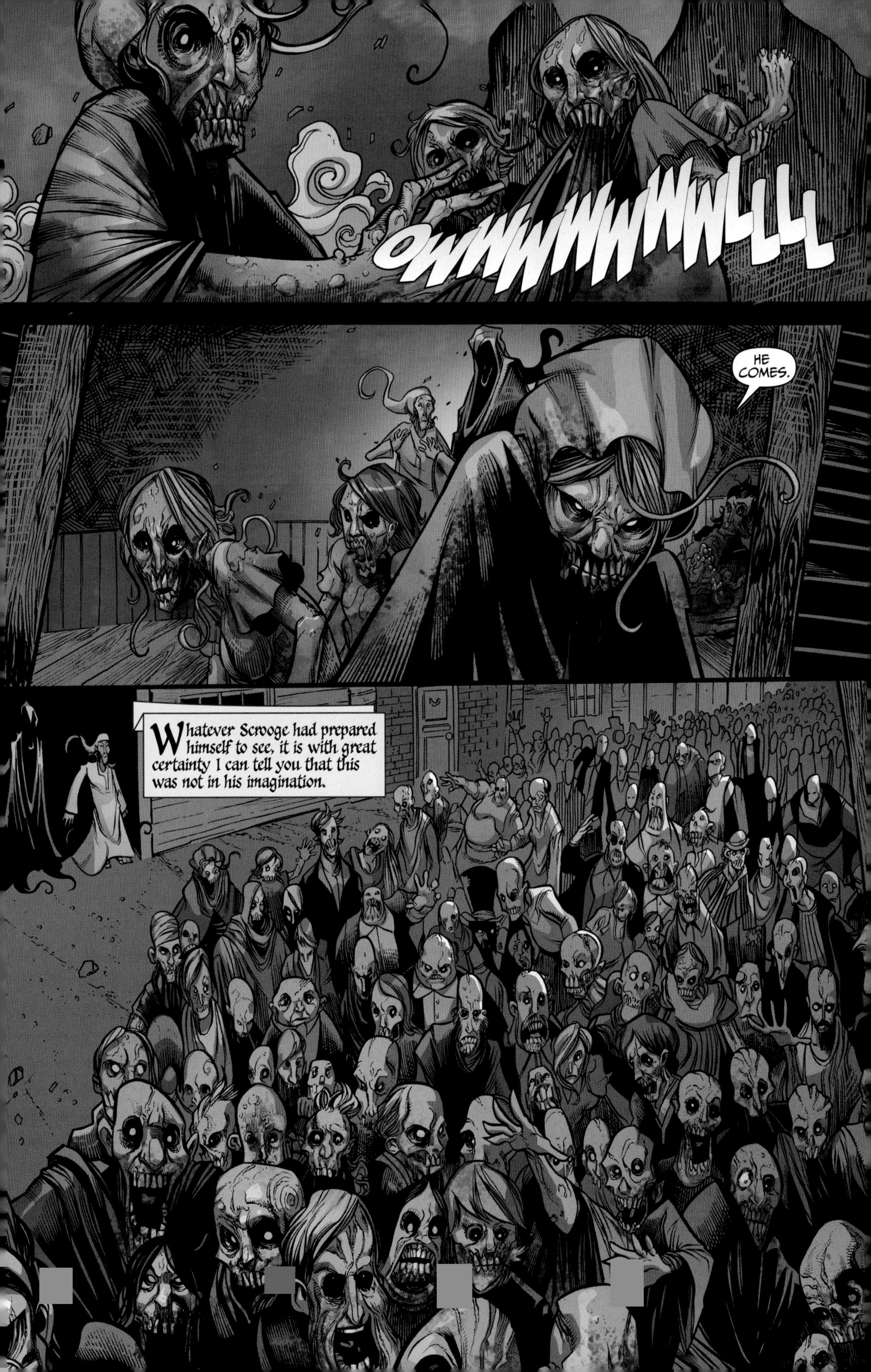
OWWWWWWWLLLL
HE COMES.
Whatever Scrooge had prepared himself to see, it is with great certainty I can tell you that this was not in his imagination.

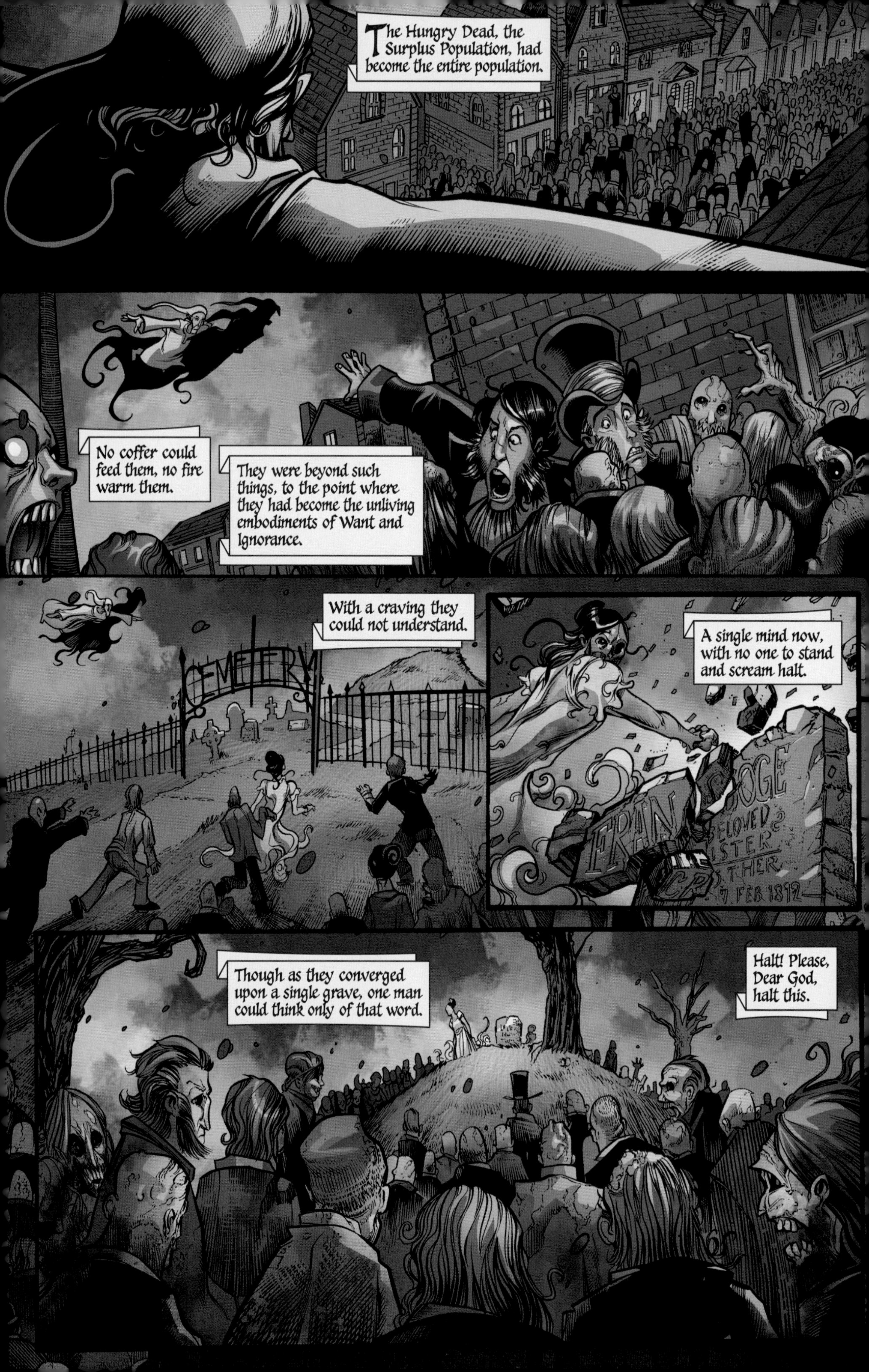
The Hungry Dead, the Surplus Population, had become the entire population.
No coffer could feed them, no fire warm them.
They were beyond such things, to the point where they had become the unliving embodiments of Want and Ignorance.
With a craving they could not understand.
CEMETERY
A single mind now, with no one to stand and scream halt.
Though as they converged upon a single grave, one man could think only of that word.
Halt! Please, Dear God, halt this.

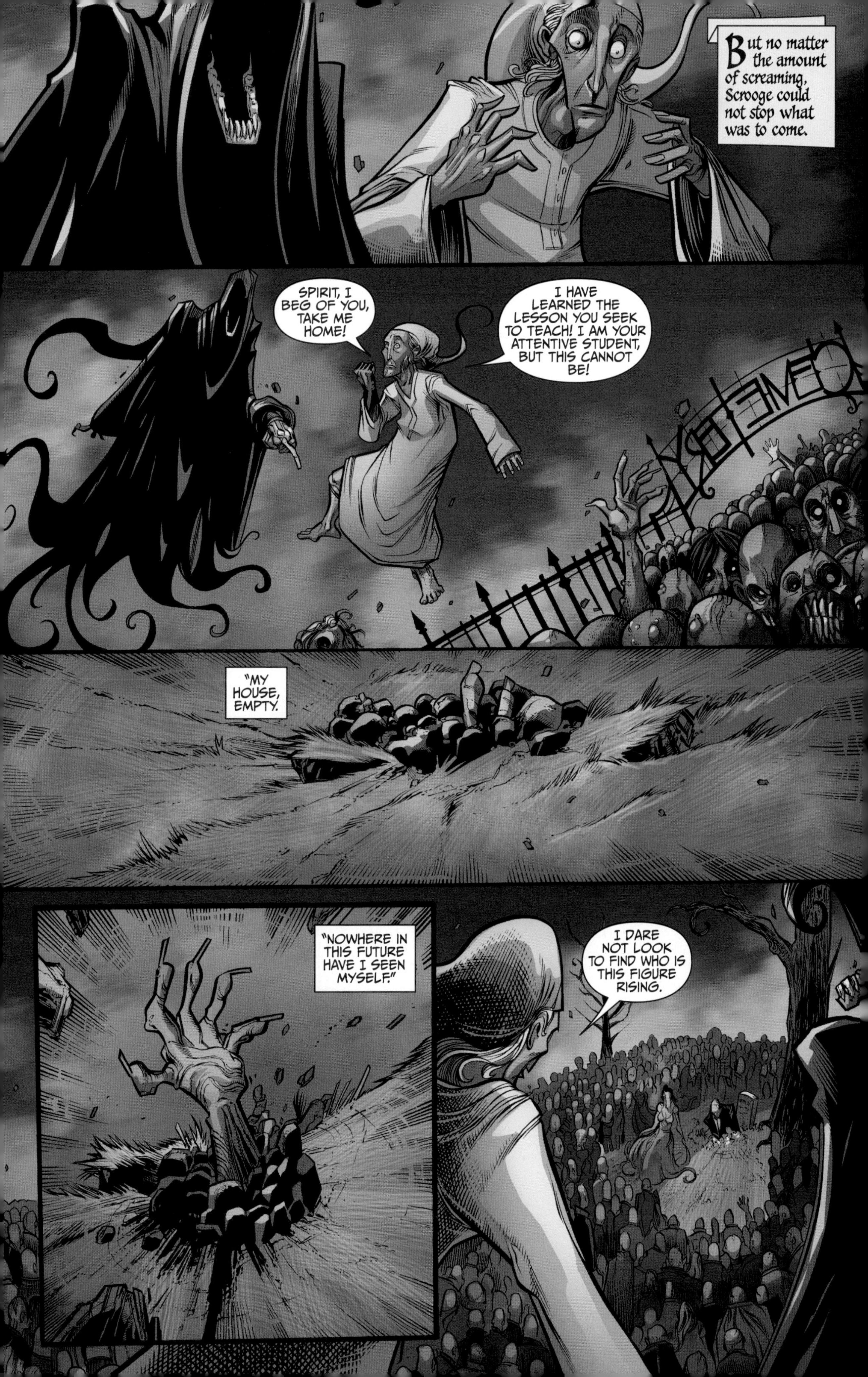
But no matter the amount of screaming, Scrooge could not stop what was to come.
SPIRIT, I BEG OF YOU, TAKE ME HOME!
I HAVE LEARNED THE LESSON YOU SEEK TO TEACH! I AM YOUR ATTENTIVE STUDENT, BUT THIS CANNOT BE!
CEMETERY
"MY HOUSE, EMPTY.
"NOWHERE IN THIS FUTURE HAVE I SEEN MYSELF."
I DARE NOT LOOK TO FIND WHO IS THIS FIGURE RISING.

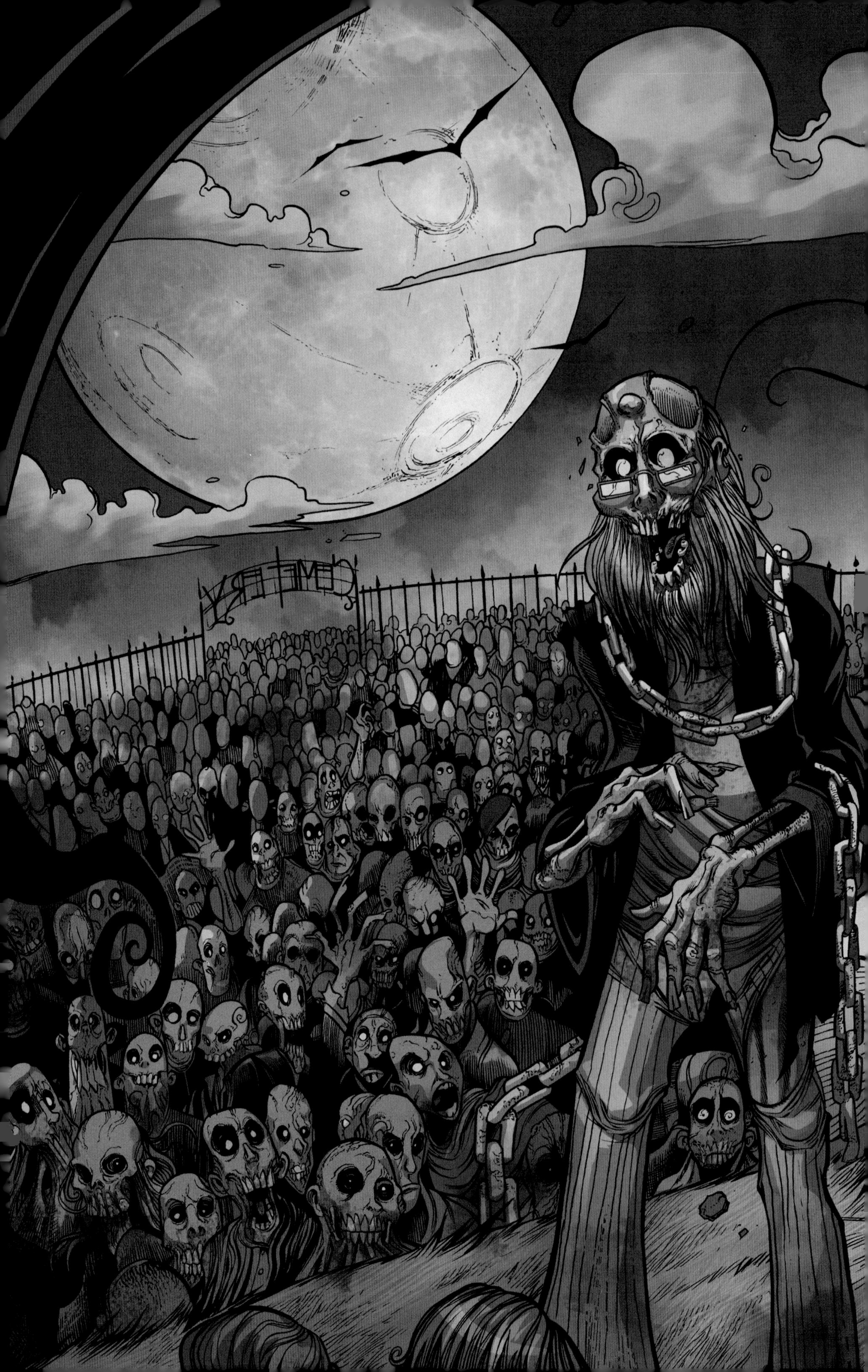
CEMETERY

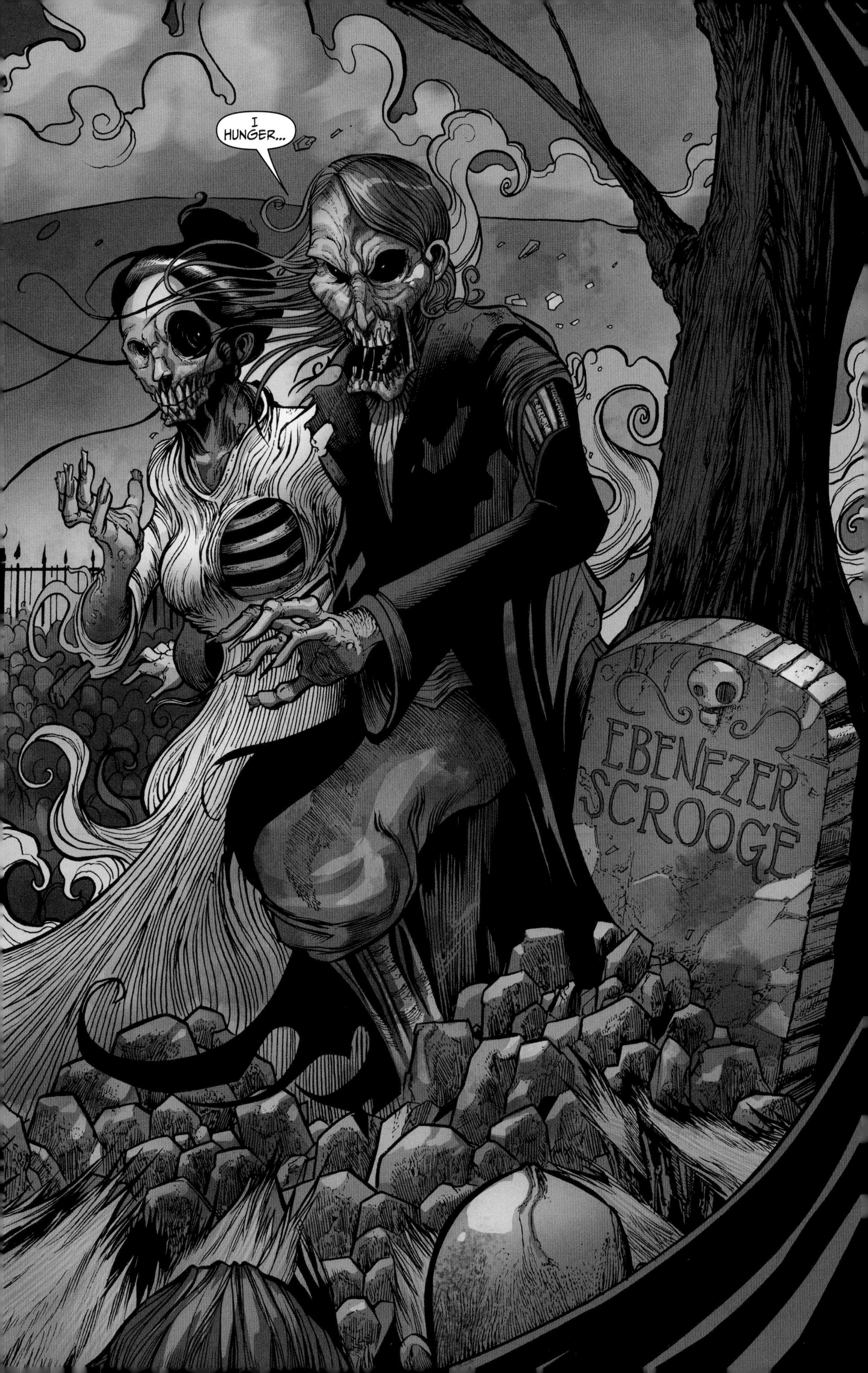
I HUNGER...
EBENEZER SCROOGE

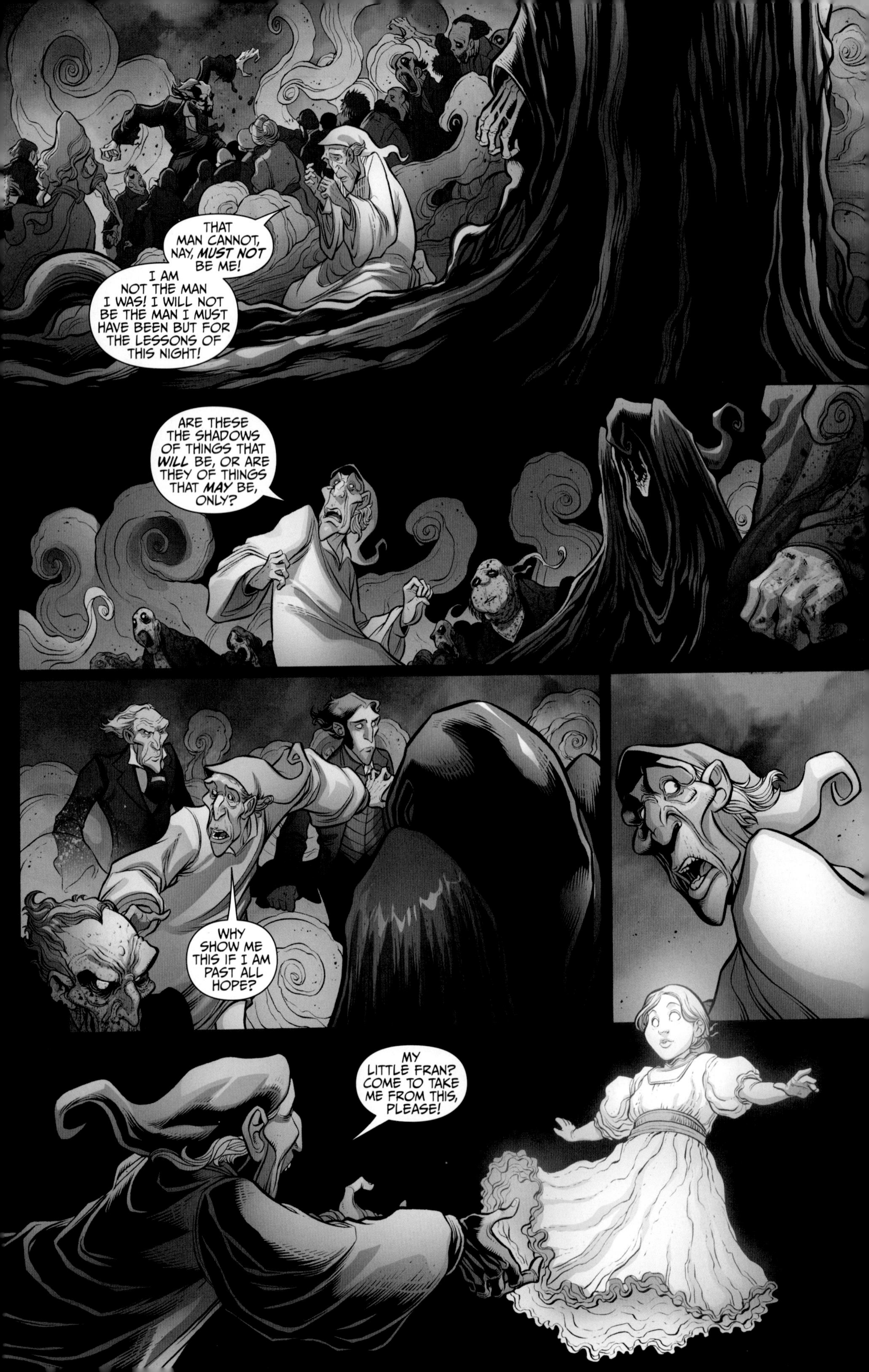
THAT MAN CANNOT, NAY, ***MUST NOT*** BE ME!
I AM NOT THE MAN I WAS! I WILL NOT BE THE MAN I MUST HAVE BEEN BUT FOR THE LESSONS OF THIS NIGHT!
ARE THESE THE SHADOWS OF THINGS THAT ***WILL*** BE, OR ARE THEY OF THINGS THAT ***MAY*** BE, ONLY?
WHY SHOW ME THIS IF I AM PAST ALL HOPE?
MY LITTLE FRAN? COME TO TAKE ME FROM THIS, PLEASE!

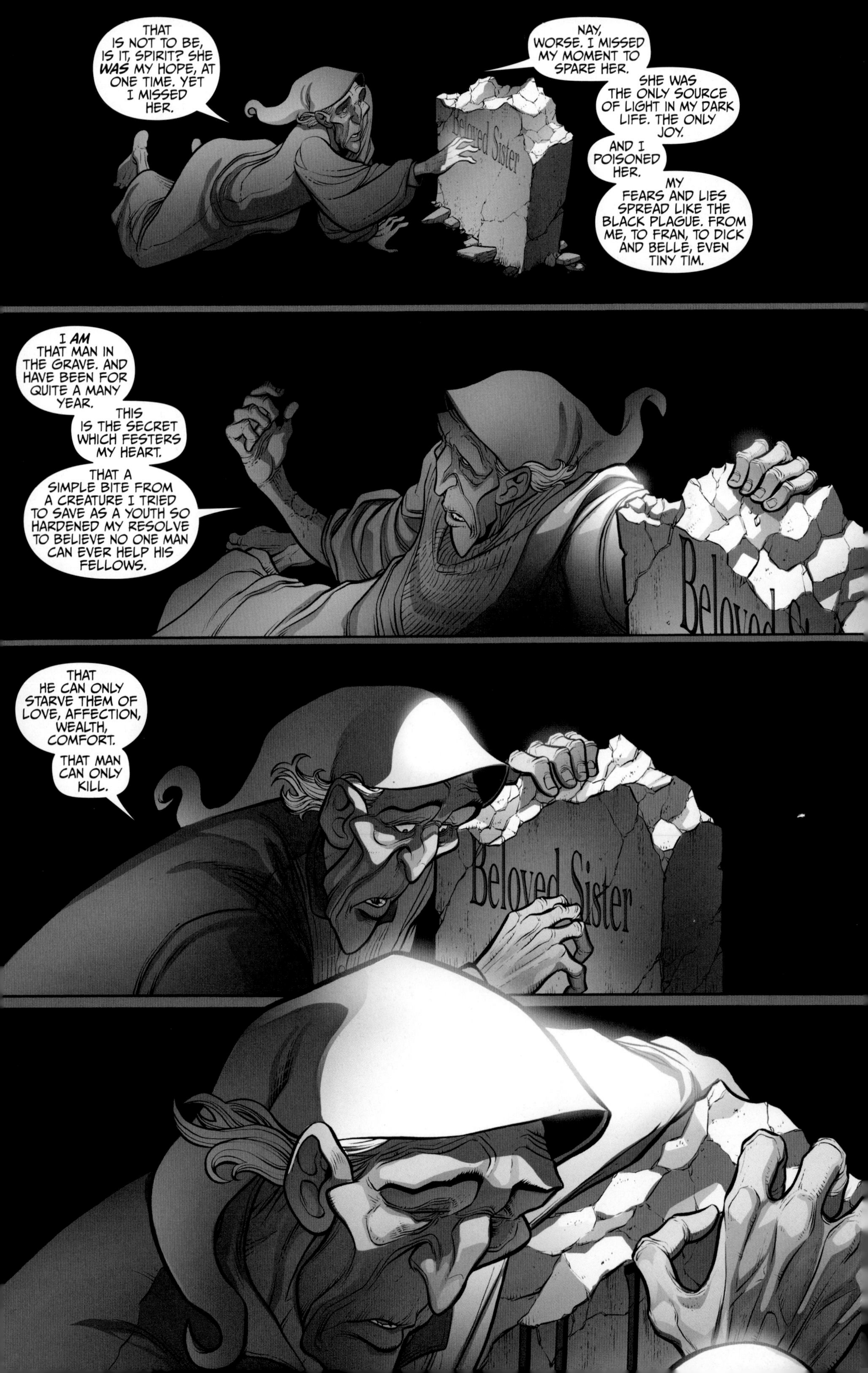
THAT IS NOT TO BE, IS IT, SPIRIT? SHE **WAS** MY HOPE, AT ONE TIME. YET I MISSED HER.
Beloved Sister
NAY, WORSE. I MISSED MY MOMENT TO SPARE HER.
SHE WAS THE ONLY SOURCE OF LIGHT IN MY DARK LIFE. THE ONLY JOY.
AND I POISONED HER.
MY FEARS AND LIES SPREAD LIKE THE BLACK PLAGUE. FROM ME, TO FRAN, TO DICK AND BELLE, EVEN TINY TIM.
I **AM** THAT MAN IN THE GRAVE. AND HAVE BEEN FOR QUITE A MANY YEAR.
THIS IS THE SECRET WHICH FESTERS MY HEART.
THAT A SIMPLE BITE FROM A CREATURE I TRIED TO SAVE AS A YOUTH SO HARDENED MY RESOLVE TO BELIEVE NO ONE MAN CAN EVER HELP HIS FELLOWS.
THAT HE CAN ONLY STARVE THEM OF LOVE, AFFECTION, WEALTH, COMFORT.
THAT MAN CAN ONLY KILL.
Beloved Sister

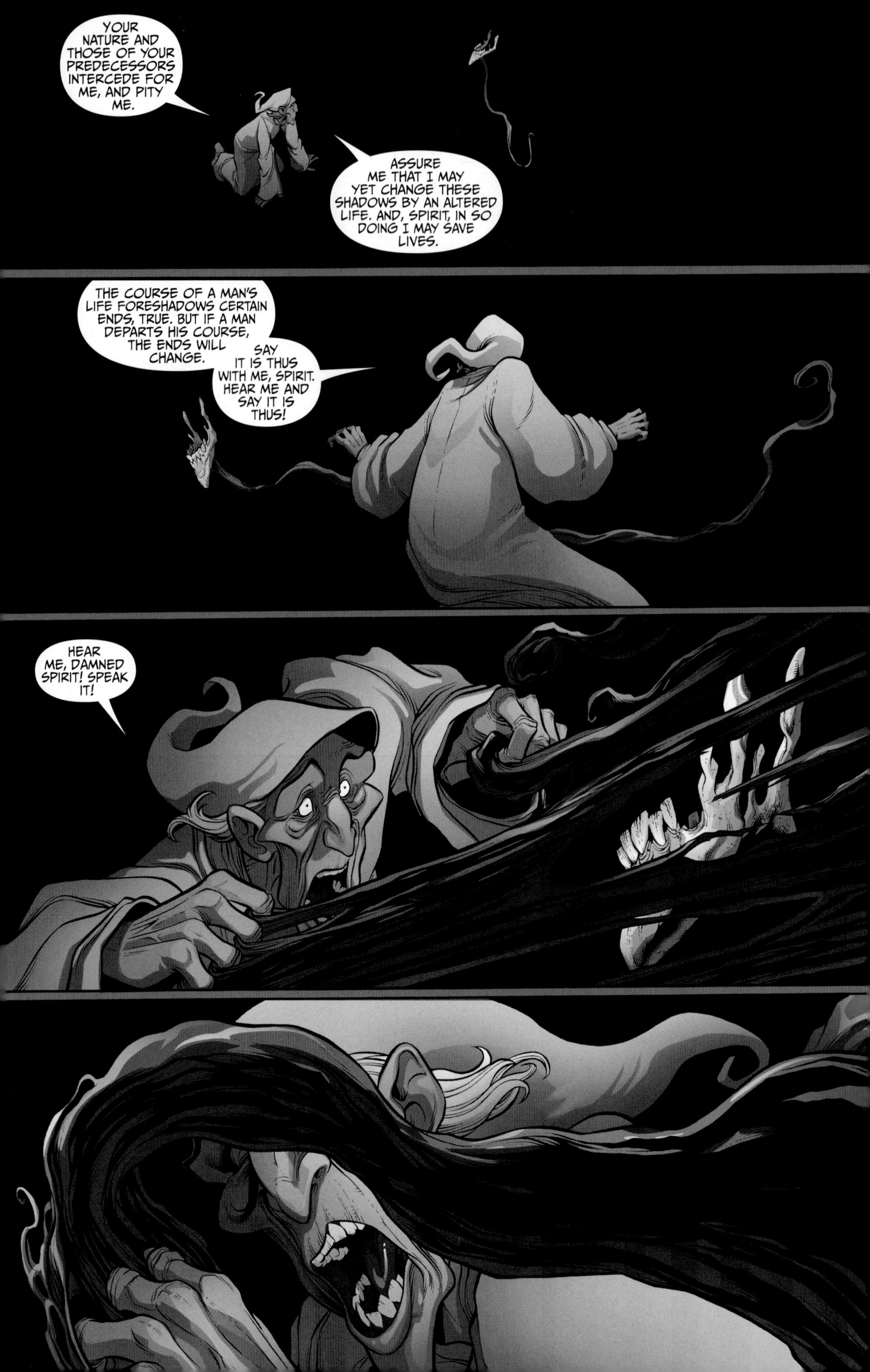
YOUR NATURE AND THOSE OF YOUR PREDECESSORS INTERCEDE FOR ME, AND PITY ME.
ASSURE ME THAT I MAY YET CHANGE THESE SHADOWS BY AN ALTERED LIFE. AND, SPIRIT, IN SO DOING I MAY SAVE LIVES.
THE COURSE OF A MAN'S LIFE FORESHADOWS CERTAIN ENDS, TRUE. BUT IF A MAN DEPARTS HIS COURSE, THE ENDS WILL CHANGE.
SAY IT IS THUS WITH ME, SPIRIT. HEAR ME AND SAY IT IS THUS!
HEAR ME, DAMNED SPIRIT! SPEAK IT!

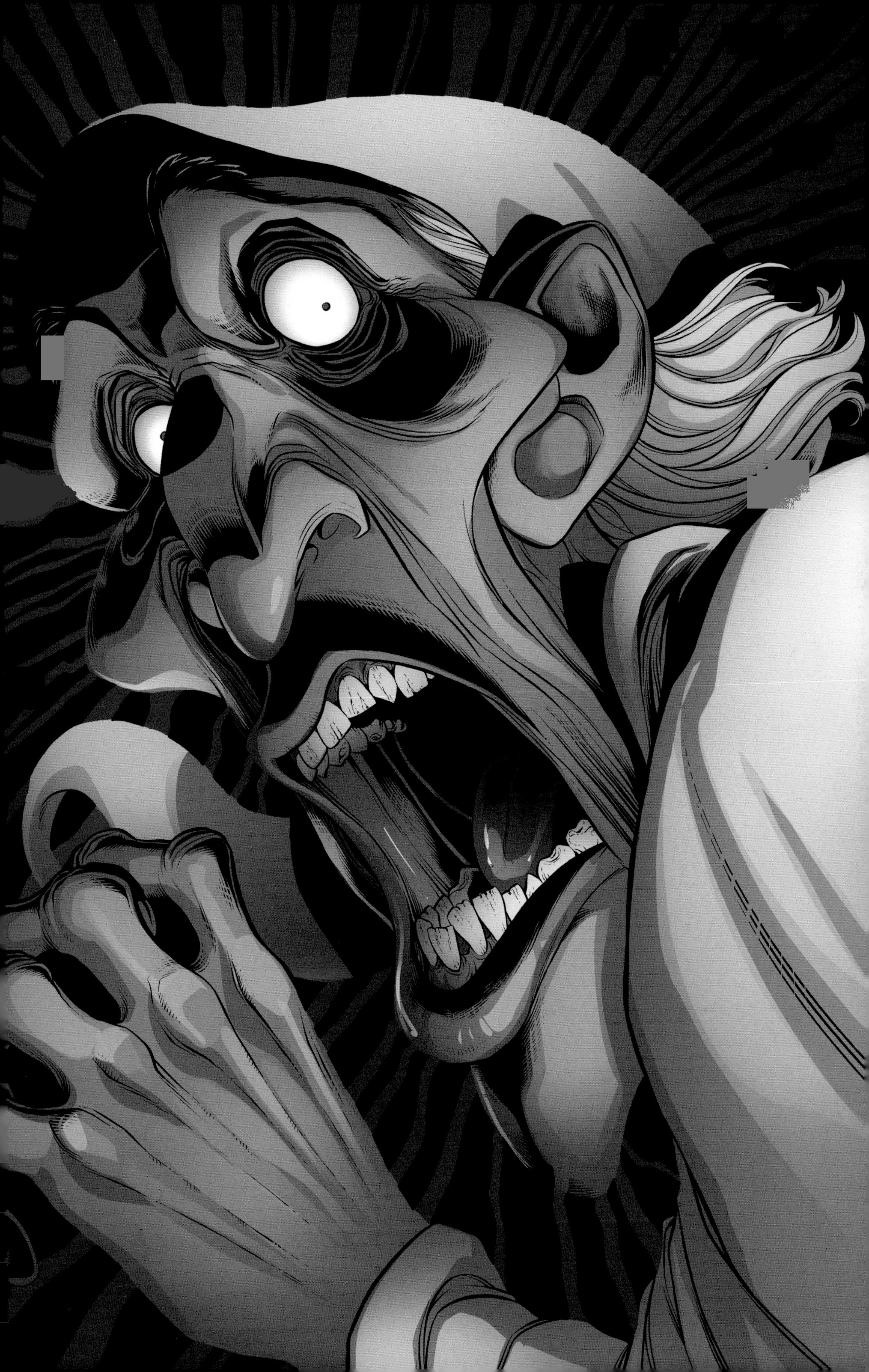

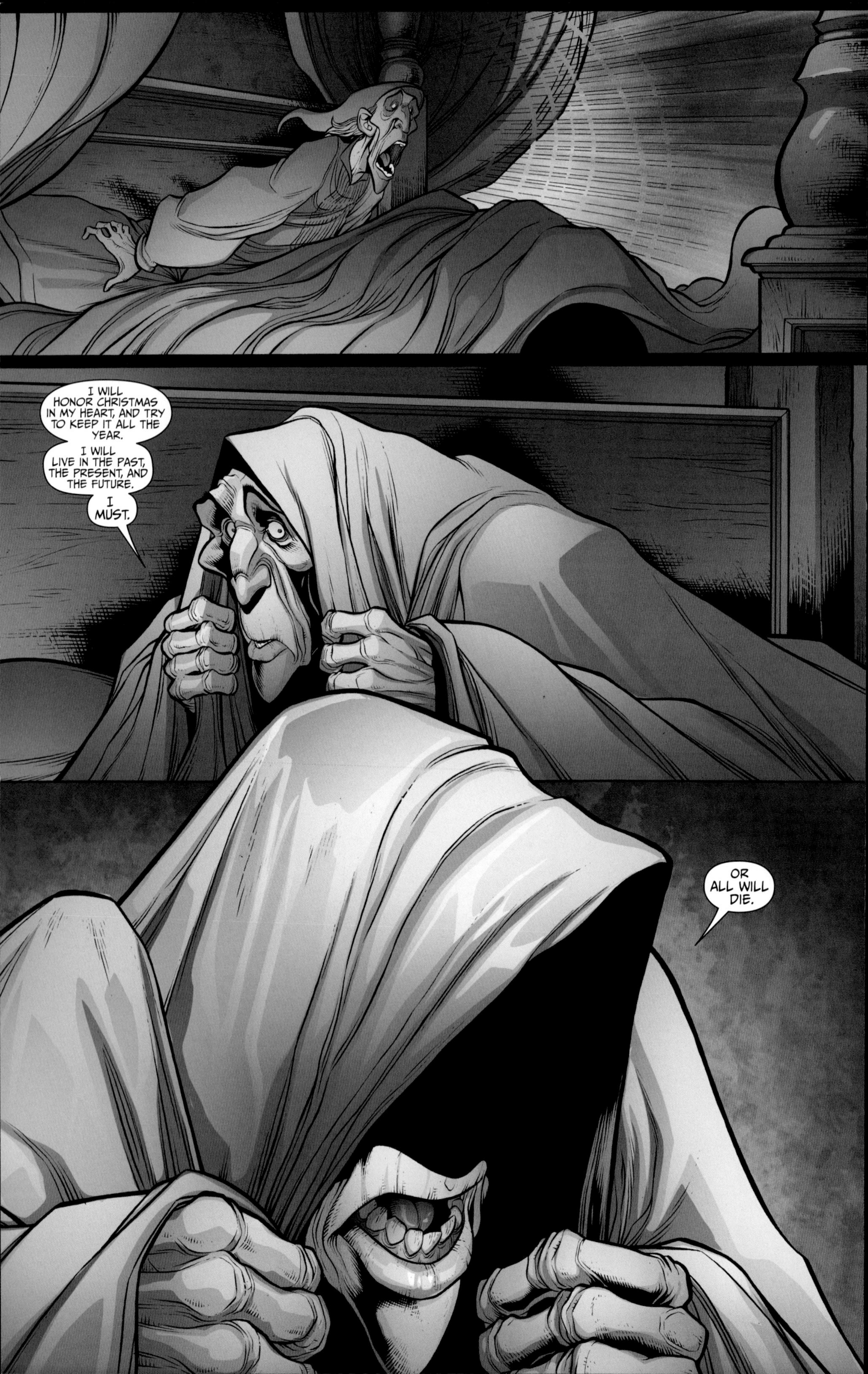
I WILL HONOR CHRISTMAS IN MY HEART, AND TRY TO KEEP IT ALL THE YEAR.
I WILL LIVE IN THE PAST, THE PRESENT, AND THE FUTURE.
I MUST.
OR ALL WILL DIE.

STAVE 5:

The End of It

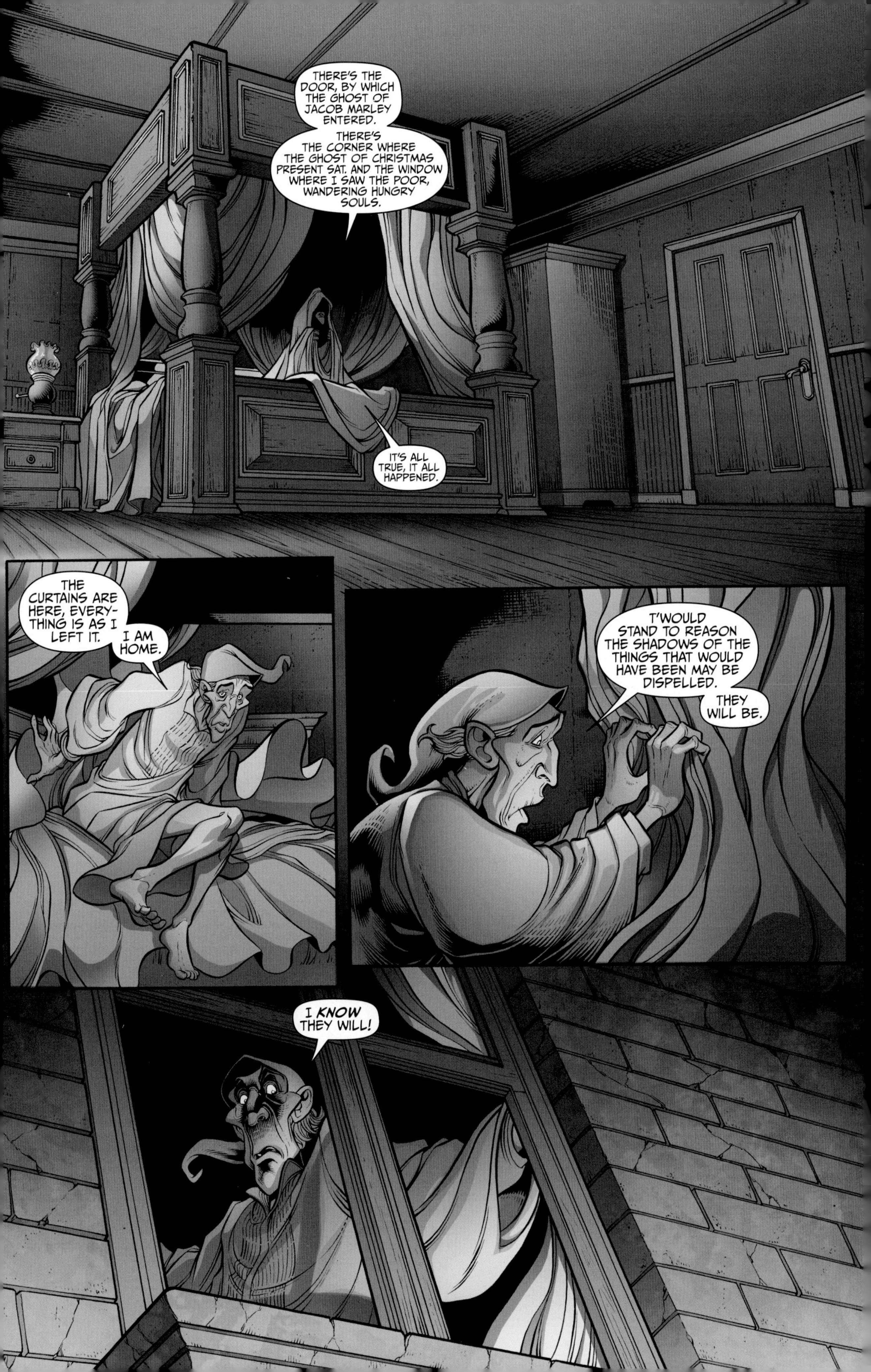
THERE'S THE DOOR, BY WHICH THE GHOST OF JACOB MARLEY ENTERED.
THERE'S THE CORNER WHERE THE GHOST OF CHRISTMAS PRESENT SAT. AND THE WINDOW WHERE I SAW THE POOR, WANDERING HUNGRY SOULS.
IT'S ALL TRUE, IT ALL HAPPENED.
THE CURTAINS ARE HERE, EVERY-THING IS AS I LEFT IT.
I AM HOME.
T'WOULD STAND TO REASON THE SHADOWS OF THE THINGS THAT WOULD HAVE BEEN MAY BE DISPELLED.
THEY WILL BE.
I *KNOW* THEY WILL!

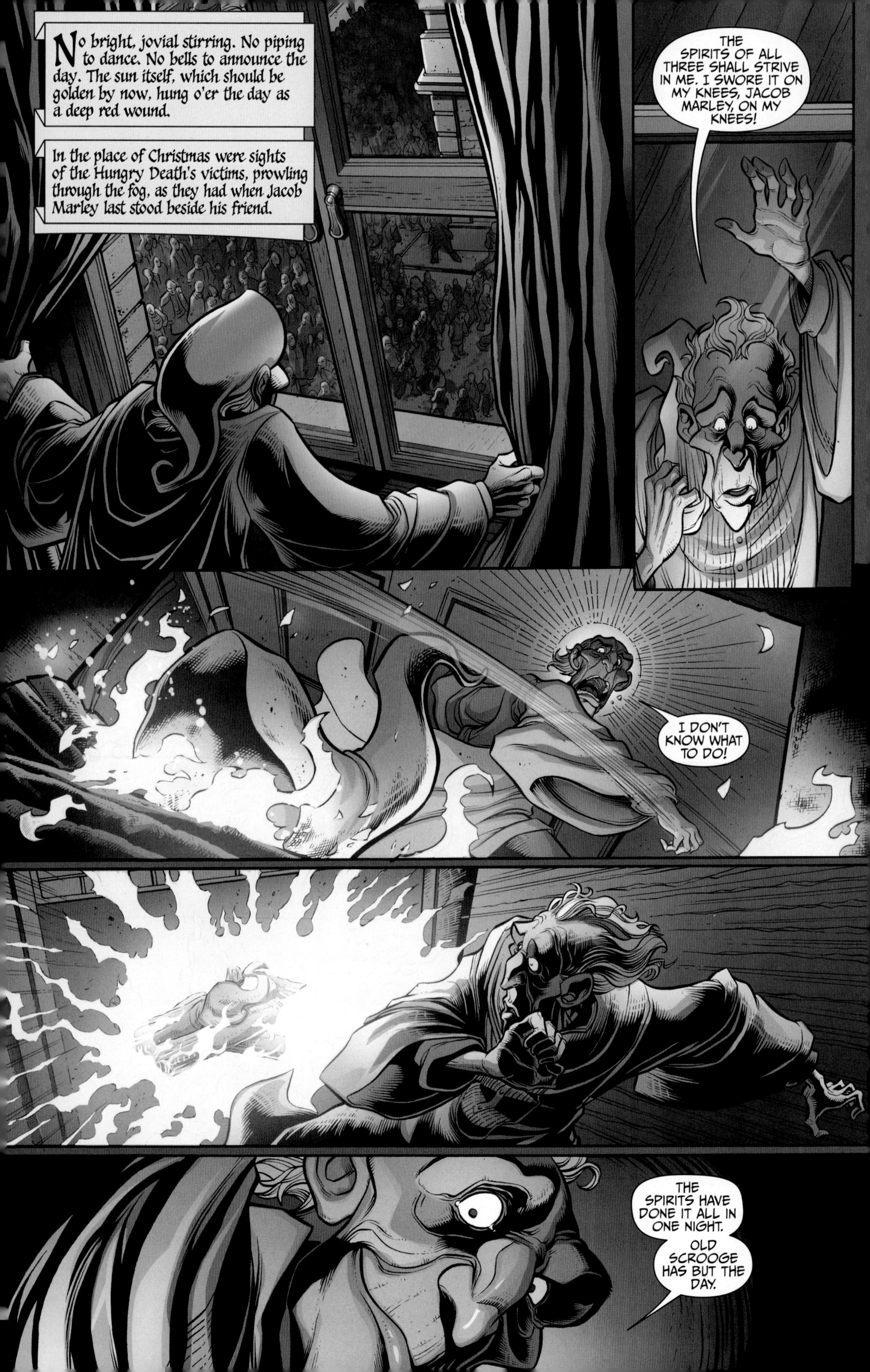
No bright, jovial stirring. No piping to dance. No bells to announce the day. The sun itself, which should be golden by now, hung o'er the day as a deep red wound.
In the place of Christmas were sights of the Hungry Death's victims, prowling through the fog, as they had when Jacob Marley last stood beside his friend.
THE SPIRITS OF ALL THREE SHALL STRIVE IN ME. I SWORE IT ON MY KNEES, JACOB MARLEY, ON MY KNEES!
I DON'T KNOW WHAT TO DO!
THE SPIRITS HAVE DONE IT ALL IN ONE NIGHT.
OLD SCROOGE HAS BUT THE DAY.

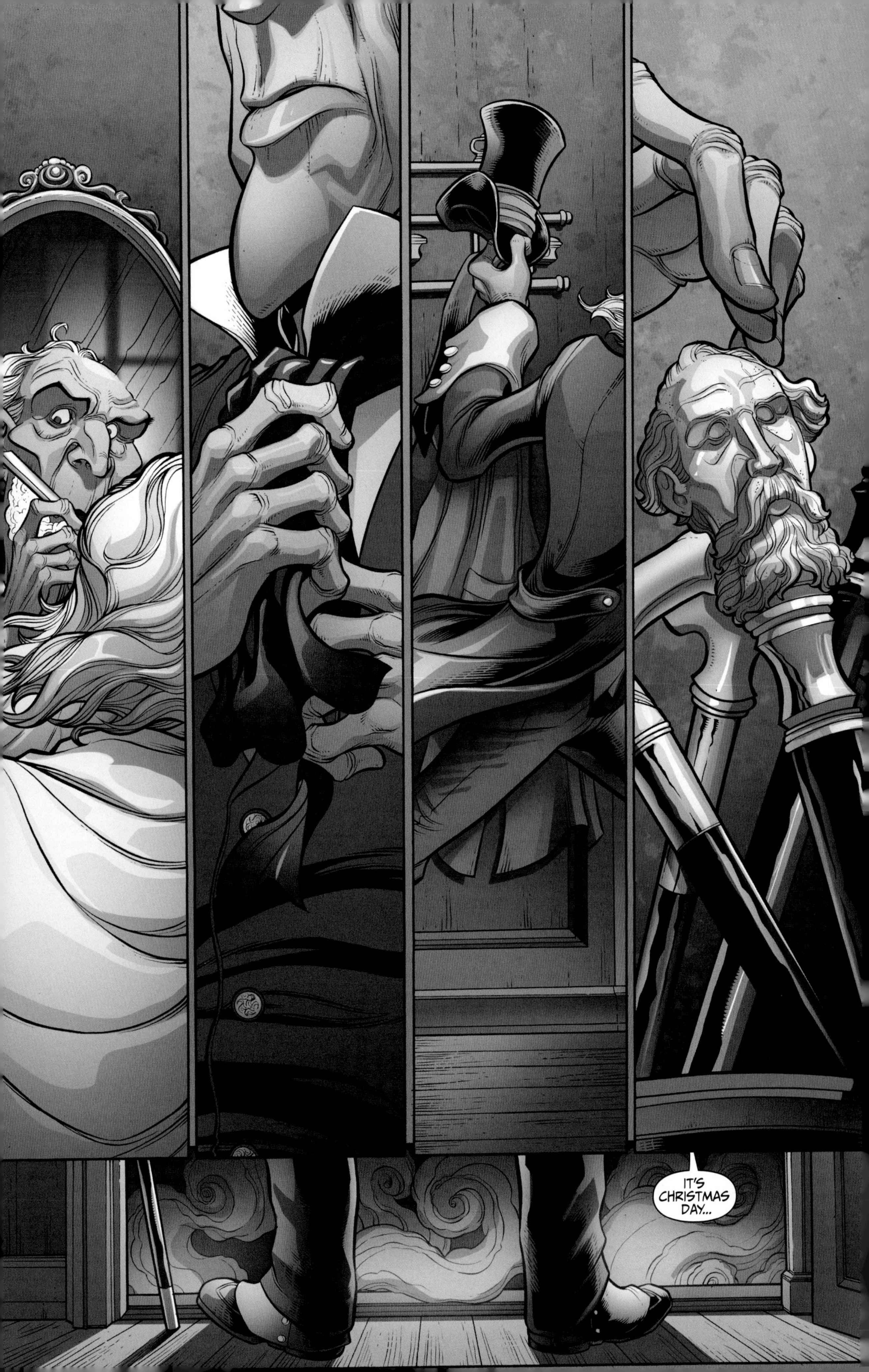
IT'S CHRISTMAS DAY...

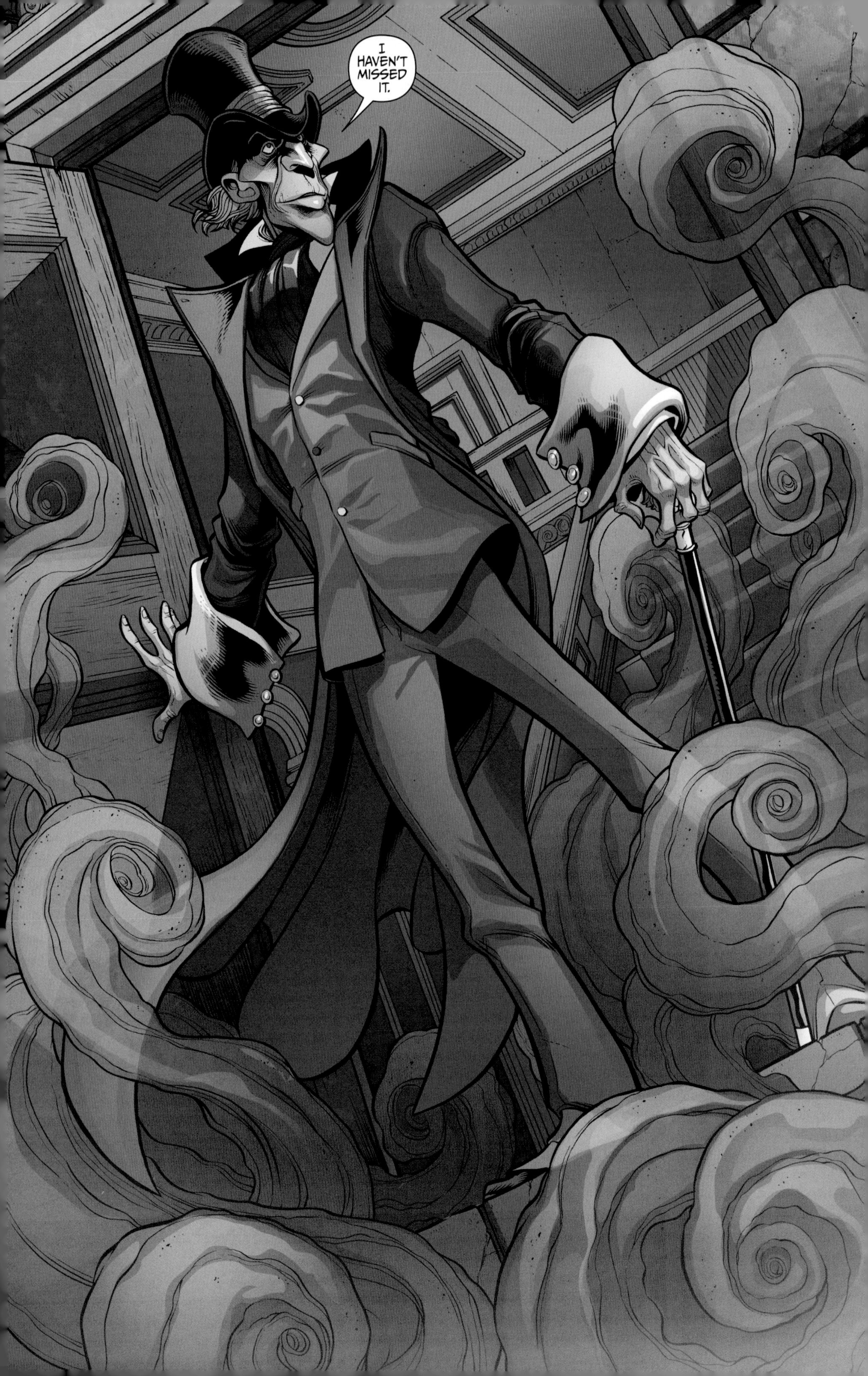
I HAVEN'T MISSED IT.

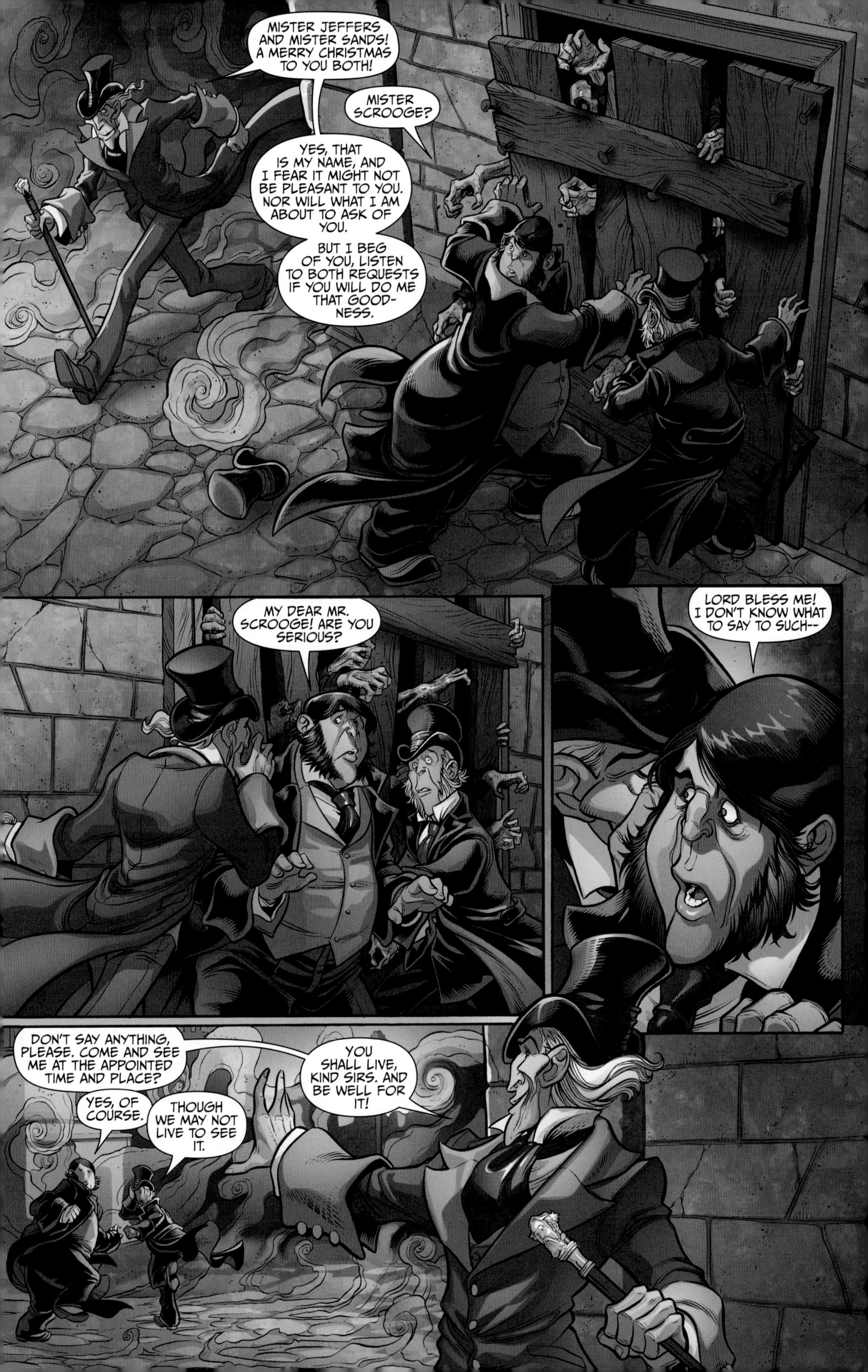
MISTER JEFFERS AND MISTER SANDS! A MERRY CHRISTMAS TO YOU BOTH!
MISTER SCROOGE?
YES, THAT IS MY NAME, AND I FEAR IT MIGHT NOT BE PLEASANT TO YOU. NOR WILL WHAT I AM ABOUT TO ASK OF YOU.
BUT I BEG OF YOU, LISTEN TO BOTH REQUESTS IF YOU WILL DO ME THAT GOODNESS.
MY DEAR MR. SCROOGE! ARE YOU SERIOUS?
LORD BLESS ME! I DON'T KNOW WHAT TO SAY TO SUCH--
DON'T SAY ANYTHING, PLEASE. COME AND SEE ME AT THE APPOINTED TIME AND PLACE?
YES, OF COURSE.
THOUGH WE MAY NOT LIVE TO SEE IT.
YOU SHALL LIVE, KIND SIRS. AND BE WELL FOR IT!

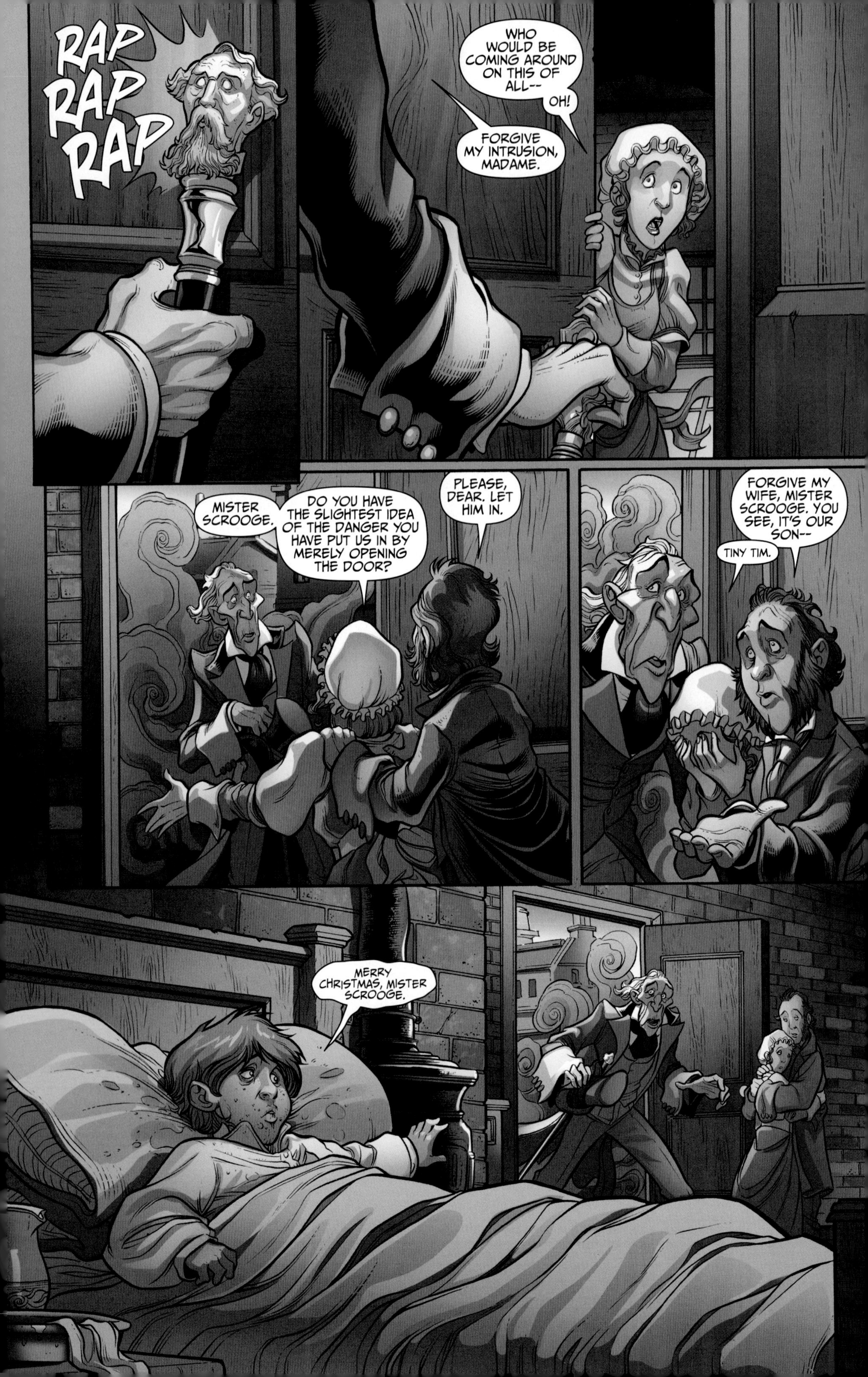
RAP
RAP
RAP
WHO WOULD BE COMING AROUND ON THIS OF ALL--
OH!
FORGIVE MY INTRUSION, MADAME.
MISTER SCROOGE.
DO YOU HAVE THE SLIGHTEST IDEA OF THE DANGER YOU HAVE PUT US IN BY MERELY OPENING THE DOOR?
PLEASE, DEAR. LET HIM IN.
FORGIVE MY WIFE, MISTER SCROOGE. YOU SEE, IT'S OUR SON--
TINY TIM.
MERRY CHRISTMAS, MISTER SCROOGE.

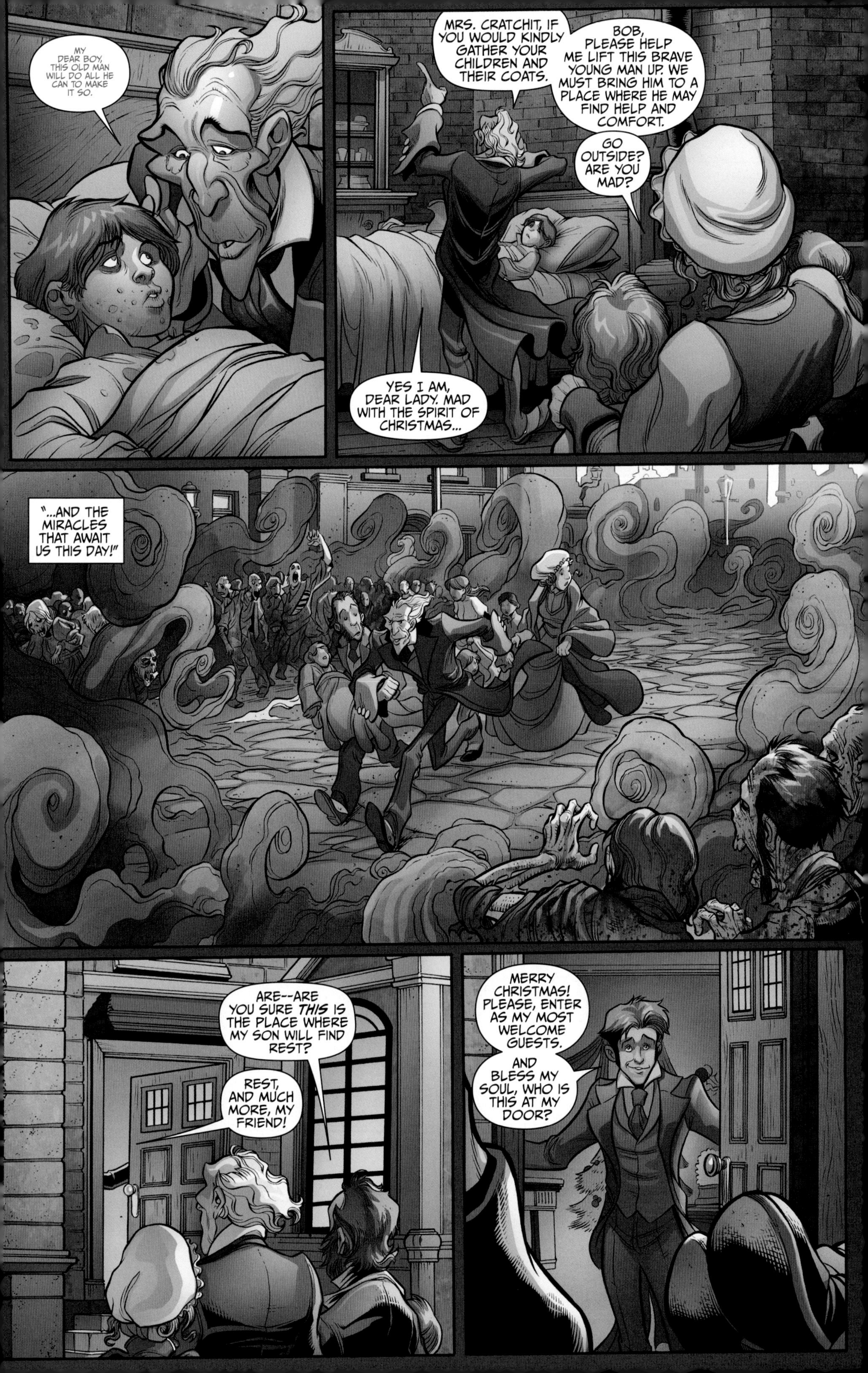
MY DEAR BOY, THIS OLD MAN WILL DO ALL HE CAN TO MAKE IT SO.
MRS. CRATCHIT, IF YOU WOULD KINDLY GATHER YOUR CHILDREN AND THEIR COATS.
BOB, PLEASE HELP ME LIFT THIS BRAVE YOUNG MAN UP. WE MUST BRING HIM TO A PLACE WHERE HE MAY FIND HELP AND COMFORT.
GO OUTSIDE? ARE YOU MAD?
YES I AM, DEAR LADY. MAD WITH THE SPIRIT OF CHRISTMAS...
"...AND THE MIRACLES THAT AWAIT US THIS DAY!"
ARE--ARE YOU SURE *THIS* IS THE PLACE WHERE MY SON WILL FIND REST?
REST, AND MUCH MORE, MY FRIEND!
MERRY CHRISTMAS! PLEASE, ENTER AS MY MOST WELCOME GUESTS.
AND BLESS MY SOUL, WHO IS THIS AT MY DOOR?

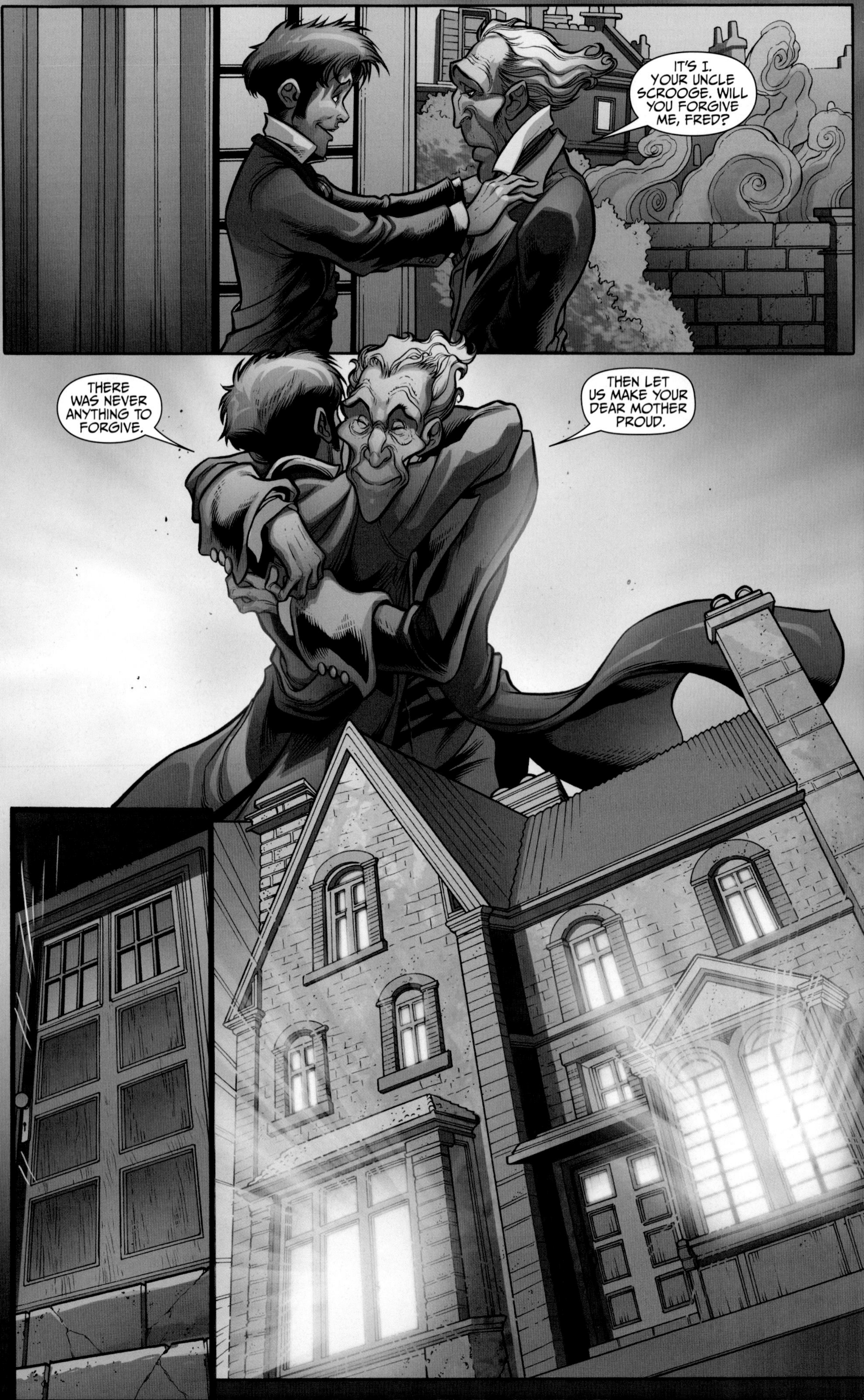
IT'S I. YOUR UNCLE SCROOGE. WILL YOU FORGIVE ME, FRED?
THERE WAS NEVER ANYTHING TO FORGIVE.
THEN LET US MAKE YOUR DEAR MOTHER PROUD.

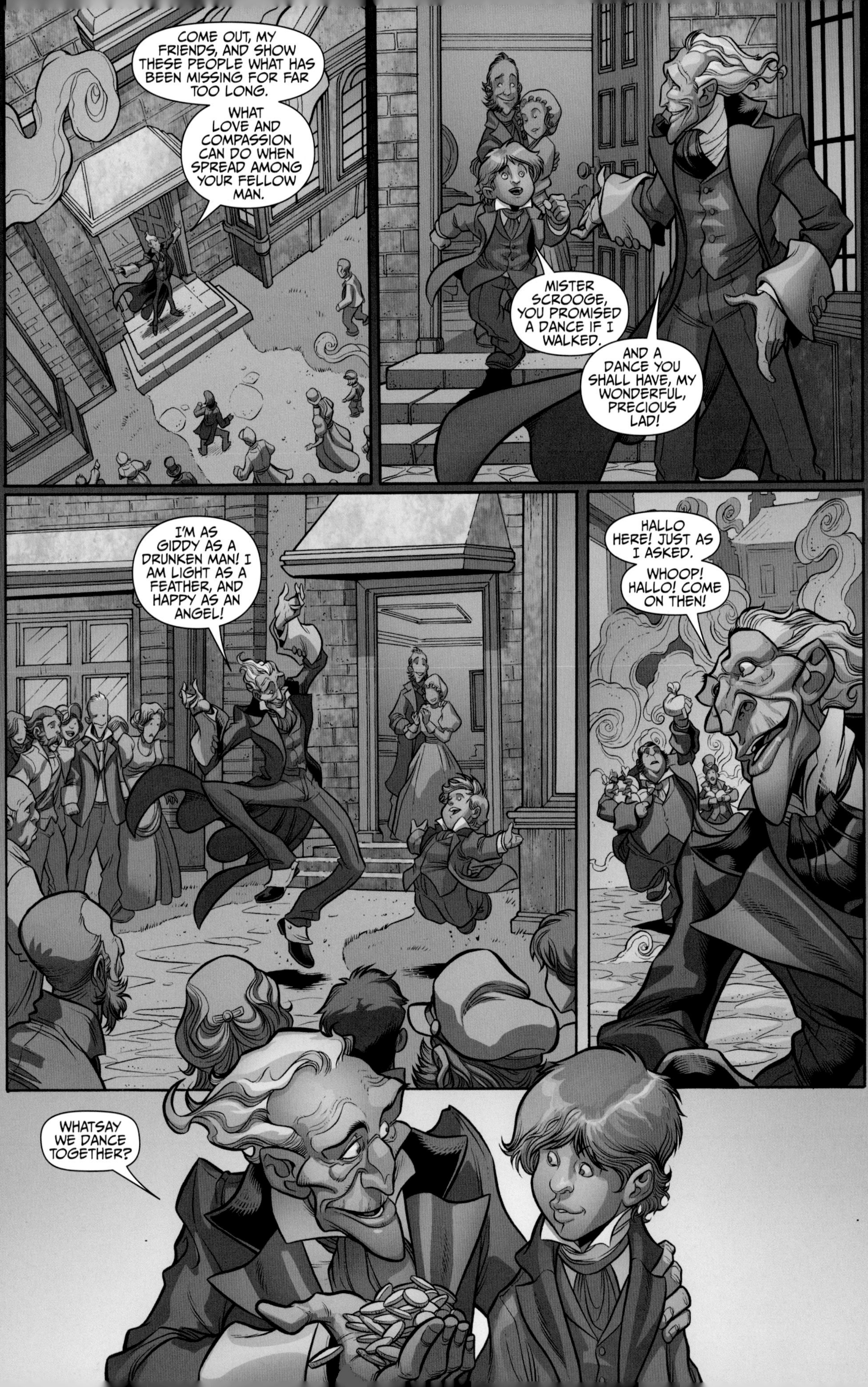
COME OUT, MY FRIENDS, AND SHOW THESE PEOPLE WHAT HAS BEEN MISSING FOR FAR TOO LONG.
WHAT LOVE AND COMPASSION CAN DO WHEN SPREAD AMONG YOUR FELLOW MAN.
MISTER SCROOGE, YOU PROMISED A DANCE IF I WALKED.
AND A DANCE YOU SHALL HAVE, MY WONDERFUL, PRECIOUS LAD!
I'M AS GIDDY AS A DRUNKEN MAN! I AM LIGHT AS A FEATHER, AND HAPPY AS AN ANGEL!
HALLO HERE! JUST AS I ASKED.
WHOOP! HALLO! COME ON THEN!
WHATSAY WE DANCE TOGETHER?

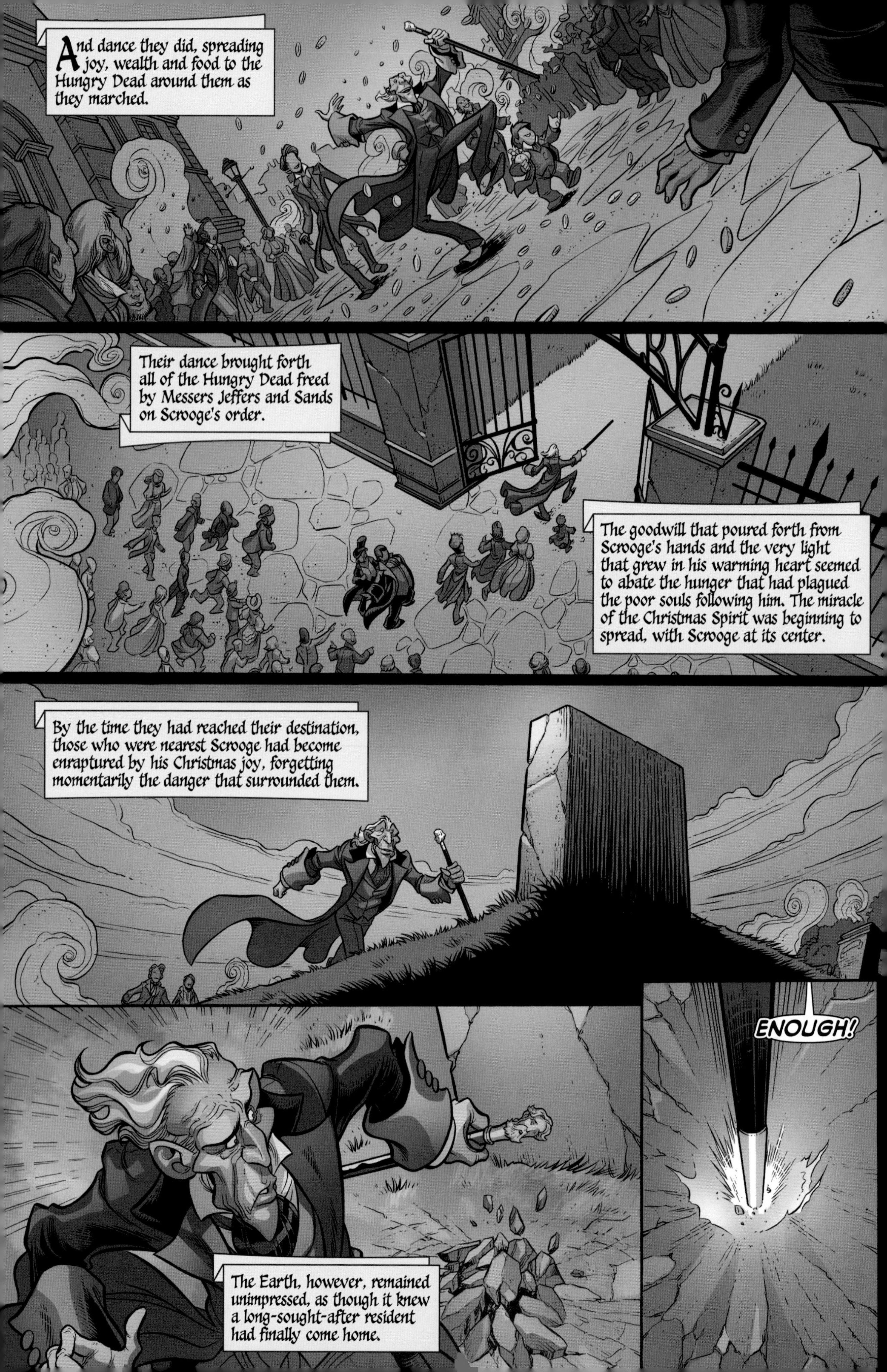
And dance they did, spreading joy, wealth and food to the Hungry Dead around them as they marched.
Their dance brought forth all of the Hungry Dead freed by Messers Jeffers and Sands on Scrooge's order.
The goodwill that poured forth from Scrooge's hands and the very light that grew in his warming heart seemed to abate the hunger that had plagued the poor souls following him. The miracle of the Christmas Spirit was beginning to spread, with Scrooge at its center.
By the time they had reached their destination, those who were nearest Scrooge had become enraptured by his Christmas joy, forgetting momentarily the danger that surrounded them.
The Earth, however, remained unimpressed, as though it knew a long-sought-after resident had finally come home.
ENOUGH!

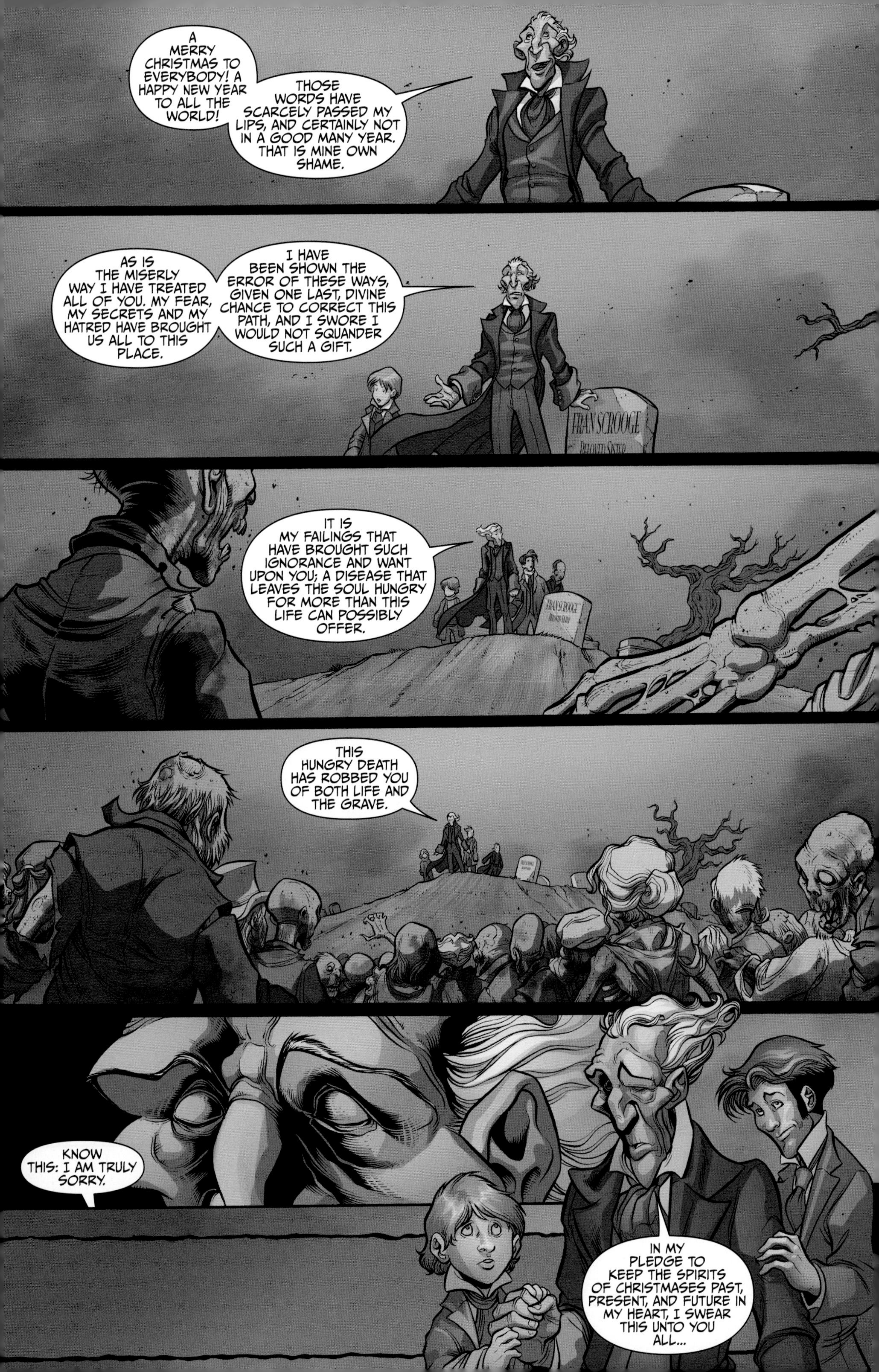

A MERRY CHRISTMAS TO EVERYBODY! A HAPPY NEW YEAR TO ALL THE WORLD!
THOSE WORDS HAVE SCARCELY PASSED MY LIPS, AND CERTAINLY NOT IN A GOOD MANY YEAR. THAT IS MINE OWN SHAME.
AS IS THE MISERLY WAY I HAVE TREATED ALL OF YOU. MY FEAR, MY SECRETS AND MY HATRED HAVE BROUGHT US ALL TO THIS PLACE.
I HAVE BEEN SHOWN THE ERROR OF THESE WAYS, GIVEN ONE LAST, DIVINE CHANCE TO CORRECT THIS PATH, AND I SWORE I WOULD NOT SQUANDER SUCH A GIFT.
FRAN SCROOGE
IT IS MY FAILINGS THAT HAVE BROUGHT SUCH IGNORANCE AND WANT UPON YOU; A DISEASE THAT LEAVES THE SOUL HUNGRY FOR MORE THAN THIS LIFE CAN POSSIBLY OFFER.
THIS HUNGRY DEATH HAS ROBBED YOU OF BOTH LIFE AND THE GRAVE.
KNOW THIS: I AM TRULY SORRY.
IN MY PLEDGE TO KEEP THE SPIRITS OF CHRISTMASES PAST, PRESENT, AND FUTURE IN MY HEART, I SWEAR THIS UNTO YOU ALL...

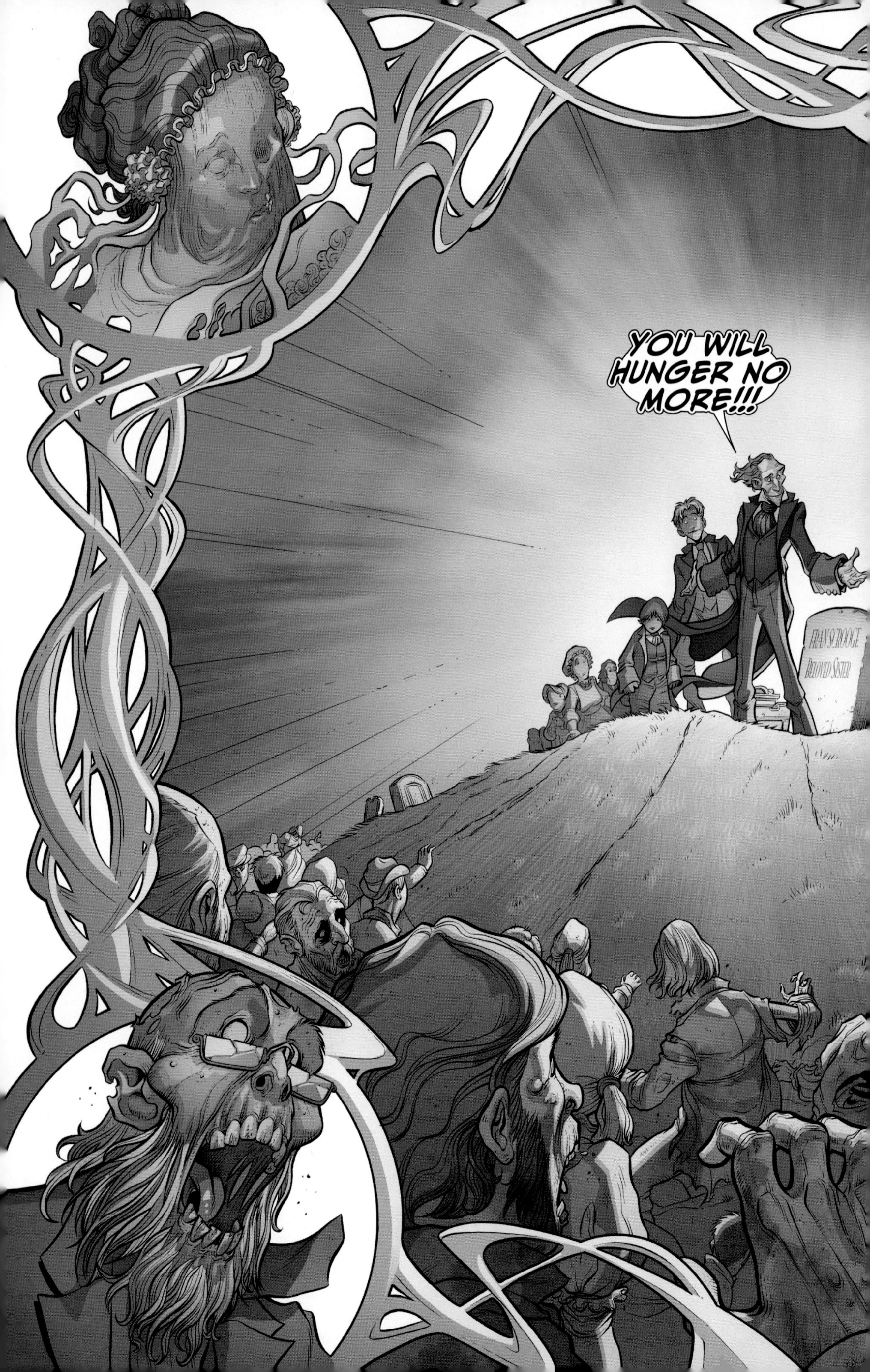
YOU WILL HUNGER NO MORE!!!
FRAN SCROOGE
BELOVED SISTER

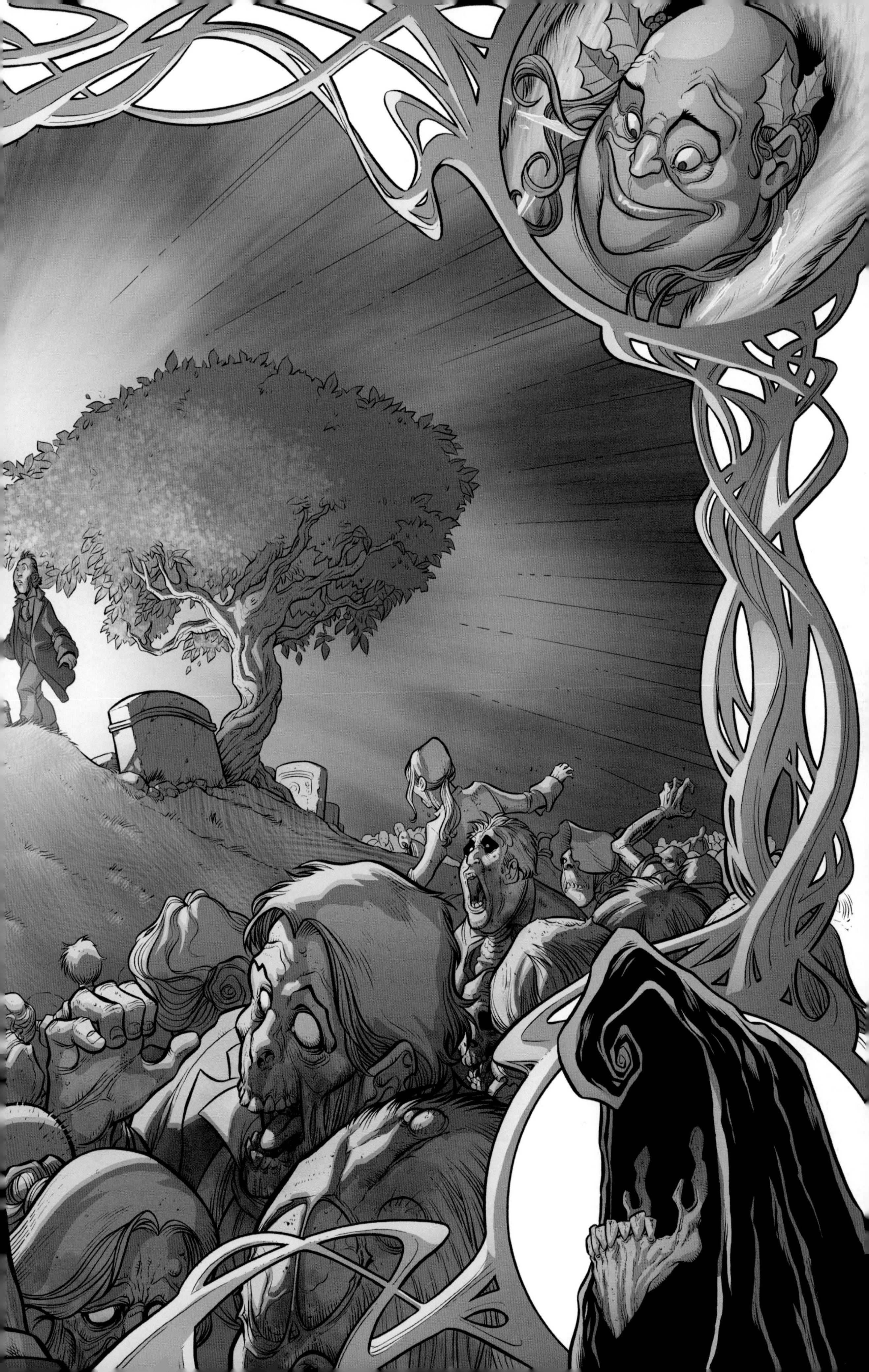

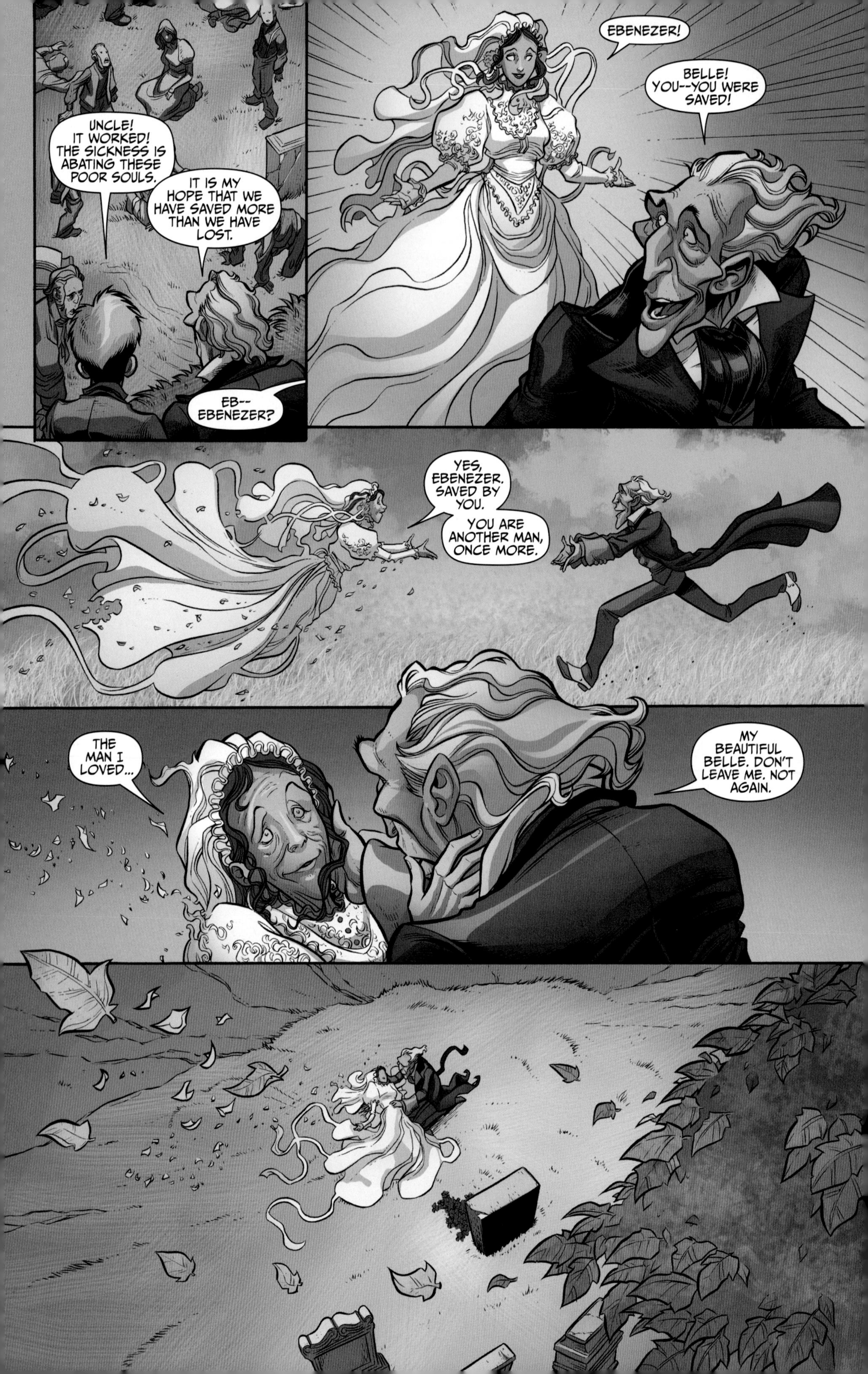
UNCLE! IT WORKED! THE SICKNESS IS ABATING THESE POOR SOULS.
IT IS MY HOPE THAT WE HAVE SAVED MORE THAN WE HAVE LOST.
EB-- EBENEZER?
EBENEZER!
BELLE! YOU--YOU WERE SAVED!
YES, EBENEZER. SAVED BY YOU.
YOU ARE ANOTHER MAN, ONCE MORE.
THE MAN I LOVED...
MY BEAUTIFUL BELLE. DON'T LEAVE ME. NOT AGAIN.

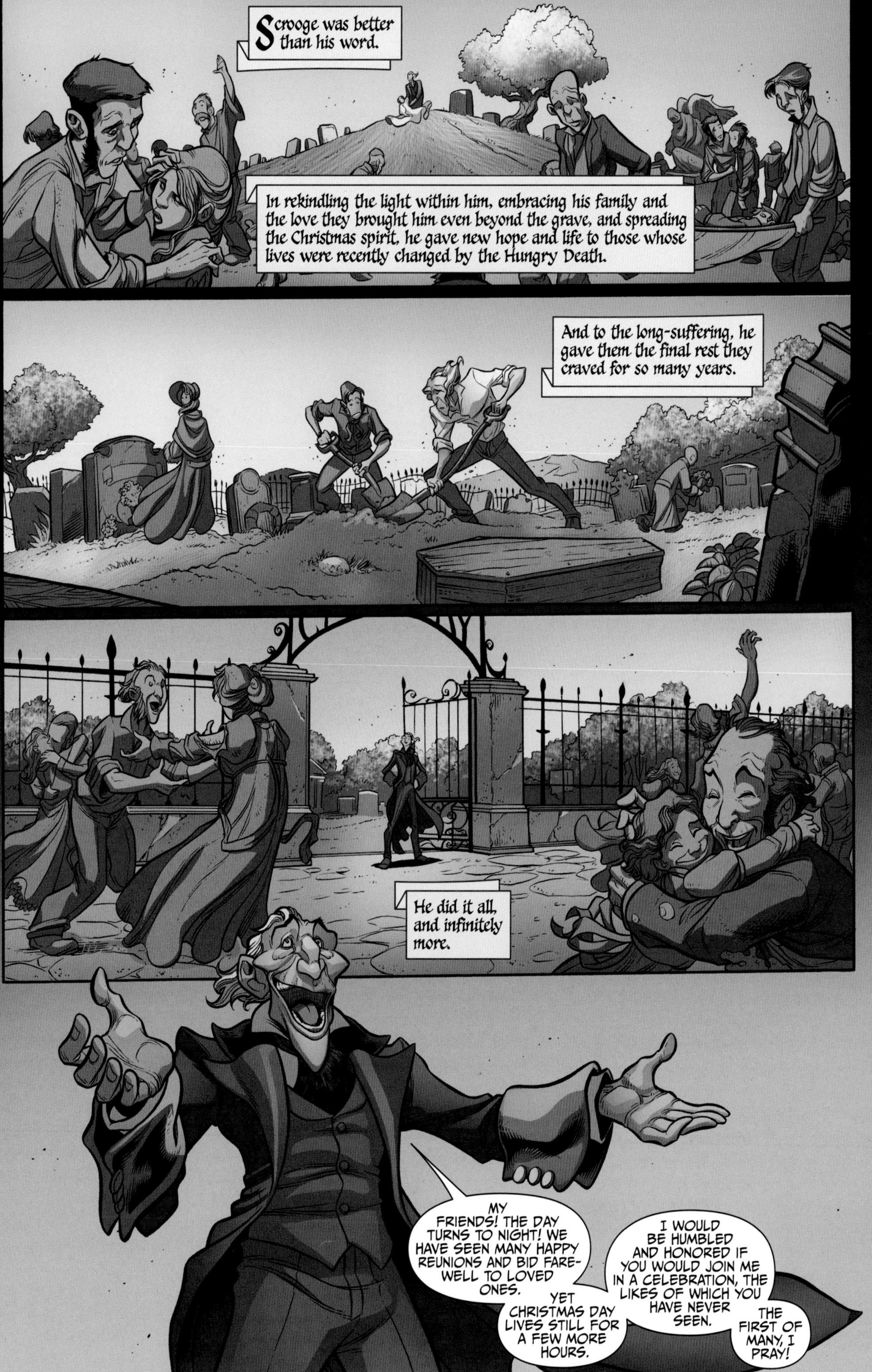
Scrooge was better than his word.
In rekindling the light within him, embracing his family and the love they brought him even beyond the grave, and spreading the Christmas spirit, he gave new hope and life to those whose lives were recently changed by the Hungry Death.
And to the long-suffering, he gave them the final rest they craved for so many years.
He did it all, and infinitely more.
MY FRIENDS! THE DAY TURNS TO NIGHT! WE HAVE SEEN MANY HAPPY REUNIONS AND BID FARE-WELL TO LOVED ONES.
YET CHRISTMAS DAY LIVES STILL FOR A FEW MORE HOURS.
I WOULD BE HUMBLED AND HONORED IF YOU WOULD JOIN ME IN A CELEBRATION, THE LIKES OF WHICH YOU HAVE NEVER SEEN.
THE FIRST OF MANY, I PRAY!

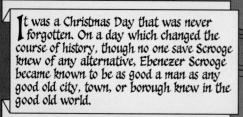

It was a Christmas Day that was never forgotten. On a day which changed the course of history, though no one save Scrooge knew of any alternative, Ebenezer Scrooge became known to be as good a man as any good old city, town, or borough knew in the good old world.

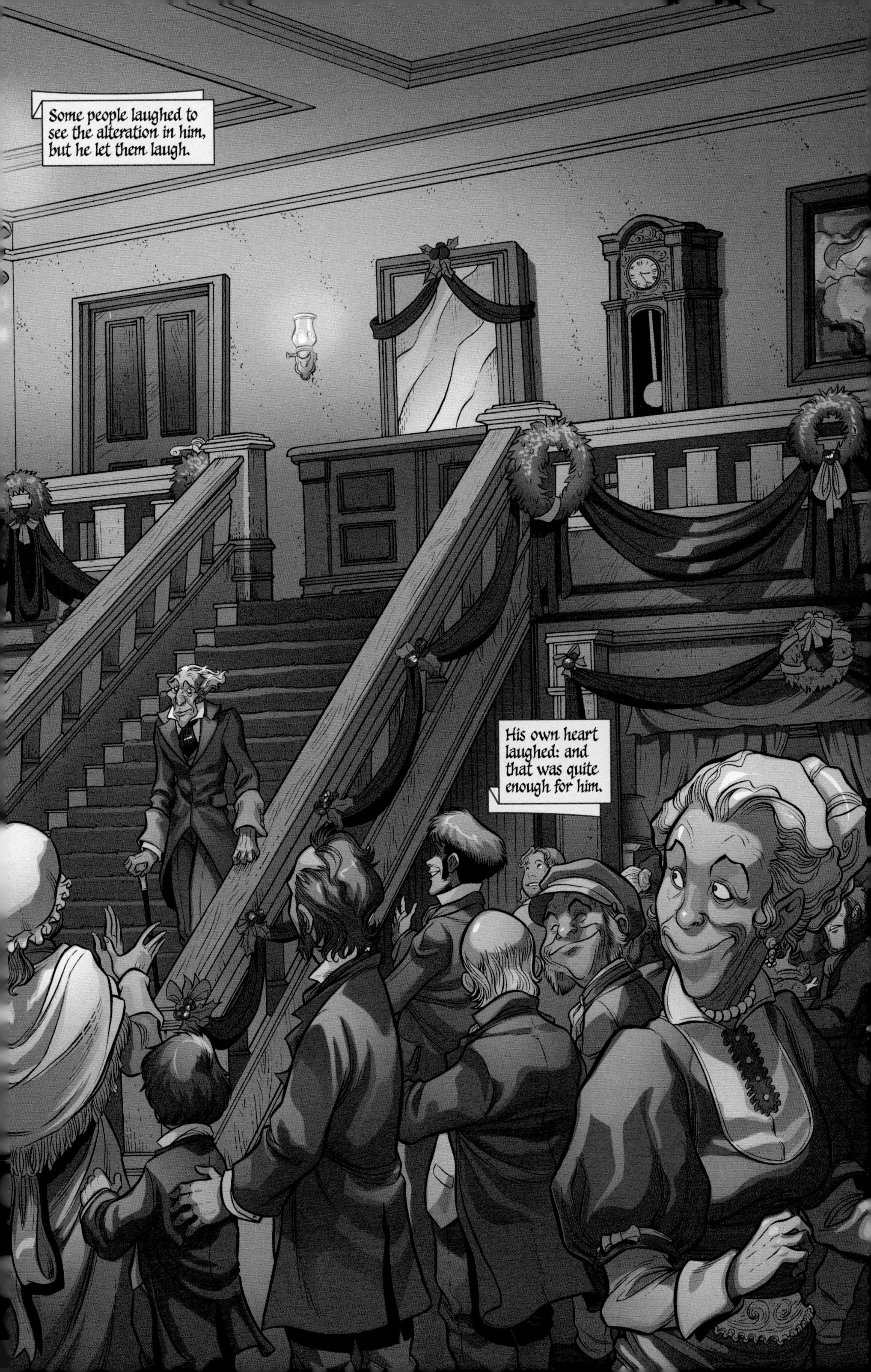
Some people laughed to see the alteration in him, but he let them laugh.
His own heart laughed: and that was quite enough for him.

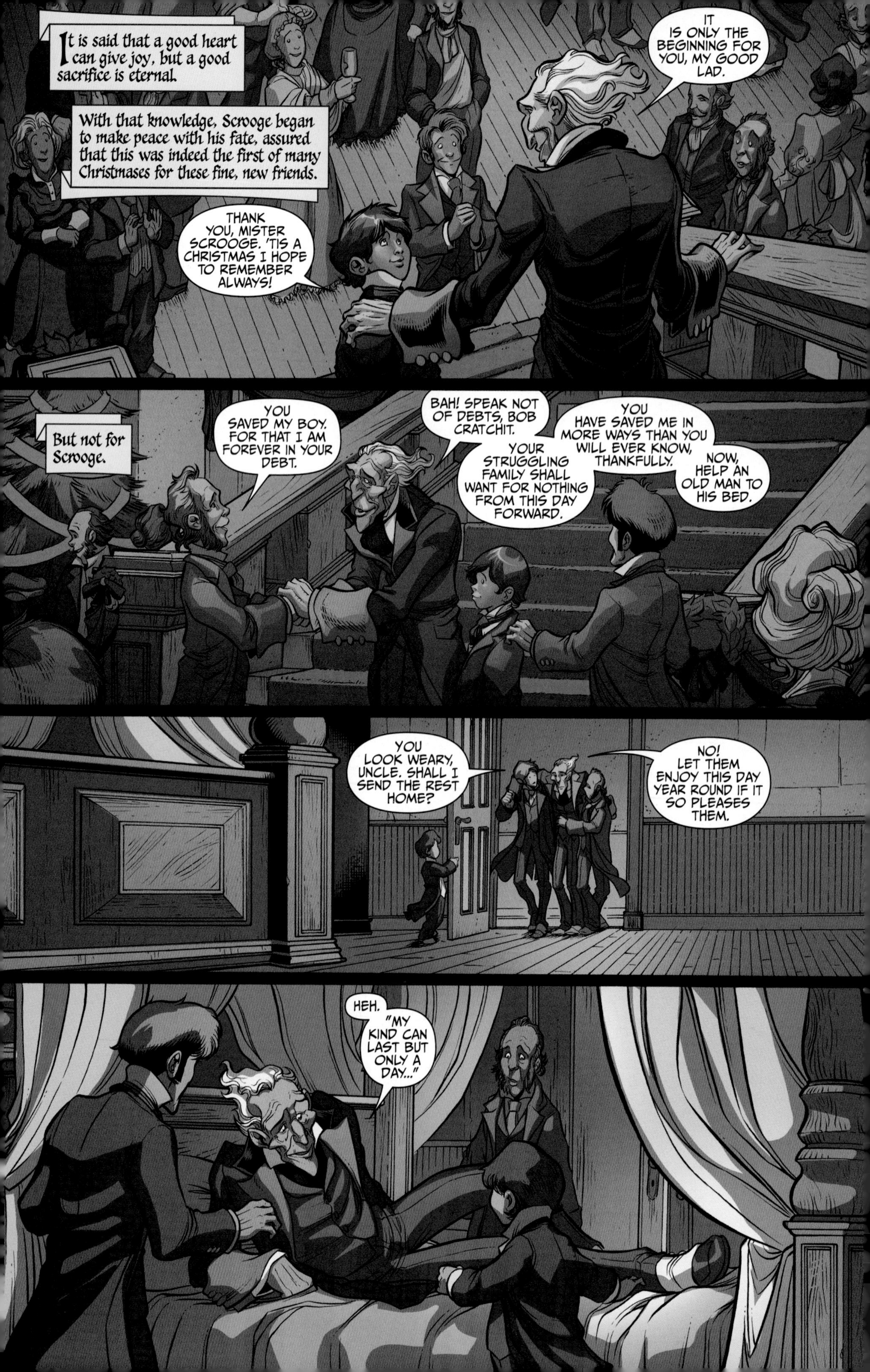
It is said that a good heart can give joy, but a good sacrifice is eternal.
With that knowledge, Scrooge began to make peace with his fate, assured that this was indeed the first of many Christmases for these fine, new friends.
IT IS ONLY THE BEGINNING FOR YOU, MY GOOD LAD.
THANK YOU, MISTER SCROOGE. 'TIS A CHRISTMAS I HOPE TO REMEMBER ALWAYS!
But not for Scrooge.
YOU SAVED MY BOY. FOR THAT I AM FOREVER IN YOUR DEBT.
BAH! SPEAK NOT OF DEBTS, BOB CRATCHIT.
YOUR STRUGGLING FAMILY SHALL WANT FOR NOTHING FROM THIS DAY FORWARD.
YOU HAVE SAVED ME IN MORE WAYS THAN YOU WILL EVER KNOW, THANKFULLY.
NOW, HELP AN OLD MAN TO HIS BED.
YOU LOOK WEARY, UNCLE. SHALL I SEND THE REST HOME?
NO! LET THEM ENJOY THIS DAY YEAR ROUND IF IT SO PLEASES THEM.
HEH. "MY KIND CAN LAST BUT ONLY A DAY..."

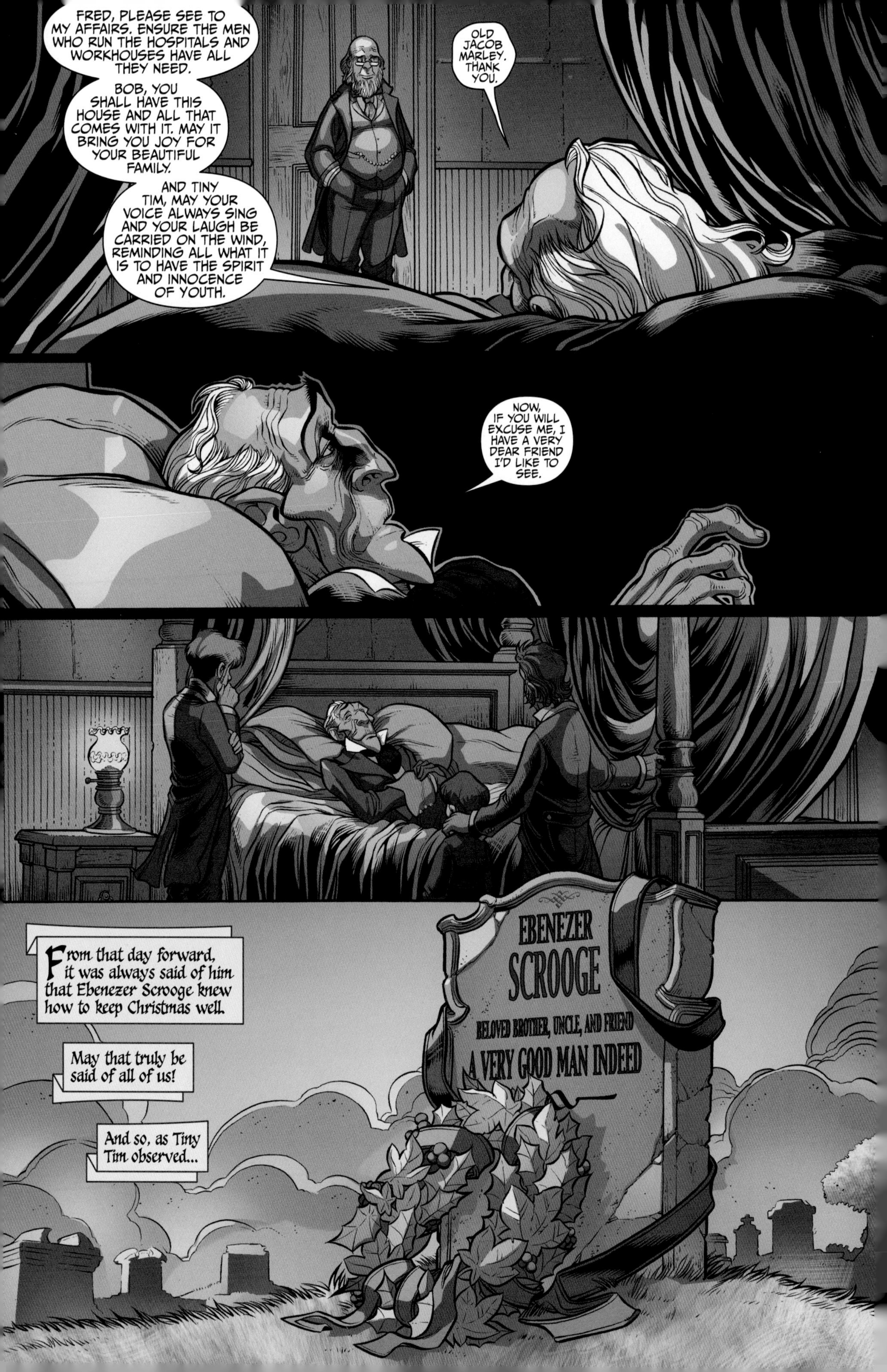
FRED, PLEASE SEE TO MY AFFAIRS. ENSURE THE MEN WHO RUN THE HOSPITALS AND WORKHOUSES HAVE ALL THEY NEED.
BOB, YOU SHALL HAVE THIS HOUSE AND ALL THAT COMES WITH IT. MAY IT BRING YOU JOY FOR YOUR BEAUTIFUL FAMILY.
AND TINY TIM, MAY YOUR VOICE ALWAYS SING AND YOUR LAUGH BE CARRIED ON THE WIND, REMINDING ALL WHAT IT IS TO HAVE THE SPIRIT AND INNOCENCE OF YOUTH.
OLD JACOB MARLEY. THANK YOU.
NOW, IF YOU WILL EXCUSE ME, I HAVE A VERY DEAR FRIEND I'D LIKE TO SEE.
From that day forward, it was always said of him that Ebenezer Scrooge knew how to keep Christmas well.
EBENEZER
SCROOGE
BELOVED BROTHER, UNCLE, AND FRIEND
A VERY GOOD MAN INDEED
May that truly be said of all of us!
And so, as Tiny Tim observed...

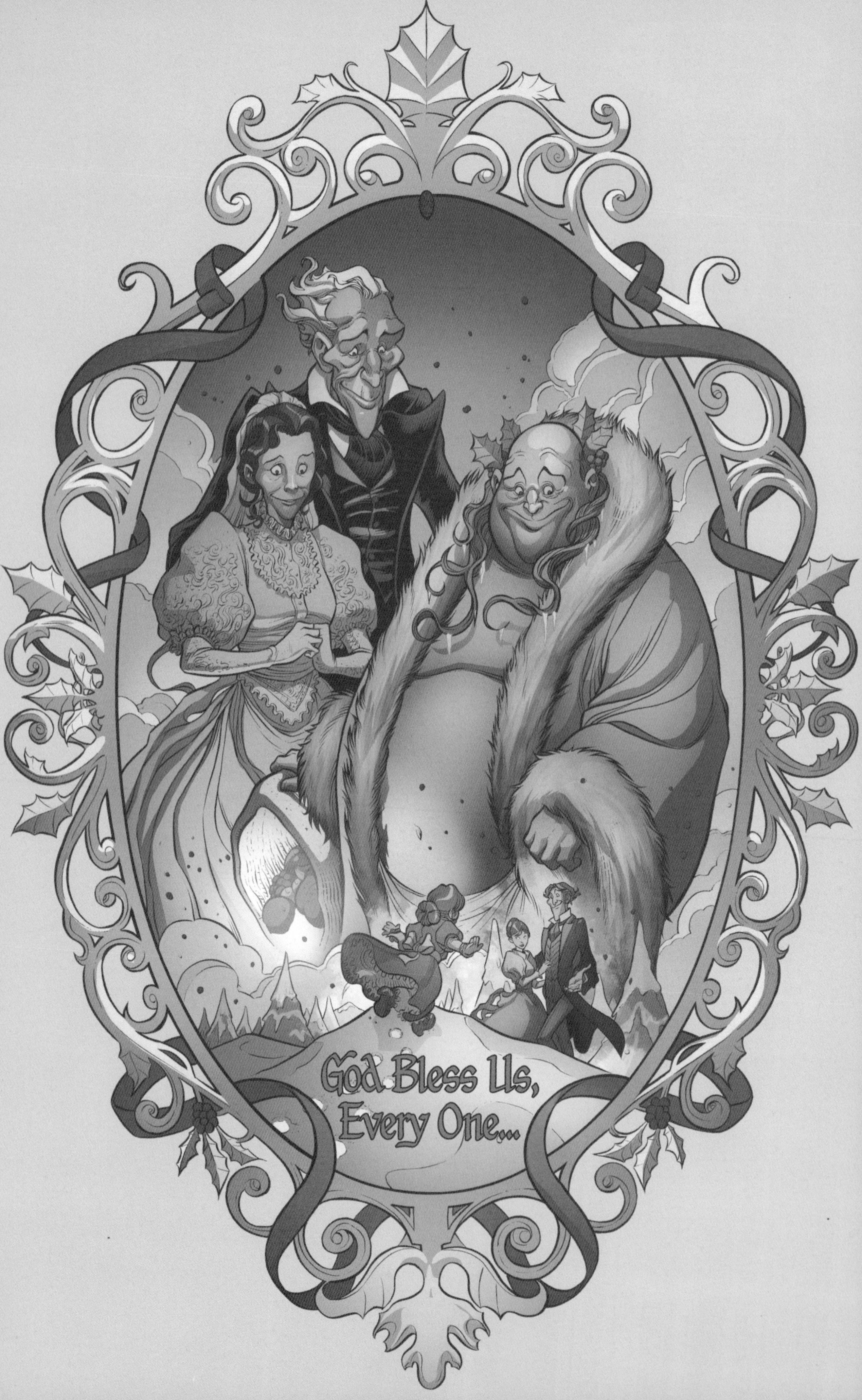
God Bless Us,
Every One...

BRINGING ZOMBIES CHRISTMAS CAROL TO (UN)LIFE

Jim McCann: This book has been quite a unique process for all involved, I must say. From a personal perspective, I wanted to keep as much of the Gothic and incredible text and scenes that Dickens has in the original work (which he, himself, called "A Ghost Story of Christmas"), while adding our own horror elements to twist this tale a bit on its undead ear.

David Baldeon: Jim's script is all about mood and terror, and the main goal is to make the pages look creepy and give them the classic Victorian terror feel...with the additional challenge of providing the whole book with a very particular style and look that measures up to a fantastic script.

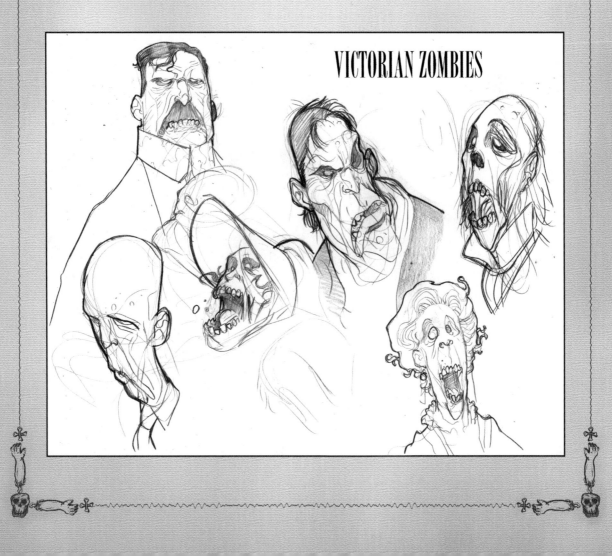

VICTORIAN ZOMBIES

EBENEZER SCROOGE

Obvious as it may seem, the cornerstones of this project are the zombies and Mr. Ebenezer Scrooge himself. His design and acting throughout the pages would completely define the style and feel of the book, and that was very much the idea when designing his look. And as for zombies...Well, the trick was to answer the question "How cool can your typical Victorian character look when necrotized?"

Jim McCann: David's designs are perfect! Much of the original text is narration and descriptive, and David's art gets across so much of that in his expressions and scenery. His design for Scrooge is spot on and the zombies are just incredible in the way that they are both Victorian (nice bonnet, undead lady) and monstrous at the same time. And I don't think anyone has ever seen the Spirits of Christmas as he's designed them. Each is more amazing than the last, in beauty and terror.

Can you tell this is like a Christmas present for me?!

REANIMATING CHRISTMAS PAST

David Baldeon: The Ghost of Christmas Past has very close ties to Scrooge in Jim's version of the tale. She was not going to be a random beatific spirit, but a very well defined character with a lot of pathos and pain to her, embodying a lot of the drama that would eventually turn Scrooge into the man who starts the book. With that and Mr. Kaluta's version from the covers in mind, the design had to be as terrifying as, in a twisted way, it was beautiful. And so Christmas Past is no more simply a guide to Scrooge's life but an actual, painful part of it. The design had to get all that through and at the same time connect with the graphic elements defining our version of Christmas Carol. Her appearance as part of the mist that heralds the Hungry Death was almost a no-brainer.

Jim McCann: The Ghost of Christmas Past has always fascinated me because she is the Spirit that has the most

nebulous description in Dickens' text, so we had a lot of room to play with in designing her and in telling her own story. Making her the love that Scrooge lost was an idea that clicked in my head and David and Jeremy really nailed it. I love David's Mucha-inspired, yet still Victorian, design. She's so hauntingly beautiful and scary at the same time.

Jeremy Treece: Young Ebenezer was a very essential part of my run on Jim's version of a Christmas Carol. I wanted to capture what I knew of him from the versions I grew up with on television. He was said to have been a devilishly handsome fellow, and I wanted to cross that thought with David Baldeon's great vision for the aged Scrooge.

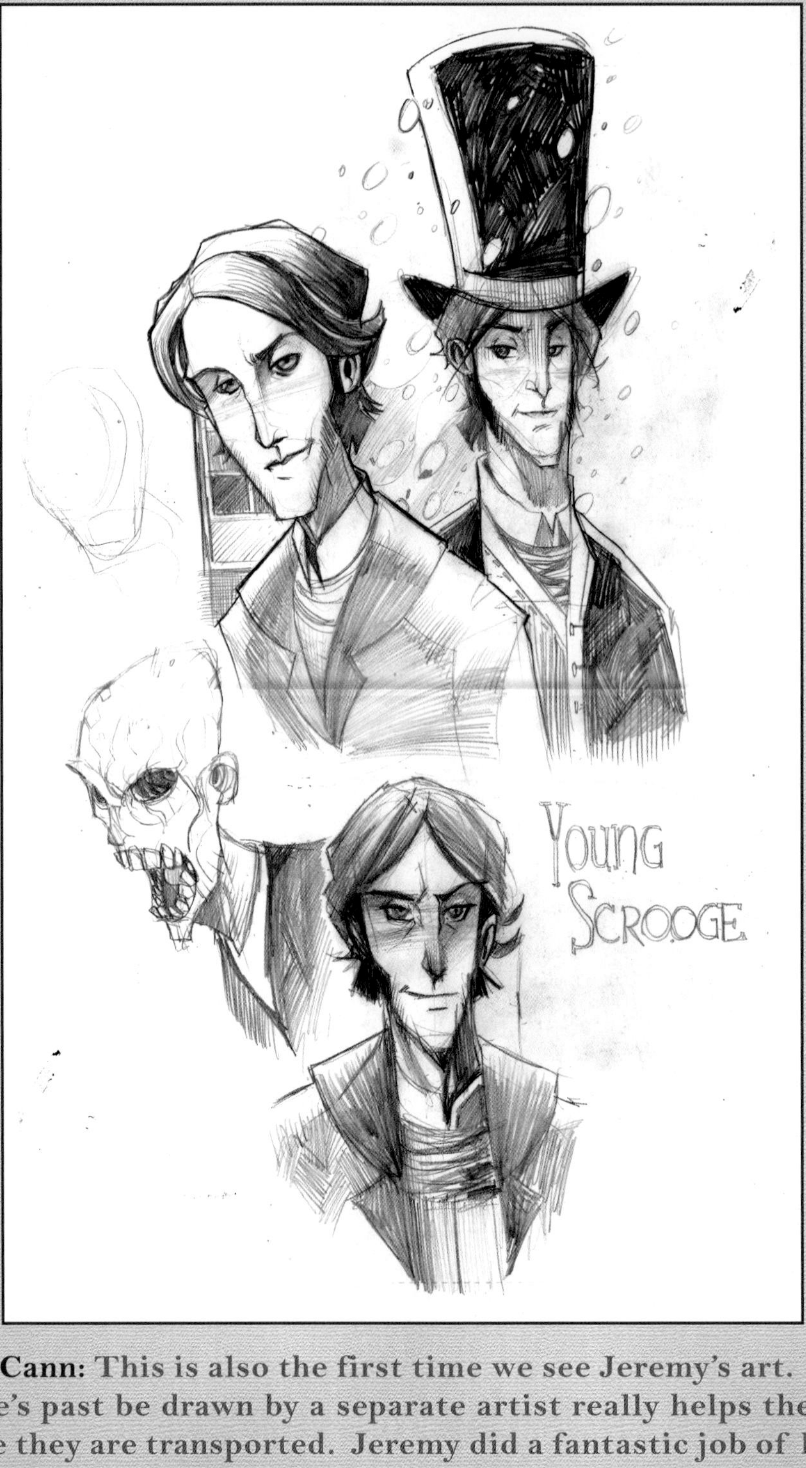
YOUNG
SCROOGE

Jim McCann: This is also the first time we see Jeremy's art. Having Scrooge's past be drawn by a separate artist really helps the reader feel like they are transported. Jeremy did a fantastic job of keeping in the tone of the book while adding his own twist!

TEARING OPEN A CHRISTMAS PRESENT

David Baldeon: The Ghost of Christmas Present ended up being, to me, the embodiment of the tone of the whole series. Fun, flamboyant and incredibly creepy and eerie. Almost all of the classic versions of Present obviously use Santa Claus as their main inspiration. Our goal being to give an unseen twist to the tale, Christmas Present turned into an overacted and slightly dangerous version of Bacchus. Too fun to be safe, so to speak. Prone to laughter but with a psychotic undertone.

Again, Jim's script clearly laid the foundations for the whole look of the character. Many of the images described went beyond simple terror to tread very unsettling ground, which was really fun to draw and quite a challenge to portray correctly. And his transformation throughout the issue was quite something too! Plus, Jim and John were kind enough to let me go with my first idea of the floating fat man that I've wanted to draw ever since I first watched Dune!

Jim McCann: This is the issue where I threw out the entire second half of what I had planned. The culprit? David Baldeon. His design for Christmas Present was so unique that I felt like I was going on the journey along with Scrooge. I stuck with many of the locations mentioned in the text, but the way events unfold was absolutely David's design of this Spirit. The image of Ignorance and Want, the way this Spirit was a floating fat man in an oversized robe, the way he could go from jovial to dark fury in a panel...I was absolutely inspired, and what more could a writer ask for from a truly remarkable artist?!

PLOTTING CHRISTMAS FUTURE

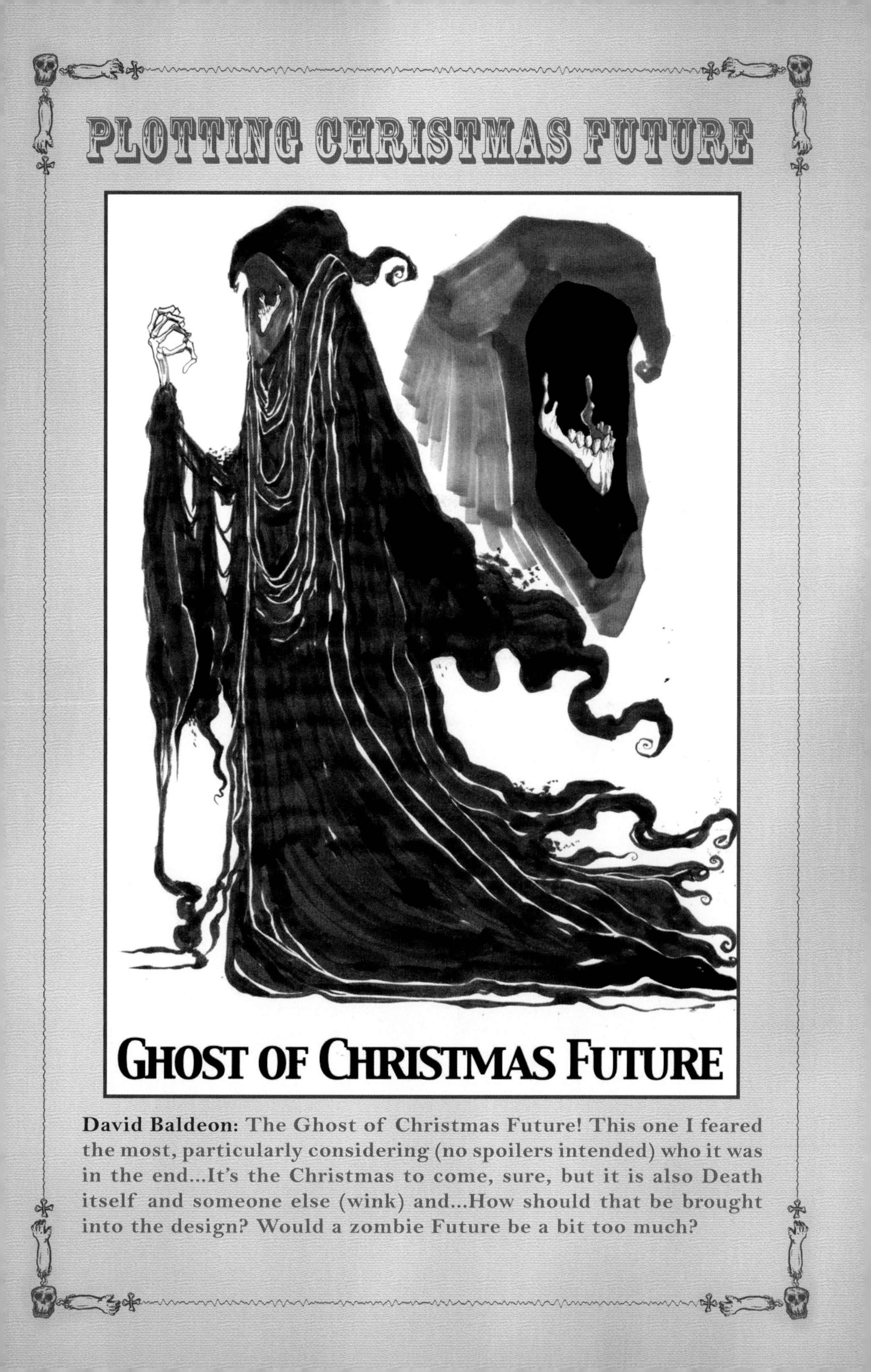

GHOST OF CHRISTMAS FUTURE

David Baldeon: The Ghost of Christmas Future! This one I feared the most, particularly considering (no spoilers intended) who it was in the end...It's the Christmas to come, sure, but it is also Death itself and someone else (wink) and...How should that be brought into the design? Would a zombie Future be a bit too much?

One influence was my first Grim Reaper from the movies: Monty Python's Death from *The Meaning of Life*, that both scared and amused me in my childhood. I have always remembered its imposing look, its shrugging shoulders up to the head. But Christmas Future being who it is in our version, and our version being a zombie one, there was something missing. I did not want a skull in the hood, nor a zombie face, and a pitch-black hood looked cool but somehow overused. Once again, the old design principle came to mind: less is more. This is a zombie book. Zombies bite. What about a ghostly, bone-clean jaw hanging in the darkness of the hood? This was a very particular looking jaw that had to be there, and the combination of that and the hood's curly end incorporated the two principal design traits that would give a visual clue about the Ghost's identity without giving it away too much.

Jim McCann: This issue was tough because it departed in visuals so much from the source material (there were no zombies in Dickens' future, as far as I know!), yet what Dickens had Scrooge experience in this ghastly vision of his future-or lack thereof-was ripe with possibilities. It took the longest to arrange the visuals and weave them in and out of the original while still making sense with the story we were telling. Fortunately, what David and Jeremy turned in was amazing!

The design for The Spirit Of Christmases That Will Never Be is stunning and David did a great job of making this one a heavy mass, something you can't escape. This is in stark contrast to the previous Spirits, who floated about.

And Jeremy...he nailed everything I threw at him, from Hungry Dead Tiny Tim to the Rise of Ebenezer Scrooge. It's not easy to do crowd scenes and in this issue we have the most ever; Jeremy didn't cut a single corner or back away from them. Every zombie is different, every refugee in Scrooge's house has their own look and feeling. This team truly worked their tails off here.

Speaking of teamwork — I think special consideration needs to be given to page 5. BOTH art teams worked on that page to transition us to the future. It was something I wrote in the script, not sure if *I* could get away with it, and then John Denning, our amazing editor, said "Let's go for it." Now go back and look at that page again to really appreciate the seemless way both pencillers, inkers, and colorists for these sections worked in lockstep to make true comic book magic!

daddy?

Jeremy Treece: This issue was all about the Cratchit family for me. Playing with the solemnness of a father refusing to give up his family, and then realizing there is no other choice. I loved creating the scenes from the moment Bob loses hope, to the death kiss, and then how easily the family moves on from the corpse to march into the cemetery. I went for an edgier, more gritty future than what I had illustrated in the second issue to bring all these feelings across.

THE END OF IT

Jim McCann: The End of It. And so it truly is. This was by far the most challenging Stave to write. Scrooge had it easy in Mr. Dickens' tale- he just needed to buy a prize turkey, have a dinner with his nephew, and play a good-natured prank on poor Bob Cratchit. And it was all wrapped up in 7 pages. Not so much in our version. We have this whole Hungry Dead plague to cure before there can be punch and feasts. But looking at the text, I knew we could have Ebenezer leave the same mark on Christmas he had in the original, but with an added punch. I hope Mr. Dickens will forgive me the liberty I took in changing the ending, but it seemed fitting in our version to make the man Scrooge a forever-changed spirit — the Spirit Of All Christmases Yet To Come. His sacrifice saved everyone and himself, and the world was better for it. And zombie-free once more! Wshew!

Jeremy Treece: This book was very interesting to work on. I was contacted by editor John Denning asking me if I'd like to participate in this book. I looked at David's art already in the works, and was just blown away, immediately afterwards I was sold. David's work really set the stage for me and something that I wanted to achieve was an easy transition between the two styles. I think David and I really succeeded in doing so, and Jim kept throwing us curveballs to challenge us as we went. The whole experience was amazing, and I'm glad I was there for the ride!

Jim McCann: This stave had less words per-page than any because this whole team, by this point, was in complete lock-step. Who needed narration when you could tell how nervous and excited Scrooge was while he shaved and got dressed? The vivid colors of the party and all of the expressions made me wish I could be in Scrooge's house that night. Fun fact — something that I wanted to put in but didn't want to crowd the art with Scrooge's monologue

— in this version, the Scrooge left his house to the Cratchit family, who continued to throw an all-day gala in Scrooge's honor that would make even the Fezziwigs proud.

David Baldeon: I'll admit it, I had not read the original Dickens story. My idea of A Christmas Carol was that of the kind, family-friendly, cheesy redemption of a grumpy old man. Yeah, there were ghosts but...

And then I got Jim's first script as I read the original Dickens story and found that it was indeed a story of redemption...through terror. Scrooge's voyage is a merciless tale, full of stress and horror. Good old Ebenezer really suffers in Dickens' story, and his turning back into a decent human being is, never mind the fantastic elements, a believable one. He starts a despicable creature, and the harsh truth about him, his past and his future make him cry, scream and learn. And yeah, it was ALL there in Jim's script. With zombies. And far from being a simple gimmick, the Hungry Dead were seamlessly woven into the story, giving it a whole new dimension and a second level of reading that, frankly, made me wonder why the heck Dickens had not used them in the first place. That was a feeling I had through the whole series, particularly after reading the beautiful, dramatic ending that Jim has given us: "Why wasn't this in the original?"

The whole proccess was an adventure and a challenge. Beyond the superficial fun of drawing Victorian zombies, it was clear that the series needed the visuals to be stretched to a limit, particularly when it came to Scrooge. He had to be different, he had to be something apart from what might be expected. He's not simply a grumpy senior, his lack of humanity was at the core of the conflict of the tale...I found myself focusing on his acting, on his interior drama, on his body language. A version of Ebenezer Scrooge based mostly on Iggy Pop! Who would have thought?

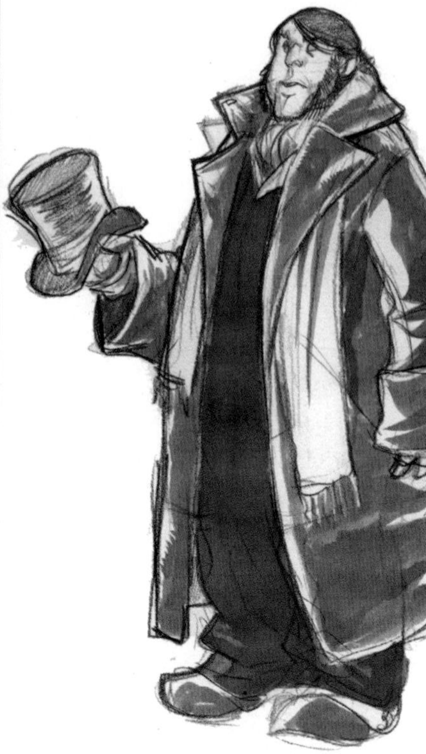

Issue #5 has been a particularly difficult one because I've grown really, really fond of the series and of our Scrooge. I feel really sorry that I cannot draw him again, not in one of those marvelous scenes Jim writes for him. It's certainly been a great voyage, an unexpected one...But most decidedly an awesome experience Definitely not a humbug.

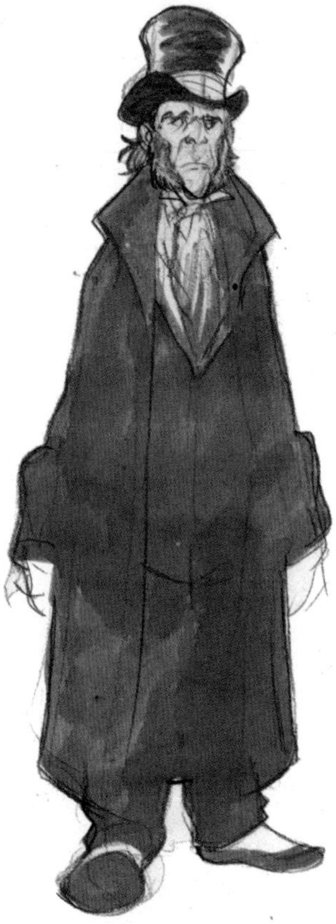

Jim McCann: I couldn't be happier with the way this all turned out. I sincerely hope you have enjoyed reading it as much as we have enjoyed creating it. Many thanks to Charles Dickens — the best co-writer any one could ask for really. And I'd like to thank the artistic, editorial, and design teams. God bless you, every one (you knew that was coming, right?). And if you don't have a great holiday, beware of zombies!

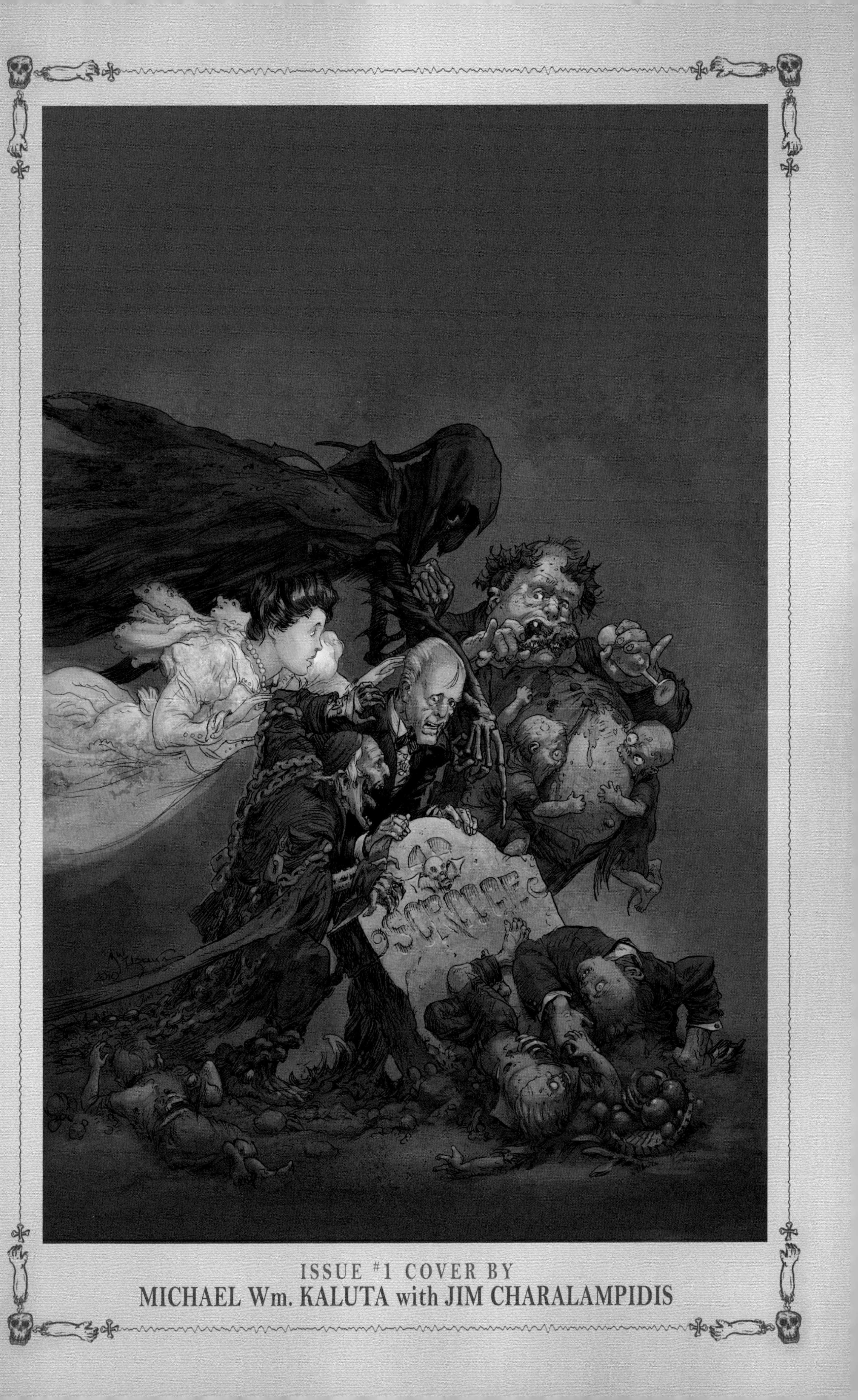
SCROOGE

ISSUE #1 COVER BY
MICHAEL Wm. KALUTA with JIM CHARALAMPIDIS

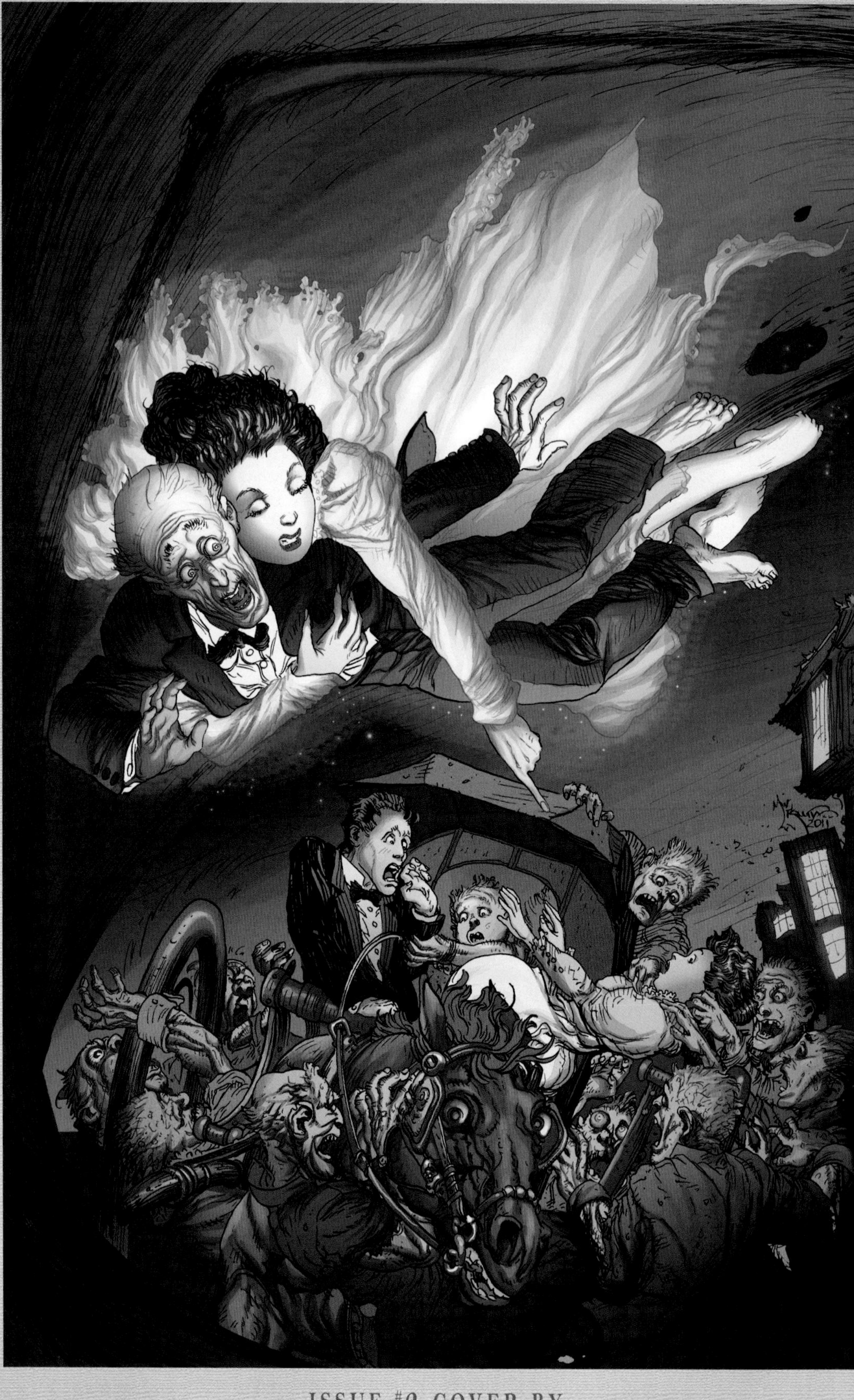

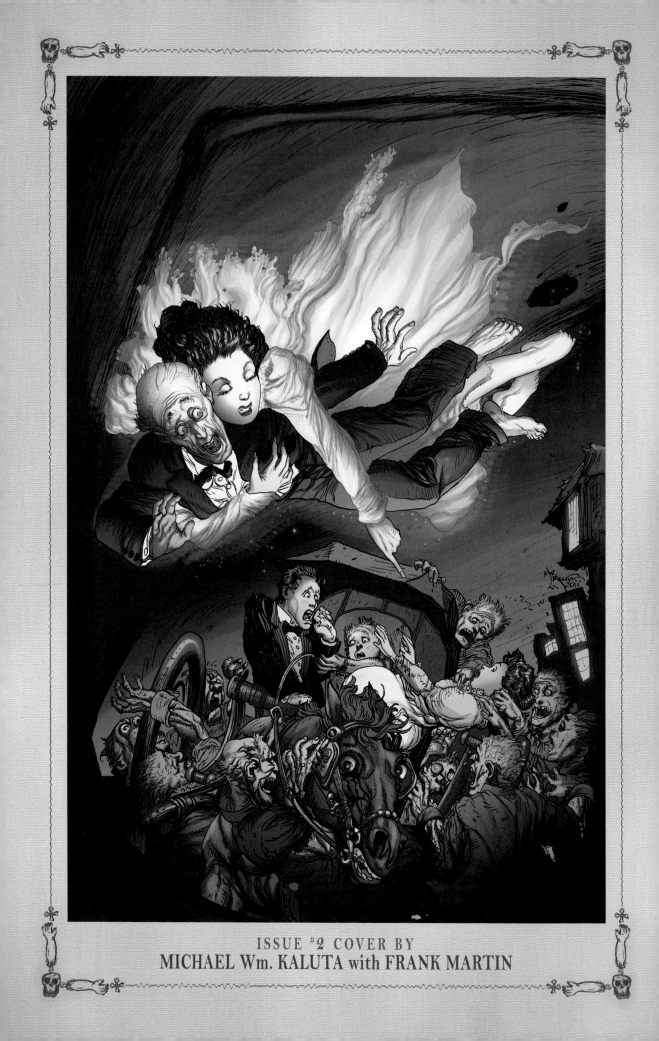

ISSUE #2 COVER BY
MICHAEL Wm. KALUTA with FRANK MARTIN

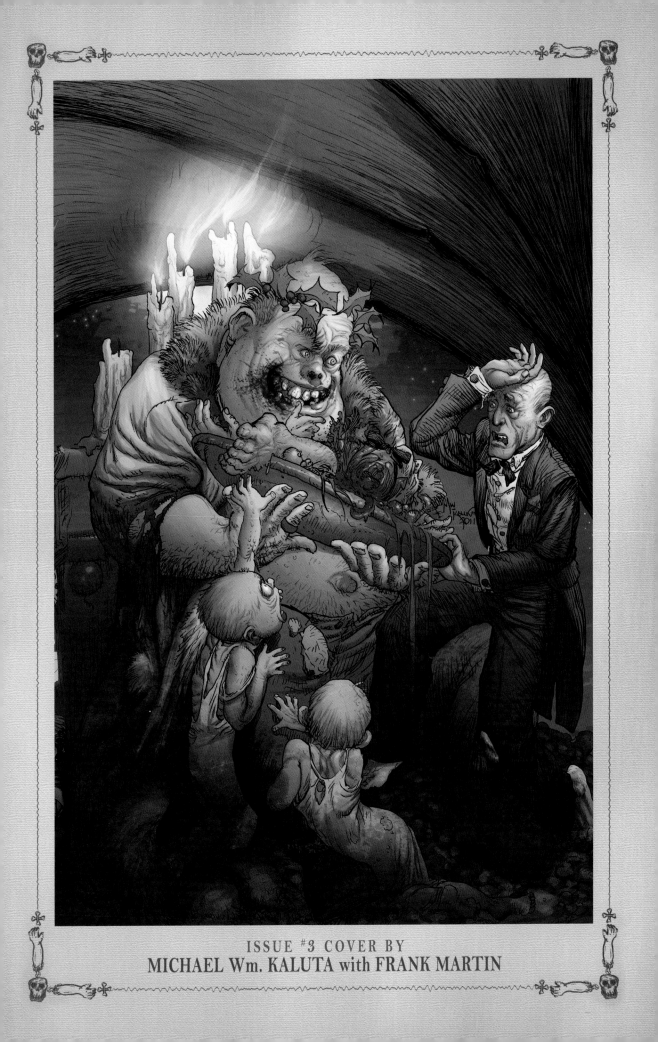

ISSUE #3 COVER BY
MICHAEL Wm. KALUTA with FRANK MARTIN

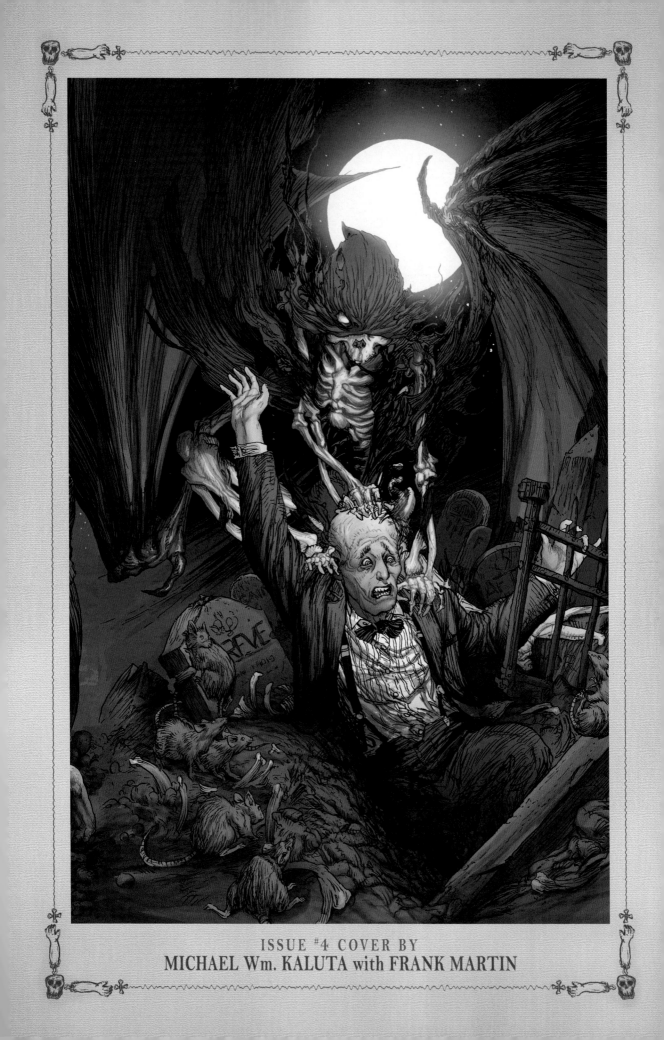

ISSUE #4 COVER BY
MICHAEL Wm. KALUTA with FRANK MARTIN

ISSUE #5 COVER BY
MICHAEL Wm. KALUTA with FRANK MARTIN

ISSUES #2-5 COMBINED COVER ART BY
MICHAEL Wm. KALUTA with FRANK MARTIN

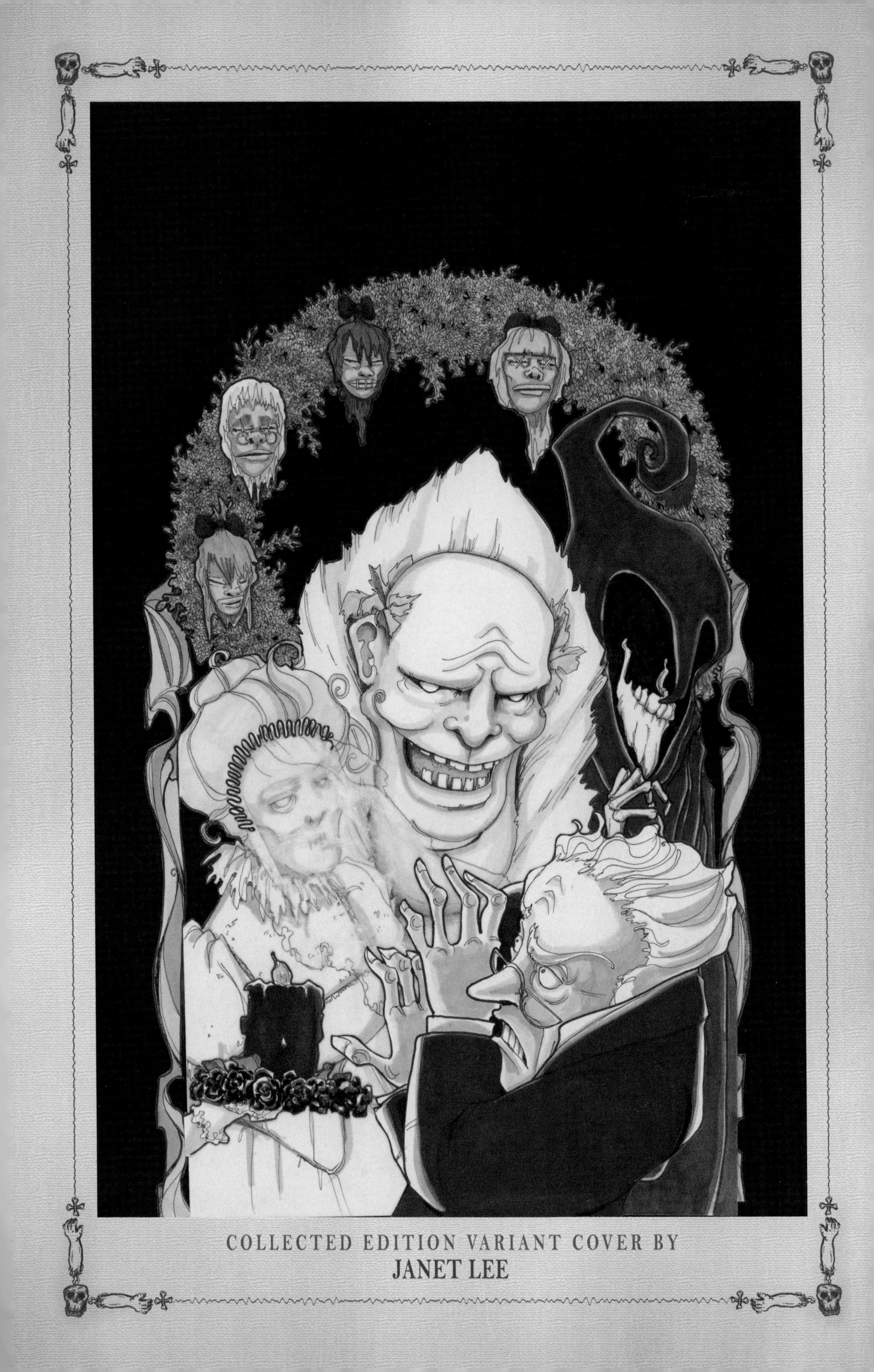

COLLECTED EDITION VARIANT COVER BY
JANET LEE